Just Good Friends

Elizabeth Stuart

Just Good Friends

Towards a Lesbian and Gay Theology of Relationships

MOWBRAY

Mowbray
A Cassell imprint
Wellington House, 125 Strand, London WC2R 0BB
PO Box 605, Herndon VA 20172

© Elizabeth Stuart 1995

First published 1995
Reprinted 1996

British Library Cataloguing-in-Publication Data
A catalogue record for this book is available from the British Library.

ISBN 0–264–67328–X   *19492820*

Printed and bound in Great Britain by
Mackays of Chatham PLC, Chatham, Kent

Contents

For Jane

My spirit in confusion,
Long years I strove,
But now I know that never
Nearer shall I move,
Than a friend's friend to friendship,
To love than a friend's love.
                    (Stevie Smith, 'Dirge')

Acknowledgements

I am very grateful to all the people with whom I discussed the issues and contents of this book. These include audiences at Lancaster University, St Martin's College, Lancaster, Leeds University, Bangor University and Manchester University; I am grateful to the Revd Bill Cave for organizing my talks and seminars at these places. The Revd Professor Andrew Linzey invited me to give a lecture as part of a series on radical theology at Mansfield College, Oxford. The Conference of Radical Baptists invited me to speak at their meeting at the Baptist Assembly in 1993. My thanks also to the Methodist, United Reformed and Roman Catholic Caucuses of the Lesbian and Gay Christian Movement for allowing me to test out ideas and gain new insights, and to the Lesbian and Gay Christian Movement as a whole for honouring me with the invitation to give their annual lecture in 1993. The Metropolitan Community Church also invited me to preach and teach during the year this book was in preparation and engaged with me on the issues it raises. I was also glad to be able to share ideas with the URC Thames North and Eastern Province Ministers' Spring School, 1994. I was delighted to be able to take part in a theological forum in New York in June 1994 with other lesbian and gay scholars, Mary Hunt, John McNeill, and Guy Ménard as part of the celebrations of the twenty-fifth anniversary of the Stonewall Riots which began the gay liberation movement; I am grateful to Dignity for financing my trip. I was also honoured by the invitation to preach in Newark Cathedral as part of the same commemorations. The Britain and Ireland

School of Feminist Theology invited me to speak at their summer school in July 1994. I was very grateful for the insights that the participants provided me into the nature of passion and to be able to share the platform with Rosemary Radford Ruether, Elaine Graham and Sheena Barnes. I am a trustee of the Institute for the Study of Christianity and Sexuality and (with Alison Webster) edit its journal. I am grateful for all the ISCS gives to those of us dealing with the difficult issues of theology and sexuality. I am also grateful to the Revd Dr Jeffrey John for offering such an incisive critique of the theology of friendship from a gay perspective. We disagree on much but we end up in much the same place. The gay historian John Boswell died tragically early while this book was in production. I want to salute his memory.

By the time this book is published I will have left my present post at the College of St Mark and St John, Plymouth, and I would like to record my gratitude to my colleagues and students for all their extraordinary support over the last eight years. It has been a pleasure to share an interest in theology and sexuality with Professor Adrian Thatcher and to be able to teach postgraduate courses on the subject with him. I am particularly grateful to my third-year undergraduates and postgraduate students for the discussions we have had on the issues dealt with in this book.

Thanks also to Penny Cassell for allowing me to use her home as a London base and to Jane Robson for reading and commenting on everything I write. The friendship of Guy Denman and Kevin Houlton meant a great deal to me during the time I was writing this book. It has been a pleasure to work with Judith Longman once again.

To quote Socrates, I am blessed with 'a passion for friends' and friends worthy of passion.

God the Father wanted order. So he invented heterosexuality, monogamy, and the family.
(Michèle Roberts, *The Book of Mrs Noah* (London: Minerva, 1987), p. 66)

There is nothing in the world
Like talking sex with God
(Thomas O'Neil, 'Sex with God', *Sex with God* (New York: Wexford Press, 1994), p. 1)

Faithful friends are a sturdy shelter;
whoever finds one has found a treasure.
Faithful friends are beyond price;
no amount can balance their worth.
Faithful friends are life-saving medicine;
and those who fear the Lord will find them.
Those who fear the Lord direct their friendship aright,
for as they are, so are their neighbours also.
(Sirach 6.14–17)

Keep your passion alive—
it will warm you when the
world around you grows cold.
It will not allow comfortable
familiarity to rob you of that
special glow that comes with
loving deeply. It can lift
you over stone walls of anger
and carry you across vast
deserts of alienation. But its
greatest gift is that of touch—
for passion cannot dwell in
solitude—it thrives best in
loving embrace. So keep your
passion alive—hold one
another as a tree holds the
Earth and your love will
bear the fruit of many,
many seasons!
(Atimah, 'Passion' in Becky Butler, *Ceremonies of the Heart: Celebrating Lesbian Unions* (Washington: Seal Press, 1990), p. 287)

Preface

The American psychologist M. Scott Peck has defined mental health as 'an ongoing process of dedication to reality at all costs'.[1] The Christian Churches do not have a very good record of dedication to the reality of sexuality and relationships and this has had a disastrous effect upon the mental health of thousands of men and women. Among these victims have been lesbian, gay and bisexual people. However, a growing number of gay, lesbian and bisexual Christians, influenced by liberation movements within and outside of the Church, are now refusing to be victims; we are claiming our place in the Church and finding a voice in theological and ecclesiastical discourse. We believe we can detect the traces of God in our own experience and we want to offer it to the Church in order to help it develop a mentally (and physically) healthy theology of sexuality. This book is written in such a spirit. I know that some people may interpret this book as an attack on marriage and heterosexuality. But to do so would be wrong. I am the product of a marriage still going strong after fifty years. I know that heterosexual relationships in general and marriage in particular can be beautiful relationships in which both partners grow, heal and flourish in the warmth of each other's enduring love; but I also know that marriage as an institution is in crisis. What I suggest in this book is that lesbian and gay people may have some important insights to contribute to creative theological reflection upon that crisis—most notably in the expansion of the understanding of friendship to include our most intimate and committed relationships. Feminist theology and philosophy, especially in the persons of Mary Hunt and Janice Raymond, has reclaimed friendship, particularly women's experience of friendship, as the central relationship on which to build a theological and ethical system. My concern is different from theirs in as much as I want to demonstrate what a noble history such an idea has in the Christian tradition, and I want to discuss what effect adopting such a model would have on our understanding of 'sexual' relationships.

As will become obvious some people are deeply uncomfortable with making the concept of friendship central to a Christian understanding of sexuality and relationships. There are several reasons for this. Some Christians are worried that there is no precedent in scripture or tradition for replacing marriage with friendship as the central model of sexual relating. One of my chief purposes in this book is to prove that this is not so. There is a con_nuous thread of sexual subversion that runs throughout the Hebrew scriptures, like an underground stream that bursts to the surface in the Christian gospels, sweeping away dominant models of relating and replacing them with models based upon friendship. This is not to say, of course, that marriage was abolished but its centre of gravity should have been transformed from hierarchy to mutuality and should have ceased to be the sole bond of passion.

The second reason why some people react so strongly against a theology of sexuality based on friendship is that we all struggle with an unconscious fear of equality and mutuality in our relationships. I shall argue later in the book that we are socialized into believing that the very nature of relationship, particularly sexual relationship, involves domination and submission, although these days some of us go to great lengths to disguise these dynamics with the language of equality. The concept of friendship strikes at the heart of this assumption and leaves us foundering, for we have to take responsibility for learning to treat our lovers with justice and mutuality, with no clearly defined role patterns to fall into. It is easier not to be friends.

This leads to the third difficulty with a theology of friendship, the problem of boundaries. We may have many friends; does the theology of friendship mean that all these people become potential sexual partners? Does defining my primary relationship in terms of friendship erect a sufficiently strong boundary around it to allow it to grow unthreatened? I shall argue that it is in its soft boundaries that the real strength of friendship lies. It involves the acknowledgement that our sexuality and passion are operative in all our friendly relationships and therefore liberates sexuality from the privatized realm of the couple to take its place at the heart of all relationality as a force for social as well as personal transformation. We seek to achieve in our most intimate relationships what we seek to achieve in our wider relating; they are part of the same process. It should also ensure that all relationships are judged by the same standards of justice. Violence and friendship are incompatible, whether that friendship is incarnate in marriage or in my relationship with my students. Sexual relationships are not privileged relationships in which injustice, violence and other forms of abuse are more tolerable than in other relationships.

The most important advantage of the theology of friendship is that it is inclusive—it can include within it lesbian and gay relationships, marriages, heterosexual cohabitation and the experience of single and celibate people. We can all have friends, and all friendships are embodied and expressions of our passion. It enables Christianity to face up to the reality of people's diverse and complex experience of relationships, something Christian theology is unable to do whilst it clings to the idealization of marriage. This is not to argue, however, that 'anything goes', that all friendships or indeed more than one friendship can involve 'sexual activity'. What constitutes 'sexual activity' is an extremely difficult question and, contrary to much Christian thinking, sexual activity, whether that be a hug, a kiss, or penetrative intercourse, does not have a universal meaning: the meaning is only incarnated in the context. In the theology of friendship sexual 'acts' are not the central concern, justice and mutuality are the keys to right relationship. The theology of friendship demands that people take responsibility for all their friendships, that they learn to balance them and that emotional and physical intimacy is negotiated between friends in the context of the web of friendships that surrounds and sustains them, and in the context of structural sin. We are broken-hearted, vulnerable people which means, I shall argue, that in order to achieve the radical, passionate vulnerability which is the yearning of all friendship we have to concentrate our attention and commitment and create a safe environment in which it can grow and flourish. But I shall argue that to take these relationships and claim them to be something ontologically different to friendship as a whole is a huge mistake. The model of friendship therefore demands that people act justly, that they think seriously about their relationships and that personal desire is always tempered by an acknowledgement of responsibility to others, whilst recognizing that just relationships based upon mutuality which overflow with love are not confined to heterosexual marriage.

This is not a book about whether Christians should accept and affirm lesbian, gay and bisexual people and their relationships. Many, perhaps too many, books have been written on that subject. The debate still goes on. Indeed, it is part of my argument that the debate will be self-perpetuating and perhaps forever deadlocked because as Christians we are still not sure about whether sex and passion are inherently evil or not. Despite the lip service we all pay these days to the goodness of the body, Augustine's voice still whispers in our ear. This book starts from the assumption that lesbian and gay people are not 'disordered' or 'handicapped' by virtue of their sexuality, nor are their relationships inherently wrong. In starting from this position I am not seeking to pretend that the Christian debate about homosexuality is already resolved or that it does not matter. I will continue to participate in that debate. But those of us whose lives are the subject of such debate cannot put them on hold whilst it runs its course. We have wrestled with the issues and we have to live our lives according to our formed consciences. You could, if you so desired, regard this as a 'what

if?' book. What if lesbian and gay people and their relationships
are equal in the sight of God to heterosexual people—what
might heterosexual people learn from them? I, like thousands
of other Christians, do not believe the 'what if?' is necessary: for
us the question is resolved, but I acknowledge, as I believe every
Christian theologian should, that I am not infallible; in the end I
may be wrong. The current state of official church debate on
homosexuality is generally stalemate. Apart from the Roman
Catholic Church and a number of fundamentalist Churches,
most Churches in Europe and North America have adopted a
de facto moratorium on official pronouncements on issues of
sexuality. A number of Churches have commissioned reports
on sexuality which have followed a general pattern of acknowledging legitimate Christian differences on issues like homosexuality, but in the end they recommend or merely suggest
that the Church should 'affirm grace against law . . . take risks of
acceptance rather than those of rejection . . . seek for humility
rather than a righteousness tending towards self-righteous-
ness'.[2] However, it has proved virtually impossible for such
reports to be adopted as official policy of the Church concerned, and amidst some extremely violent debate the reports
have often been referred to local congregations for study.
These attempts to encourage the widest possible debate and
to reach a consensus are honourable (although perhaps not
realistic), but in the meantime lesbian and gay people are
expected to exist in some kind of limbo, waiting for others to
make up their minds about us. This book will not explore in
any depth the various official church statements on homosexuality. Others have undertaken this task.[3] My concern is
different.

I have no doubt that the World Council of Churches' report
on sexuality is right that 'the fact that the churches are so greatly
exercised on the subject suggests that God is calling us to
rethink it',[4] but if we really do believe that human beings are
made in the image and likeness of God then when we seek to
do theology around certain people's lives our first duty is to
go to them and listen to the way that they make sense of the

experience of God in their lives. It is not simply a matter of receiving evidence from them, as some church bodies have begun to do in connection with homosexuality. It is about giving priority to their theology as the people who know most about the subject and have to live it every moment of their lives. In a case of right idea, wrong order, the United Reformed Church in Britain, after having commissioned two reports on homosexuality which fundamentally contradicted each other, recently invited the United Reformed Caucus of the Lesbian and Gay Christian Movement to compile its own report. In this book I seek to offer a theology of sexuality based upon lesbian and gay experience, to start in a different place to all church documents on sexuality, and most other works on the subject. Perhaps in lesbian and gay experience we can find a new model of understanding sexuality that will catch the theological imagination of many in the Churches, speak to their experience and break the impasse at least at a local level.

In this book I criticize the Church for idealizing/idolizing marriage and I have tried not to fall into the trap of idealizing lesbian and gay relationships, as I think some lesbian and gay theologians have done as an understandable reaction against the dismissal and degradation of our relationships which we have to live with daily.

James Nelson has said that 'as never before we need gracious theologies' of sexuality,[5] by which he means theologies of sexuality which begin with genuine belief in the goodness of bodies, passion and sexuality in themselves, rather than 'works-justification' theologies which justify the existence and enjoyment of these things only if they produce children or some other 'goods'. This book attempts to do such a theology. One of its most important arguments is that we should not isolate or confine our passion to one area or activity of our lives but recognize its existence in everything we do. We need to find an overarching ethic that does not separate out our 'sexual' relationships from others but demands the same standards of behaviour in all our encounters. In chapter 1 I set out the theological basis of the book. In chapter 2 I explore different understandings of friendship, with particular attention to lesbian and gay experience of friendship. The tradition of passionate friendship between members of the same sex is examined to demonstrate how recent and how false the distinctions between friendship and 'sexual' relationships are. In chapter 3 I begin to ask questions about the meaning of so-called 'sexual' acts. In chapters 4 and 5 I examine the Church's idealization and idolization of marriage and argue that the traditions in which the Church roots itself contain the seeds of subversion of this idol, potentially able to replace it with an all-embracing model of friendship which includes all relationships. In chapters 6 and 7 I begin to explore the ethical implications of developing a theology of relationships on the basis of friendship. The implications of living in a relational system of structural sin are discussed. I set out an agenda for the Church at the close of chapter 7. The last chapter consists of a short discussion on the metaphor of God as friend.

In what I consider to be one of the most beautiful pieces of theology written in the last thirty years, the lesbian feminist theologian Carter Heyward manages to express the connections that exist between all our relationships because the same passion flows beneath them all, although it may be expressed in a variety of different ways. She expresses what I hope this book is about:

> To say I love you is to say that you are not mine, but rather your own. To love you is to advocate your rights, your space, your self, and to struggle with you, rather than against you, in our learning to claim our power in the world.
>
> To love you is to make love to you, and with you, whether in an exchange of glances heavy with existence, in the passing of a peace we mean, in our common work or play, in our struggle for social justice, or in the ecstasy and tenderness of intimate embrace that we believe is just and right for us—and for others in the world.
>
> To love you is to be pushed by a power/God both terrifying and comforting, to touch and be touched by you ... To love you

is to sing with you, cry with you, pray with you, and act with you to re-create the world.

To say 'I love you' means—*let the revolution begin!*[6]

Elizabeth Stuart
Plymouth
September 1994

Notes

1 M. Scott Peck, *The Road Less Travelled* (London: Arrow, 1990), p. 52.
2 *Homosexuality: A Christian View* (London: United Reformed Church, 1991), p. 6.
3 For an overview and analysis of various Church pronouncements and reports on homosexuality, see Denise and John Carmody, 'Homosexuality and Roman Catholicism', and Marvin M. Ellison, 'Homosexuality and Protestantism' in Arlene Swidler, *Homosexuality and World Religions* (Valley Forge: Trinity Press International, 1993), pp. 135–80 for a North American angle. For a British perspective see Peter Coleman, *Gay Christians: A Moral Dilemma* (London: SCM, 1989).
4 Robin Smith, *Living in Covenant with God and One Another* (Geneva: World Council of Churches, 1990), p. 3.
5 James Nelson, *Body Theology* (Louisville: Westminster/John Knox Press, 1992), p. 70.
6 Carter Heyward, *Our Passion for Justice: Images of Power, Sexuality and Liberation* (New York: The Pilgrim Press, 1984), p. 93.

1   Weaving theology

This book is going to offer a theology about sexuality starting from the experience of lesbian and gay people. In the last fifty years a great deal has been written about homosexuality and Christianity. By far the vast majority has been written by people who would describe themselves as heterosexual and they have also usually been men. Homosexuality has been treated as a problem within the domain of Christian sexual ethics. Those of us who are lesbian, gay or bisexual have sat on the sidelines watching scholars tackling each other for the ball of our lives. When the fundamentalist gets hold of it he kicks it into the goal marked 'perversion deliberately chosen, explicitly condemned by God's word, get cured or get out of the Church'. When the conservative gets hold of it he kicks it into the goal marked 'not deliberately chosen, probably born that way, but activity still condemned by God's word—it is OK to be it, not OK to engage in genital acts'. The angst-ridden liberal kicks the ball back and forwards, up and down the pitch; finally he stands in the middle and declares that, whereas scripture and tradition undoubtedly condemn homosexual acts, they did not know as much about homosexuality as we do today; so although the Church has a duty to uphold the ideal of heterosexual marriage, because that is what scripture and tradition do, homosexual relationships might be looked upon as falling short of this ideal but not sinful as such because they can't help it. He then scuttles off the pitch before the crowd and players can get him. The radical bounces the ball up and down on his head, doing amazing tricks whilst he explains: 'Yes, marriage is the ideal, but lesbian and gay people are perfectly capable of marriage.' He has read his feminist theology, he knows all about the patriarchal context of the scriptures and Christian history and how the worst thing patriarchy can imagine is a man playing 'the role of a woman' in sex. He knows lesbian and gay people, he knows they are as capable of forming committed stable relationships as any heterosexual couple. What is the difference between them and straight couples who cannot have children? 'They are just like us, so let's welcome them into the institution of marriage.' He awaits the adoration of the crowd but the only sounds are of splatters of rage coming out of the fundamentalist and the conservative, and the anxious perspiring of the liberal in the changing-room. The radical cannot understand it: he is hurt, he has risked his reputation, even his career, to speak out for lesbian sisters and gay brothers. He turns to the crowd: 'What *do* you want then?' he shouts in exasperation. And with one voice the answer booms: 'Can we have our ball back please?' We are tired of other Christian people kicking around the ball of our lives. We are tired of being treated as a 'problem' reduced to a small part of the Christian ethics curriculum. Lesbian and gay people are the latest in a now fairly long line of people claiming the right to do theology for themselves about themselves.

In the 1960s, Latin American Catholics began to wake up to and draw attention to the fact that the theology which has been preached at them for hundreds of years was a theology constructed in Europe, and later North America, by white, celibate, comfortably off men. It had nothing to do with their daily fight against injustice, poverty and death, except in so far as it preached Jesus the passive lamb led to slaughter without opening his mouth, or Jesus the king, the man of power who legitimates the power of all rulers and therefore presented them with a model of living which exacerbated rather than eased their suffering. So they began to do theology from the basis of their own experience, and liberation theology was born. For those of us in the Roman Catholic tradition the Second Vatican Council promised to change everything about our Church. We were told that 'we are the Church', that the Church is the pilgrim people of God journeying towards the truth, not the kingdom of static perfection it had previously claimed it was, and that the laity were as much part of the Church as the Pope. Indeed one of the Council documents said of the laity:

> To the latter [their pastors] the laity should disclose their needs and desires with that liberty and confidence which befits children of God and brothers of Christ. By reason of the knowledge, competence or pre-eminence which they have the laity are empowered—indeed sometimes obliged—to manifest their opinion on those things which pertain to the good of the Church.[1]

I sometimes think that some members of the Vatican hierarchy must regret that such positive things about the laity were ever said because some of us took it seriously and have been the bane of their lives ever since. Black theology, Asian theology, feminist theology, womanist theology (black feminist theology) all emerged in the 1960s and 1970s. People about whom the Churches had spoken, and done theology about or for, began to do it for themselves.

Now at last lesbian women and gay men have begun to do theology for themselves, most of them in the USA.[2] This book will draw upon the work already done by lesbians and gay men and add some insights of its own. It is written first because I believe lesbian, gay and bisexual people have a right to have their voices heard. If anyone is an expert on the subject of homosexuality they are. Second, I believe that lesbian, gay and bisexual people may have a great deal to teach the Church on this issue; indeed they may have a model for understanding sexuality that could offer healing, liberation, justice and inclusion to all in the Churches and beyond, where up until now there has often only been pain, anger, confusion and exclusion. The French gay philosopher Foucault argued that wherever there was a dominant discourse there would be a reverse discourse. These reverse discourses use the assumptions of the prevailing discourse to argue against a conclusion from the dominant discourse. This is the way of all liberal and much radical theory and theology. A perfect example of this is the ordination of women to the priesthood in the Anglican Communion. The dominant discourse argued along the lines that since a priest is an icon of Christ and Christ was male, women cannot be priests. Opponents of this view spent a great deal of time arguing that women could represent Christ and therefore could be priests. Very few people thought to question the basic assumption that priesthood is a good and necessary function in the Church; very few voices were heard suggesting that the whole concept of a priestly caste might be patriarchal. Some suggested that the ordination of women would herald the end of the clerical caste, but there is little evidence of this happening in Churches where women have been ordained for many years. Apparently when Captain Cook arrived at a certain island in the course of his travels he discovered that the indigenous people, whilst able to relate to him and his sailors, literally could not see the ship these had arrived in because they had no intellectual model of a ship such as Cook's. Stories like this remind us that human beings construct reality and that this is a process of constant change. As Vincent Scully has said, 'Human beings see selectively, not empirically. They see what the conceptual structure of their culture permits them to see, and they only see new things when their existing cultural model is broken.'[3] In 1977 the British theologian Dennis Nineham, commenting on the demythologizing movement that was sweeping through Western theology, noted that 'it is at the level of the *imagination* that contemporary Christianity is most weak. Men find it hard to believe in God because they do not have available to them any lively imaginative picture of the way a God and the world as they know it are related.'[4] Since then, of course, feminist theologians, theologians of ecology and others have provided very many imaginative models which have been largely ignored by the theological establishment, which if it is looking for anything at all, is looking for 'some *doctor angelicus*—or should we rather say some prophet?'[5] (a man of course) and can't see what is under their noses. Jim Cotter has noted:

> The person who cannot walk in familiar territory is compelled to live elsewhere, searching, raising questions, learning new languages. All this is vital to the well-being of those back home, however unwelcome and disturbing travellers' tales may be.[6]

The space of the marginalized is often a space where imagination can flourish outside the restricting dictates of the mainstream. Raymond Williams recognized that it is only those whose voices have been drowned out by the dominant culture who will have the motivation to develop a new language, new symbols, new discourses. The very narrowness of the dominant culture and its discourses leaves plenty of space for such work to be done.[7] There people have to make sense of their own reality and on the issue of sexuality, lesbians, gay men and bisexuals have been doing just that. Lesbian, gay and bisexual people are producing imaginative new models to understand sexuality and where God is in it. They are the prophets and the 'angelic doctors' who might be able to help us make a leap of imagination beyond the dominant discourse and beyond the reverse discourse to understand not only what God is up to in sexuality but what God is up to on a much larger scale.

Where do we begin? ① Problems with theology

There is an old joke about a tourist in Ireland who gets lost and approaches a local to ask directions for Dublin. 'Well', says the local, 'if I were going to Dublin I sure wouldn't start from here.' I believe that most Christian attempts to think about sexuality have started in the wrong place and hence got hopelessly lost or stuck in cul-de-sacs. As James Nelson has noted: 'A theology of (or about) sexuality tends to argue in a one-directional way: What do scripture and tradition say about our sexuality and how it ought to be expressed? What does the church say, what do the rabbis say, what does the pope say?'[8]

Starting with scripture and tradition may seem perfectly

logical and this is exactly the starting-point for fundamentalists, conservatives and liberals. We then witness an unholy tussle with the texts as each group seeks to claim them as their own, each regarding the scriptures as the primary source of Christian authority. In order for such a tussle to take place with the passion and sincerity it almost always has, the participants have to avoid certain uncomfortable facts or questions. So it is rare to find those engaged in seeking to do theology around sexuality acknowledging the extent to which the reader of the text, any text, brings to that text a hermeneutical agenda which affects even the most apparently scientific exegesis. There is no neutral, objective approach to the scriptures, which is why two people can extract diametrically opposed interpretations from one text. It is even rarer to find a willingness to question the status of the writings which have been labelled Scripture.

> He plants a cedar and the rain nourishes it. Then it can be used as fuel. Part of it he takes and warms himself; he kindles a fire and bakes bread. Then he makes a god and worships it, makes it a carved image and bows down before it ... He feeds on ashes; a deluded mind has led him astray, and he cannot save himself or say, 'Is not this thing in my right hand a fraud?'
>
> (Isaiah 44.14–15, 20)

Most of the Hebrew prophets railed against idolatry because the people of Israel seemed to have a disposition to succumb to it, despite its complete illogicality, to which Isaiah draws attention. Christians have made an idol out of the Bible. Like the deluded and blind idol-makers of Isaiah we have forgotten the process that went into the forming of the canon of scripture. From a wide variety of writings some were selected and some rejected, often after heated argument and indecisiveness. We easily forget that the Hebrew canon was not fixed until the first century CE and that even then Hellenistic and Palestinian Jews followed a different canon, a pattern that replicates itself today among Reformed Churches on the one hand and the Roman and Orthodox Churches on the other. We also forget that it was not until 382 CE that a council set the canon of the Christian scriptures. Yet the Bible itself cautions us against making an idol of it. It is an anarchic collection which makes no claim for itself, in which different theologies and versions of events sit next to one another without embarrassment, where echoes of polytheism seep through the ideological monotheism, and the rock face of patriarchy is broken by obscure hints of other woman-centred traditions. The New Testament books, particularly the epistles, offend the modern reader by being unashamedly addressed to someone else. They also remind us of the fact that the early community of faith was not a monolithic structure of belief enjoying perfect unity and agreement but a constellation of communities with different structures and beliefs. For example, Dennis Smith and Hal Taussig have shown how in the early Church different communities celebrated the Eucharist in very different ways and gave it different meanings to reflect the radical impact of the Christ-event on those particular communities, and that these meanings are reflected in the various accounts of the Last Supper.[9] It is also important to remind ourselves that the formation of a canon was an essential part of the fight to define orthodoxy, to distinguish between right and wrong belief. The canon, like most of the creeds, Church councils, the office of bishop and the primacy of Rome, developed in a search for a system of authority to resolve conflict. In conflict there are winners and losers. Now the Church has traditionally taken an optimistic, evolutionary view of history, believing that the Holy Spirit has guided her actions, so all the winners have been spirit-led and all the losers deluded and deceived. There is something decidedly incongruous about a community which focuses itself on a person who stood with the outcast, the disenfranchised, the marginalized, and died at the hands of the powerful majority, taking this view of Church history. The miracle of the modern ecumenical movement was that Churches created out of division, which had for hundreds of years labelled each other heretical or schismatic and sometimes claimed the authority of Holy Spirit for themselves alone, began to reconsider and recognize the presence of the Spirit in their former adversaries.

Objections to the ecumenical movement were always grounded in fear of where it might lead, fear of losing any sense of authority or certainty. If yesterday's heretic is today my friend and has something to teach me, what about all the other heretics down the ages? Where will it end?

In the gospels of Luke and John Jesus promises his followers that he will not leave them desolate but will send the Holy Spirit/Paraclete to them to enable them to continue the work that he began. In both gospels it is clear that this is the same Spirit of God that has been incarnate in Jesus. Indeed in John Jesus literally exhales the Spirit into his friends (20.22). It is easy to miss a similar episode in Mark's crucifixion narrative: 'Then Jesus gave a loud cry and breathed his last. And the curtain of the temple was torn in two, from top to bottom' (15.37–38). Christopher Burdon has pointed out that the Greek word translated here as 'breathed his last', *exepneusen*, literally means 'the spirit went out':

> Perhaps Mark intends us to see in this not only the human death of Jesus but also the release of the Spirit that had descended on him at the Jordan; from Golgotha it goes out into all the world. It is released from his body, and it is released from that counterpart of his body, the Temple, which had claimed to enclose the holy presence of God. [10]

The incarnation continues not in a book, not in one person, not even a select group of followers (neither Luke nor John limits the transfer of the Spirit to the twelve) but in a community of people whose only common experience was that of having been changed in some way by the person of Jesus of Nazareth. Luke gives us a two-volume work to emphasize the point that the incarnation goes on. He draws close parallels between the early Christians' ministry and that of Jesus. Both Luke and John are also clear that there is no particular advantage in having known the human Jesus: the Spirit is poured out on all those who are changed by him after his death. But what happens when the community begins to disagree within itself? The first major case study Christian history presents us with is the Gentile question. Even though the accounts of this saga presented to us by Luke and Paul are written with hindsight, and obscure to a greater and lesser extent respectively the anguish and friction caused by this question, we might usefully draw upon it, for the earliest Church had no canon of scripture, no highly developed creeds or system of hierarchy. In that sense they were in the same position as those of us today who can no longer accept on trust that the 'good guys' of the past were always the ones that won. Luke's attempt to convince us that the matter was settled amicably by a council at Jerusalem and that Peter had already accepted the truth anyway is unfortunately blown apart by Paul's own writings which reveal constant tension and argument between those who accepted his views and those who stood with Peter and James. He does not demonstrate any confidence that the issue has been dealt with and resolved. He had to argue his corner to the end of his days. There were no mechanisms of authority in place to make decisions on these matters. Paul won in the end but it was a victory not won on argument but on experience, and it was a victory that could only be hailed with hindsight. The authors of Deuteronomy faced a very similar problem: How do you distinguish between true and false prophets? Their answer is as frustrating as it is wise: 'You may say to yourself, "How can we recognise a word that the Lord has not spoken?" If a prophet speaks in the name of the Lord but the thing does not take place or prove true, it is a word that the Lord has not spoken' (Deuteronomy 18.21–22).

The message is 'wait and see', and note that no time limit is given on that. This is effectively what the early Church had to do on the Gentile question—wait and see—whilst different factions lived by the vision which they believed to be true and held each other in a fragile sort of communion. Paul and the Gentile mission succeeded whilst the Jewish mission did not and eventually the question mark faded in the face of reality. In the earliest days of the Church when Christians constituted a weak minority, grounded only in a common experience of transformation through the person of Jesus of Nazareth whose mission was now entrusted to them, community, unity, friendship with one another seems to have been the most important consideration. Even though they found themselves living with what I call 'the tension of the ascension'—the tension caused by being left no blueprint, no authority structure, just a small amount of teaching, a brief life history and themselves—they mattered to one another, did not give up on one another, because the Spirit was among them. They clung together in a fragile sort of communion, trusting that the truth would emerge in due time. The eschatological vision of the early community was crucial in this regard. The absolute truth was not something expected to be revealed in the present, it was for the future.

M. Scott Peck, in his study of the way communities develop, notes that in the process of becoming a community and maintaining community most groups go through a stage of chaos when conflict emerges.[11] There are two ways out of this situation; one is to escape into organization. Organizations are hierarchical with firm boundaries and define themselves in terms of those they exclude; conformity is all. The alternative to organization is emptiness, a period when people commit themselves to one another despite being in disagreement, listen to one another and let go of some of their expectations and preconceptions. It seems that the early Church managed to move from chaos into emptiness over the Gentile question but in subsequent periods of chaos fell into organization. One might say that the tortuous efforts of the House of Bishops of the Church of England to keep opponents and supporters of the ordination of women together in one Church are made in the spirit of true community and should be applauded for that. The problem is that they are trying to create community in a structure which is already organizational. Community is based upon consensus, realism, soft boundaries and celebration of diversity.

The point to grasp is that when they faced the Gentile question all the early Christians had were each other, their shared experience of being transformed through an encounter with Christ and their conviction that the Spirit was among them somewhere. Each faction believed that their approach to the question was inspired by the Spirit, and they fought for it, drawing upon the tradition of their ancestors in the faith as well as their own experience. They did not succumb—or rather no one let them succumb—to the temptation of making idols out of themselves and claiming unique authority. Poor Paul, who certainly felt he ought to have the respect at least of the communities he had founded, was constantly disappointed! And Peter and James undoubtedly expected Paul to defer to their position as friends of the living Jesus. Nobody was obliging anybody else.

As soon as parts of the Church slipped into organization and became obsessed with orthodoxy and creating standards and structures to judge and maintain orthodoxy (however urgent and necessary this may have been perceived to be), they at least partially lost themselves. The fruits they bore testify to this fact. They often became a gross parody of the saviour they proclaimed. Reform movements sprang up with regularity but none recalled the Church back to before the development of all its systems of authority. Perhaps the time is ripe to attempt such a project now. For those of us who cannot buy into the package of fundamentalism, who have been schooled in the science of biblical criticism and taught the hermeneutic of suspicion from liberation and feminist theologians, need a new place to do theology. We cannot start with blind faith in the winners of past struggles or white, Western, male prelates. We simply cannot see, as Pope John Paul II evidently can, that the 'splendour of truth' shines out of an obvious and absolute natural law which the Church is charged to guard.[12] We have to start somewhere else.

We start with ourselves. Returning to the accounts of the giving of the Spirit in Luke and John we notice that this took place in both cases when the disciples were gathered together. In John, Jesus appears 'among them' and breathes the Spirit into them. Luke associates the giving of the Spirit with the Feast of Pentecost, the Feast of Weeks which celebrated the grain harvest and the giving of the promised land. It is interesting, however, that by the second century CE the content of the feast had changed and it became a celebration of the giving of the law on Sinai. It is unclear whether this change had happened by the time Luke wrote Acts, but it is significant that on the day the Jews celebrate the giving of law, some of it written by Yahweh on tablets of stone from the midst of fire (Deuteronomy 5), Christians are supposed to celebrate the coming of the Spirit of God among people. It is in the midst of people, finite frail creatures, that the Spirit dwells, between them. So when we begin to do theology, we must start with our own experience because it is in our interaction with life around us that revelation occurs. But this does not mean that my individual experience is the truth. It is in the sharing of experience with others and the subjection of my experience to analysis and question by others, using the tools of many different types of knowledge like sociology, psychology, history and so on, and in the meeting and conversation between my experience and your experience, that new understandings emerge. The lesbian feminist theologian Carter Heyward points out the word 'authority' comes from the Latin verb *augere*, which means 'to cause to grow', 'to augment that which already is'. It is not a possession but a dynamic power, the power of God's presence.[13] This is the power represented by Jesus' gentle breath in John, and wind and fire in Luke; it is the power that is felt when a group of people find connections between their stories which make sense of their experience. Mary Grey calls this process a 'new awareness' or 'dawning of a different consciousness',[14] and it will be familiar to anyone who has been part of a consciousness-raising group or taken part in the method of doing theology used in Christian base communities. I think the metaphors of spinning and weaving are helpful here. We take our own experience, share it, analyse it and spin it into threads of knowledge which can be woven with the threads of others. We cannot know whether a pattern will emerge. If it does, we may claim it as a moment of revelation, a pattern, a map, a trace of the divine.

But what if the pattern that emerges from one group does not match the pattern of another, so when put together they clash, with no continuity, no relationship between the two? Here we need to remind ourselves of how the early Church dealt with the Gentile question. Two tapestries emerged there with distinctive and clashing patterns. They could not unpick or burn each other's tapestries. They held them together and each lived by their own pattern, fully aware that it was not in anybody's power to choose between the two. That would happen in good time. I always think that Christian debate on issues like sexuality might be much more constructive if both sides began every book, every speech, every conversation by acknowledging that they might be wrong. We can only weave what we find, but we might be weaving a false trail—our neighbour may be right. This is why we must always be prepared to listen to our neighbour and why we have a duty to scrutinize our neighbour's tapestry and speak out if we are convinced that it will lead not to a God of justice but down a road of injustice. We are not God. The incarnation of God may continue among us, but it is always greater than us. We might also take a lesson from the author of Mark's gospel. Mark's Jesus is a wild person who streaks through the gospel leaving chaos in his wake. He is uncatchable: he cannot be pinned down, he is always ahead. We have an unhappy urge to pin God, Christ, the Spirit down. When I look at a crucifix I am always reminded of what the Victorians did to butterflies. They caught them, killed them and pinned them to bits of wood. The resurrection, whatever else it is, is a message that you cannot do that to God. As Luce Irigaray has put it: 'Paralysis was never his rhythm.'[15] God cannot be pinned down. And yet we desperately want to do this. We want the security of knowing where God is. We want a comforter, a teddy bear who is always there, something to cling to in times of stress. But this is not the God revealed in Christ. As R. S. Thomas has put it: 'He is such a fast God, always before us and leaving as we arrive ...'[16] 'Do not cling to me', John's Jesus tells Mary (20.17). This God is not contained, not locked away in books or the past, but blows through our lives, always ahead of us, always summoning us to follow. Nor does she dance in a straight line. She takes us backwards, forwards, sideways, she spirals and encircles. When we weave our webs of theology we are not weaving shrouds to wrap the dead body of God in, nor are we capturing her, sewing her into the patterns we create. In a very real sense we are weaving the tracks of a God who has already moved on, the trails of the trail-blazer. So all our theology is partial, transitional and at best but a shadow of the truth.

Weaving with the ancestors

G. K. Chesterton once said of Catholics that they 'give votes to the most obscure of all classes, our ancestors'. Beginning with ourselves does not mean that we abandon the Bible or tradition. It is simply that we refuse to make idols of them. We refuse to lock God into them. In recent years Christian feminism has challenged us all with the patriarchal nature of so much of the scripture and how that scripture has been used to humiliate, oppress and enslave women. The exposure of these 'texts of terror', to use Phyllis Trible's phrase, has done more than anything else to knock this particular idol off its pedestal. The past is where we have come from. It has formed and shaped us; we are its children. We ignore it at our peril, for those who do not learn from the mistakes of the past are destined to repeat them. We also believe, of course, that the Spirit has been blowing through history for thousands of years, inspiring the spinning and weaving of tapestries of theology. These past patterns can help us make sense of our own, can challenge us to question the patterns we create. In other words a secondary mode of revelation is created. Revelation occurs between persons, but it can also occur when those persons, having taken their experience and analysed it using tools available to them, then take it to the past, take it to their ancestors for their comments and wisdom. This is about entering into a relationship with the past, not treating the past as an infallible parent but as a friend. The gay theologian Gary David Comstock describes the dynamics of this relationship in relation to the Bible:

> Instead of making the Bible into a parental authority, I have begun to engage it as I would a friend—as one to whom I have made a commitment and in whom I have invested dearly, but with whom I insist on a mutual exchange of critique, encouragement, support, and challenge ... Although its homophobic statements sting and condemn me, I counter that those statements are themselves condemned by its own Exodus and Jesus events. Just as I have said to my friends, 'How can you express love and be a justice-seeking person and not work to overcome the oppression of lesbians and gay men?' In my dialogue with the Bible I ask, 'How can you be based on two events that are about transforming pain, suffering, and death into life, liberation, and healing, and yet call for the misery and death of lesbians and gay men?'[17]

The Bible is above all else a collection of works which testify to different groups' experience of God over a very long time. There are parts which we will struggle with and ultimately reject, and parts we will welcome. The same holds true for tradition. Nor do we have to confine ourselves to the winners of the past, although on the whole it is the winners whose tapestries are preserved. It is possible to pick up perhaps dim echoes of other tapestries or to stumble across long-forgotten tapestries whose designs make sense of your own or are so different that they challenge your skill. There are undoubtedly many who would like to raid their ancestors' store cupboard and hold fast to their tapestries. They prefer a religion dead, a Spirit pinned down like a butterfly. Anything to avoid having to take the risk of spinning and weaving for themselves. This is a particular temptation for those whose power has been validated by the past, yet 'he is God not of the dead, but of the living' (Matthew 22.32). We are forever the early Church, incarnating the mighty wind or the gentle breath of God, forever running to catch up with it, forever weaving theological meaning out of our experience. The thirteenth-century woman mystic Mechthild of Magdeburg knew of the delight and frustration of being the 'bride' of this fast 'beloved' God:

> I seek thee with all my might,
> Had I the power of a giant
> Thou wert quickly lost
> If I came upon Thy footprints.
> Ah! Love! Run not so far ahead
> But rest a little lovingly
> That I may catch thee up.[18]

As the prophet Habakkuk knew, those who read God's word know they have to run (2.2). There are also echoes of this experience of the divinity in other religious traditions:

> Spiderwoman is a Native American Goddess from a Hopi legend who is credited with the beginning of creation, since she wove woman and man. Spiderwoman was the first to create designs and to teach the Indian people how to weave. Every design she created had her spirit in it and every design contained a flaw so that her spirit could find its way out and be free.[19]

The myth of the Spiderwoman beautifully conveys what doing theology is all about. Theologians are spinsters and weavers. To be a believer is to be at least a spinster, to try and make sense of your personal experience, and given the opportunity believers are also weavers keen to bring their threads into relationship with those of others. The fact that the metaphor of spinster will jar with some readers because of the negative connotations this word has acquired in Western culture, draws attention to the fact that my understanding and method of doing theology emerge from my experience as a woman, and a woman who is proud to own the title of feminist.

Re-assertion of the Sophia in my the over the Logos stand.

*② *

Sophia the Spiderwoman

In her exploration of the theology of revelation, Mary Grey identifies two myths from part of the Christian tradition which offer radically different models of revelation: Logos and Sophia.[20] It is the Logos myth which has dominated Christian history. God sends his Logos, his Word, into the world to reveal what has been hidden from sinful human nature. As Grey points out, this myth has led to the identification of revelation with rationality, because *logos* also means reason, and (as men have identified themselves with the rational and women with the irrational) with maleness.

> Revelation has come to be identified with revealed truths, or rational propositions, whose authority is guaranteed by an external source, either the Bible, tradition, or the teaching magisterium of the Church ... revelation has often been thought to consist of 'timeless truths' ... When Word/Logos/Reason are made synonymous with 'order' and establishment, vast areas of human experience can be swept under the carpet.[21]

And those vast areas of human experience have included the experience of women in general, all non-white people and gay people. It is vital therefore to find a new myth, a new understanding of revelation that speaks authentically of the lives and understandings of these people. There are also other reasons why such a search is urgent. Like most feminists and ecologists, Grey is aware that the Logos myth has served to create and sustain a dualistic, patriarchal, competitive and profit-based ethic in the Western world which has brought the planet to the edge of global catastrophe and created a mindset in which exploitation and injustice can flourish. She suggests therefore that the time is ripe to re-member the Sophia myth.

Ask any student of the Bible how many creation stories there are in the Hebrew scriptures and they are most likely to reply 'two' and take you through the early chapters of Genesis distinguishing between two different accounts, one earlier than the other. In fact there are more than two creation accounts in the Hebrew scriptures:

> The LORD created me at the [or as] the beginning of his work,
>   the first of his acts of long ago.
> Ages ago I was set up,
>   at the first, before the beginning of the earth.
> When there were no depths I was brought forth,

when there were no springs abounding with water.
Before the mountains had been shaped,
  before the hills, I was brought forth—
  when he had not yet made earth and fields, or the world's first
    bits of soil.
When he established the heavens, I was there,
  when he drew a circle on the face of the deep,
  when he made the skies above,
  when he established the fountains of the deep,
  when he assigned to the sea its limit,
  so that the waters might not transgress his command,
  when he marked out the foundations of the earth,
  then I was beside him, like a master worker [or little child];
  and I was daily his delight, rejoicing before him always,
  rejoicing in his inhabited world and delighting in the human
    race.

(Proverbs 8.22–31)

The speaker is Hochma in Hebrew, Sophia in Greek: Wisdom.
A similar story is told in the book of Sirach:

'I came forth from the mouth of the Most High,
  and covered the earth like a mist...'
'Then the Creator of all things gave me a command,
  and my Creator chose the place for my tent.
He said, "Make your dwelling in Jacob,
  and in Israel receive your inheritance".'

(24.3, 8)

Wisdom literature seems to have begun to emerge in the
Jewish community during the post-exilic period, although
some of the traditions it draws upon are undoubtedly much
older. Israel shared this particular genre of writing with most of
its neighbours. The books of Proverbs, Job, Ecclesiastes in the
Hebrew canon, along with the books of Sirach and Wisdom of
Solomon in the Greek canon, are part of this tradition and there
are traces of it in other writings. Wisdom is always personified
as female. Notice how different the creation stories of Wisdom
literature are from the more well-known ones in Genesis.
There is no 'fall', no alienation between God and the human

race. Wisdom is the link between God and humanity, she inhabits both worlds and rejoices in both. In Proverbs 1 she appears at the city gates warning people of the consequences of ignoring her. In chapter 9 she invites all to a banquet with her. (Indeed, Proverbs portrays her in terms which at the very least suggest prostitution: she is a strong, alluring woman, hanging around on street corners calling and reaching out for those who pass by, scorning those who refuse.) The world-affirming spirit continues in the Wisdom of Solomon:

> ... God did not make death,
> and he does not delight in the death of the living.
> For he created all things so that they might exist;
> the generative forces [or the creatures] of the world are
> wholesome,
> and there is no destructive poison in them.
>
> (1.13–14)

Wisdom is portrayed as easily found, indeed 'she goes about seeking those worthy of her, and she graciously appears to them in their paths, and meets them in every thought' (6.16). She is immanent in creation: 'she pervades and penetrates all things' (7.24) and in every generation passes into holy souls making them 'friends of God' (7.27). She is 'a breath of the power of God' (7.25) and in the latter part of the book is identified with the presence of God moving through the history of Israel. Sophia is the presence of God immanent in creation, teaching those who seek her, she is the breath of God, the Spirit of God, journeying through creation, offering herself as food and drink to those who seek her.[22] Grey wants to reclaim the myth of Sophia as a myth which conveys the fact that revelation occurs in connectedness: it is in reconnecting with each other, with our past, with the forgotten voice of our tradition that revelation occurs; it is in listening to each other that the patterns of truth emerge. Carol Gilligan would argue that this is the way women work. They define themselves in relation to others, they are interested in interconnectedness and interdependence, whilst men have been taught to see these things as threatening.[23]

Others have also suggested that women spin and weave webs of meaning embracing paradox, whilst men tend to conceive of the world in terms of either/or.[24] It is therefore highly appropriate that Wisdom should be personified as female. It is interesting to observe what both Judaism and Christianity did with the Wisdom tradition. The dominant strand in Judaism identified Wisdom with the Torah, the law; Christianity first in Paul identified Wisdom with Jesus. In both cases the female dimension was lost and the understanding of Wisdom changed so that it conformed to the Logos myth.[25] Luke and John in particular employ Wisdom imagery in their story about Jesus; but remember that both of them, contrary to the way that they have been interpreted down the centuries, do not end the incarnation in Jesus: he releases the Spirit/Sophia back into the world.

Jesus and Sophia

Christianity centres itself on an incarnate God. Amazingly, the doctrine has survived despite hundreds of years of body-hating dominating Christianity. However, the doctrine has not survived unscathed. The association of the body and sex with sin and uncleanness led to the myth of the Virgin Birth and the cult of the submissive, obedient, Virgin Mother as the model of womanhood. It also reinforced the identification of God and the male: as Mary Daly so pithily put it, 'where God is male, the male is God'. Women found themselves placed in yet another relationship of dependency upon a man, this time Jesus their saviour. These problems and others have led feminist theologians to reconsider the whole notion of the incarnation. Some point to Jesus' radical attitude to women and argue that he deliberately subverted patriarchy, showing that strength lay in dispossession and vulnerability. But as Rita Nakashima Brock has pointed out, this understanding of Christ still presents

> a heroic Jesus who alone is able to achieve an empowering self-consciousness through a solitary, private relationship with God/ess. If Jesus is reported to have been capable of profound love and concern for others, he was first loved and respected by

the concrete persons of his life. If he was liberated, he was involved in a community of mutual liberation.[26]

It is this community of liberation, the community that nurtured and sustained Jesus, that becomes the basis of the vision of the *basileia* (kingdom) which Jesus proclaims. It is this community, rather than Jesus alone, who incarnates God's power, Christ. So the emphasis is taken off the uniqueness of Jesus and put upon the community of which he was part. This Christology complements the understanding of the Pentecost experience I developed earlier. We could either take the view that the embodiment of God began with Jesus and after Jesus' death continued in the community of Jesus' followers or, taking into account the Hochma/Sophia myth, we could argue that the Jesus story reminds us that Sophia 'pervades and penetrates all things', that God is and always has been incarnate. Meister Eckhart, the medieval theologian who was one of the 'losers' of history, being regarded as heretical, called Christ the 'Great Reminder'. Eckhart also linked the incarnation with Sophia: 'For this reason, therefore, has the Wisdom of God wanted to show our redemption by himself assuming flesh—in order that our instruction in divine, natural and moral matters would be remembered.'[27] And what is it that we have forgotten? That God's Spirit is a rapid river, unstoppable and uncontrollable, flowing into the souls of those who make space for it. It is the love which can fill every person as it filled Jesus. 'God becomes God where all creatures express God: There he becomes "God".'[28] Our bodies are temples of the Spirit. Dietrich Bonhoeffer defined the Church as Christ existing as community; wherever community exists, there is Church. There is no dualism between God and humanity/body; God is continually embodied and Jesus is the great reminder of that fact. This is the Christology which will underpin this book.

Sophia is the Spiderwoman of Native American tradition. She exists in the midst of us, teaching and inspiring us to weave, never allowing us to rest with our creation. She summons us to weave agreement among brothers and sisters, friendship

Writes largely from a gay feminist perspective though!

among neighbours and harmony between men and women (Sirach 25.1).

So it is in the spirit of the Sophia/Spiderwoman myth that I am going to try to weave together a theology about sexuality which starts from and draws upon the experience of lesbian women and gay men or, I should say, *some* lesbian woman and gay men, albeit a fairly large circle, with whom I have been privileged to do some weaving. I have also taken the weaving and shared it with some heterosexual men and women and done some weaving with them. Plenty of works have been written using the 'theology of sexuality' method that Nelson outlines. I am going to be offering what he calls a sexual theology: '[A sexual theology asks] What does our experience as human sexual beings tell us about how we read the scripture, interpret the tradition, and attempt to live out the meanings of the gospel?'[29]

I cannot claim that the theology that is going to be woven is representative of all lesbians and gay men. Whether one can talk about 'lesbian and gay' anything is a matter of debate among lesbians and gay men themselves. In the last ten years the queer movement has developed. This is a movement which seeks to unite lesbians and gay men in a political coalition which celebrates sexual difference and engages in transgressive political action. However, many lesbians are beginning to question whether the queer movement is working. Certainly in Britain it is the gay male agenda that has dominated queer action. No one can doubt that lesbians and gay men have something in common—loving people of the same sex—and are to varying degrees punished for it. This creates an important experience of solidarity and friendship which has manifested itself particularly clearly in the AIDS crisis. Yet there are vital differences between gay men and lesbians. Although gay men are dangerous anomalies under patriarchy, the fact that they are men guarantees them privilege over most women, most of the time. Gay men tend therefore to be seeking simply a place at the table of equality with heterosexual men and define their liberation purely in terms of sexual expression. Gay men are as capable of

virulent misogyny as heterosexual men. This is, of course, a
gross generalization but it points to at least a partial truth.
Lesbian women as the refugees of patriarchy have been more
concerned with working to overturn the table rather than join it,
recognizing that the complex interplay of forces are building
perpetual injustice. We have tended to see our liberation in
terms of relationship rather than sexual expression. Not all
lesbians are feminists and indeed there has been something of a
backlash against feminism in the lesbian community, but those
of us who are feminist are so for two broad reasons. There are
those whose lesbianism has emerged out of their feminist
commitment, who have come to see heterosexism as the back-
bone of patriarchy because it makes women continuously
dependent upon men. And there are those who have been
brought to a feminist commitment through their lesbianism
and their realization that homophobia has its roots in the
patriarchal fear of female sexuality. I happen to believe that the
liberation of all women is the precondition of the liberation of
gay men, and that it is therefore in gay men's interests to
support the feminist cause—and a fair number do.

No doubt the way gay men and lesbians experience sex and
sexuality is different too—although again it is dangerous to
generalize. In Western culture women are socialized into taking
a relational view of sex, whilst men are socialized into a less
relational view and this is undoubtedly mirrored in the lesbian
and gay communities. In this book I shall attempt to draw upon
differing insights from lesbians and gay men (for example, I
think gay men do challenge us to ask questions about the
'meaning' of sexual activity), but the bias of the book will be
towards the experience and analysis of lesbian feminism. I
believe that feminism gives us the necessary tools with which to
construct a new imaginative and liberating theology of sexuality based upon same-sex experience. As Audre Lorde put it,
the master's tools will never dismantle the master's house, and
there is no just liberating space in the master's house for
lesbians and gay men. In this book I will use the language
of 'patriarchy' and 'oppression' when describing the lived

experience of lesbians and gay men. Patriarchy is the name given to the web of systems which have developed in human history in which *some* male experience is made normative and most of the power to define and order reality is placed in the hands of men who are required to embody a particular construction of masculinity. It is against this particular construction that feminism works, not against men *per se*. However, this does not mean that women are or ever have been rendered utterly powerless. There are degrees of oppression, degrees of subordination and exploitation. Some argue that Western women and gay men have no right to attempt to share the language of oppression with groups such as the Jews in Nazi Germany, blacks in pre-1990s South Africa etc. However, I choose to use the language of oppression for both women and gay men because it serves to remind us of the brutality that many women and gay men suffer from, for no other reason than that they are women or gay men: rape, violence, economic exploitation, unjust treatment under the law, and psychological conditioning which convinces them of their inferiority— experiences which do link them with other oppressed groups. Some women and gay men are more cushioned against all this than others, but even they cannot escape the reality of it completely. Patriarchy is not the only evil in our world—for example, there is racism, classism, ageism, speciesism, the list is endless—but these are closely interlocked with patriarchy and based upon the common practice of making one group's experience normative. When I use the term 'patriarchy' I use it as a blanket term to include all these others.

Patriarchy is not the 'original sin'. All these 'isms' seem to spring out of a human fear of difference which probably has its roots in deep insecurity. I often preach on the theme: 'We are saved: what if we really meant what we said?' It seems to me that the assurance that Christianity claims to give us, namely that we are loved unconditionally by the divine and will be held in its love for ever, should create secure, confident and generous people who can live with and rejoice in difference. The fact that it generally does not, and often seems to create people who exhibit an almost pathological fear of difference, indicates, first, how deep our insecurities are and, second, how badly the 'good news' has been spread. However, I firmly believe that within the essence of the Christian proclamation of salvation lies the solution to oppression. We just have to learn to believe it.

I want to reiterate that the views articulated in this book are not representative of all lesbian and gay people, nor indeed of all lesbian and gay Christians. Lesbian and gay people will not need to be told that I do not represent all Christians! Of course this book is partial, non-neutral; of course many Christians will disagree with my starting-point and may regard the whole notion of Sophia myth within which I work as illegitimate. Of course I may be wrong. *All theology is partial, subjective, fallible.* We can only hope to lay hold of the shadow of the divine.

✱ Is the Sophia myth illegitimate?

Notes

1 *Lumen Gentium: Dogmatic Constitution on the Church* (21 November 1964), para. 37 in Austin Flannery OP, *Vatican Council II: The Conciliar and Post-Conciliar Documents* (Leominster: Fowler Wright, 1980), pp. 394–5.

2 Among the growing list of lesbian and gay theologians in the USA are: Carter Heyward, Robert Goss, Mary Hunt, Gary David Comstock, Beverly Harrison, Chris Glaser, J. Michael Clark and John McNeill. Mention should also be made of the gay historian John Boswell, who has undertaken important historical studies of the Church's response to homosexuality. Guy Ménard is a Canadian theologian. British theologians include Jim Cotter and Alison Webster. And from the Republic of Ireland, Bernard Lynch.

3 Vincent Scully, *The Earth, The Temple and Gods: Greek Sacred Architecture* (London: Yale University Press, 1979), p. ix.

4 Dennis Nineham, 'Epilogue' in John Hick, *The Myth of God Incarnate* (London: SCM, 1977), p. 201.

5 Nineham, *The Myth of God Incarnate*, p. 202.

6 Jim Cotter, *Yes … Minister?: Patterns of Christian Service* (Sheffield: Cairns Publications, 1992), p. 29.

7   Raymond Williams, *Problems in Materialism and Culture: Selected Essays* (London: Verso and New Left Books, 1980), pp. 38–44.

8   James Nelson, *Body Theology* (Louisville: Westminster/John Knox Press, 1992), p. 21.

9   Dennis E. Smith and Hal E. Taussig, *Many Tables: The Eucharist in the New Testament and Liturgy Today* (London: SCM, 1990).

10 Christopher Burdon, *Stumbling on God: Faith and Vision through Mark's Gospel* (London: SPCK, 1990), p. 70.

11 M. Scott Peck, *The Different Drum: Community-Making and Peace* (London: Arrow, 1988).

12 *Veritatis Splendor: Encyclical Letter Addressed by the Supreme Pontiff Pope John Paul II to All Bishops of the Catholic Church Regarding Certain Fundamental Questions of the Church's Moral Teaching* (London: Catholic Truth Society, 1993).

13 Carter Heyward, *Touching Our Strength: The Erotic as Power and the Love of God* (San Francisco: Harper and Row, 1989), pp. 72–86.

14 Mary Grey, *The Wisdom of Fools? Seeking Revelation for Today* (London: SPCK, 1993), p. 28.

15 Luce Irigaray, *Marine Lover of Friedrich Nietzsche* (New York: Columbia University Press, 1991), p. 183.

16 R. S. Thomas, 'Pilgrimages', *Frequencies* (London: Macmillan, 1978).

17 Gary David Comstock, *Gay Theology without Apology* (Cleveland: The Pilgrim Press, 1993), pp. 11–12.

18 Mechthild of Magdeburg, *The Flowing Light of the Godhead*, 2:25, cited in Carol Lee Flinders, *Enduring Grace: Living Portraits of Seven Women Mystics* (HarperSanFrancisco, 1993), pp. 61–2.

19 Rosemary Catalano Mitchell and Gail Anderson Ricciuti, *Birthings and Blessings: Liberating Worship Services for the Inclusive Church* (New York: Crossroad, 1991), p. 85.

20 Grey, *Wisdom of Fools*.

21 Grey, *Wisdom of Fools*, p. 12.

22 Asphodel P. Long, *In a Chariot Drawn by Lions: The Search for the Female in Deity* (London: The Women's Press, 1992), pp. 20–61.

23 Carol Gilligan, *In a Different Voice? Psychological Theory and Women's Development* (Cambridge, MA: Harvard University Press, 1982).

24 James Ashbrooke, 'Different voices, different genes', *Journal of Pastoral Care*, vol. 46 (Summer 1992), pp. 174–83.

25 Long, *In a Chariot Drawn by Lions*, pp. 139–80. Only the Kabbalists and some Gnostics remained faithful to the Wisdom tradition but often combined it with a dualistic understanding of human nature.

26 Rita Nakashima Brock, *Journeys by Heart: A Christology of Erotic Power* (New York: Crossroad, 1991), p. 66.

27 Matthew Fox, *Breakthrough: Meister Eckhart's Creation Spirituality in New Translation* (New York: Image Books, 1991), p. 561.
28 Fox, *Breakthrough*, p. 77.
29 Nelson, *Body Theology*, p. 21.

2 The forgotten love

How do lesbian and gay people understand their committed sexual relationships? Society as a whole presents us with two dominant models: marriage and 'living together'. The Church presents only one model: marriage. One would expect lesbian and gay people to define their relationships in one of these two ways, using the categories of the dominant discourse, which has traditionally excluded them, to create a reverse discourse in which they are included. Some gay Christian theologians have sought to argue that committed lesbian and gay relationships are marriages and should be blessed by the Church as such. Their arguments will be examined later. However, research has confirmed what has long been my experience: a great many lesbian and gay people understand their committed sexual relationships not in terms of marriage or of 'living together' like unmarried heterosexual couples, but in terms of friendship.[1] This is a perfect example of people on the margins, travelling outside the domain of the dominant discourse, weaving a new tapestry, a new model with which to understand their lives. This new tapestry is what we are going to explore.

What is friendship? The answer to this question is varied and complicated. The following is a series of snapshots showing the changing understanding of friendship.

(a) In the writings of Homer friendship is something that exists between men, men of outstanding virtue who hold each other in high social positions by speaking favourably about each other. Friendship is therefore a 'mutual admiration society' among friends seeking to retain social and political power.

(b)   According to Plato, Socrates had a very different understanding of friendship to Homer. Socrates believed friendship could exist regardless of social rank. It is a subversive relationship which creates a kind of counter-culture. In friendship we find kindred spirits, whilst society forces kin and family upon us. Friendship is idealistic; it is free and it is visionary, unlike society, which is the opposite of these things. Society works on the basis of an 'old boys' network' in which people are scratching each other's backs. True friendship is based only upon shared ideas and feelings. So in Socrates friendship is a relationship of affinity, reciprocity and mutuality based upon freedom, in which people can discover their true selves, and it stands in sharp contrast to the corrupt establishment and the family, which seeks only obedience and conformity.

(c)   Aristotle was to write the most influential theory of friendship. He dissected friendship into three types. The first kind of friendship is based upon utility. People are useful to us and to the common good. The second kind of friendship is based upon pleasure: friends are people whose company we enjoy because they are like ourselves. The third kind of friendship is the best, the most pure. This is friendship based upon character. It is a rare experience in which a person finds a 'second self'. In this relationship each loves the other for what the other is, not for profit or pleasure. Aristotle's model of friendship is hierarchical and as one moves up the hierarchy the fewer numbers are involved, so less is more. A person will only enjoy the purest friendship with one or two people during a lifetime. Friends become friends when they admire each other's goodness. Once again friendship is restricted to the good and the male.

(d)   Christian theologians in the medieval Church often presented friendship as the ideal love because it was untainted by sexual feelings, which by this time had become identified in mainstream Christianity with loss of control of the will, the cause of humanity's fall. In the twelfth century, Bernard of Clairvaux had shifted God-talk away from the language of war, kings and judges into the language of love, using the Song of Songs as an allegory telling of Christ's love for his Church. One of the most important but unusual writers on friendship in the medieval Church was St Aelred of Rievaulx. In *De spirituali amicitia*, a work modelled on Cicero's writings on friendship, which he greatly admired, Aelred took Cicero's definition of friendship as 'mutual harmony in affairs human and divine coupled with benevolence and charity', and explored the place of friendship in Christian life. He argued that the whole world was created for friendship. Human beings were created equal for friendship, because friendship can only exist between equals. At the fall, concupiscence caused private good to take precedence over common weal, and friendship was corrupted through avarice and envy. However, nature still testified to the original plan:

> What soil or what river produces one single stone of one kind? Or what forest bears but a single tree of a single kind? And so even in inanimate nature a certain love of companionship, so to speak, is apparent, since none of these exists alone but everything is created and thrives in a certain society with its own kind. And surely in animate life who can easily describe how clear the picture of friendship is, and the image of society and love? And though in all other respects animals are rated irrational, yet they imitate man in this regard to such an extent that we almost believe they act with reason. How they run after one another, play with one another, so express and betray their love by sound and movement, so eagerly and happily do they enjoy their mutual company, that they seem to prize nothing else so much as they do whatever pertains to friendship.[2]

The fall means that we can only achieve true friendship with a small number of people, and have to will ourselves to love our enemies through charity, but after the last judgement universal friendship will be restored. Aelred believed that friendship was divine love. In a reworking of 1 John 4.16, he wrote: 'God is friendship ... he that abides in friendship, abides in God, and God in him.'[3] Human friendship is the path to friendship with God:

> Friend cleaving to friend in the spirit of Christ, is made with Christ but one heart and one soul, and so mounting aloft through degrees of love to friendship with Christ, he is made one spirit with him in one kiss. Aspiring to this kiss the saintly soul cries out: 'Let him kiss me with the kiss of the mouth.' ... Man needs two elements to sustain life, food and air. Without food he can subsist for some time, but without air he cannot live even one hour. And so in order to live, we inhale air with our mouths and exhale it. And that very thing which we exhale or inhale we call breath. Therefore, in a kiss two breaths meet, and are mingled, and are united. As a result, a certain sweetness of mind is born, which rouses and binds together the affection of those who embrace ... the spiritual kiss is characteristically the kiss of friends who are bound by one law of friendship: for it is not made by contact of the mouth but by the affection of the heart ... I would call this the kiss of Christ, yet he himself does not offer it from his own mouth, but from the mouth of another, breathing upon his lovers that most sacred affection so that there seems to them to be, as it were, one spirit in many bodies.[4]

It was this model of love that Jesus embodied in his own lifetime and in particular in his relationship with the 'beloved disciple', a relationship which Aelred describes in another book as a 'heavenly marriage'.[5] Unlike other contemporary writers on this subject Aelred was not overly concerned with the dangers of friendship leading friends into sexual relationships. He refused to see beauty as 'some kind of diabolical flytrap to ensnare those so imperfect as to notice the beauty of human beings' and argued that the 'readiness to respond to beauty is an advantage' because it draws people together into friendship.[6] True friendship does not pair people off, creating factions, but builds community, so a monastery should be a school and model of friendship. For Aelred, then, friendship is a relationship between equals in which both parties have found someone

> in whom your spirit can rest; to whom you can pour out your soul; in whose delightful company, as in a sweet consoling song, you can take comfort in the midst of sadness; in whose most welcome friendly bosom you can find peace in so many worldly setbacks; to whose loving heart you can open as freely as you would to yourself your innermost thoughts; through whose spiritual kisses—as by some medicine—you are cured of the sickness of care and worry; who weeps with you in sorrow, rejoices with you in joy, and wonders with you in doubt; whom you draw by the fetters of love into that inner room of your soul, so that though the body is absent the spirit is there, and you can confer all alone, the more secretly, the more delightfully; with whom you can rest, just the two of you, in the sleep of peace away from the noise of the world, in the embrace of love, in the kiss of unity, with the sweetness of the Holy Spirit flowing over you; to whom you so join and unite yourself that you mix soul with soul, and two become one.[7]

(e)   The sixteenth-century humanist Michel de Montaigne regarded friendship as the purest and highest form of love, for true friendship has no cause or aim or advantage. It is a relationship which is impossible to construct; it is a gift of grace and occurs perhaps once in three hundred years. It is only available to men. Montaigne based his philosophy of friendship on a relationship he enjoyed with a gentleman older than himself which lasted for five years until the death of his friend. He talked about the two friends becoming one soul in two bodies the moment they met and captivated each other. Their friendship took precedence over every other commitment or loyalty.

(f)   Sir Francis Bacon was having none of this sentimental idealism. He knew the tragedy that trust could bring upon itself and believed that the only people one could really trust were not equals but inferiors because one had a hold on them which reduced the chances of betrayal. He certainly thought that friendship had no part to play in public life as it made powerful people vulnerable. Private friendship was good for three things: unburdening the soul, sharpening the intellect, and deputizing in the other's absence.

(g) The angst-ridden existentialist Søren Kierkegaard developed no theology of friendship but his comments to his closest friend Emil Boesen reveal the importance of friendship to the Danish theologian:

> You know how I am, how in conversation with you I jump about stark naked. Whereas I am enormously calculating with other people, I confide only in you ... You, my friend, the only one, through whose intercession I endured the world that in so many ways seemed unbearable, the only one left when I let doubt and suspicion like a violent storm wash away and destroy all else ... my Mt Ararat.[8]

His friend is the only one with whom Kierkegaard can be himself, the only thing he can trust—and yet for Kierkegaard the demands of God come first because only God can give complete freedom.

(h) Georg Simmel, one of the early sociologists, was unusual in that he was actually interested in friendship.

> He pictured society as a web of sociability, a subtle balance of delicate exchanges and, where other sociologists treated society as if it were the replacement for God, Simmel said it was only the name given to the comings and goings of human beings, the interchanges that simultaneously link and separate people.[9]

Sociability is a social relationship based upon play. It is in the play of friendship that people can be who they are. Friends are equal and friendship's joy is that it is purely about mutual encounter, particularly conversation. But friendship is also brittle and every conversation brings with it the risk of the death of the friendship. Simmel also believed that there is an erotic dimension to friendship, although this must not be allowed to become overtly so because the skill of friendship lies in 'constructing a relationship which never comes to an end, is never satisfied and never given up'.[10] Friendship is a necessary distraction from everyday worries; it is the place of creativity and, as such has to be taken very seriously, but not too seriously.

(i)   Psychoanalysis has had remarkably little to say about friendship. Freud's work resounds with silence on the subject. If he talked about it at all, it was appropriate only in childhood; adulthood was a time for independence. Heinz Kohut came to the conclusion that our personalities depend on 'self-others': people whom we experience as other but also as part of ourselves. In that self-other we see and learn to love ourselves as well as the other. Margaret Mahler, the children's psychoanalyst, suggested that friendship provides us with an adult version of the crucial experience of coming and going that we learn in childhood. We develop our self from being free to come and go from our mother, knowing that she will welcome us back warmly when we have gone off to explore the world. D. W. Winnicott developed a similar idea: the child learns to be alone in the presence of the mother; this is the definition and test of security. Such a relationship is a 'transitional relationship' and is repeated in adult friendships. The ability to be alone with another person, free to be yourself and to think your own thoughts is a test of maturity. In this way the adult friend is the child's teddy bear. Little comments:

> Winnicott was privately disappointed at the widespread confusion between his idea of the teddy bear and Linus' famous security blanket. The blanket, like a thumb to suck, stands for the sort of mothering—or friendship—that comforts and reassures and does nothing more ... But transitional relations assist change. They are psychological bridges that allow traffic to cross in either direction: they link the past and the future, the familiar and the strange, and they are both given and created. The teddy bear, though it is presented to the child by the mother (and the culture) becomes the child's own, highly individual creation, its way of moving on.[11]

Other psychologists have suggested that a child does not have to learn to communicate, that we are in communication, in friendship with our world through our mother in her womb. As Little has noted: 'It is as if pure friendship, instead of being the dream of ancient philosophers or the salon play of *fin-de-siècle* sophisticates in the demi-monde, is in fact the basic building block of human experience.'[12]

(j)   Graham Little, whose study of the history of friendship I have been drawing upon, has decided that there are three types of friendship. First, Social Friendship, which is broadly equivalent to Aristotle's utilitarian friendship, is light affection between people who work or play together, usually of the same social, racial or gender group, which 'never forgets that the real world is elsewhere—in power relations, structured competition, institutions, sanctioned behaviour and accepted beliefs'.[13] Second, Familiar Friendship is very much like Socrates' understanding of friendship. It 'is the attempt to reproduce for adults what an ideal family would be for children ... It is opposed to the requirements of society, or is at least a haven from them.'[14] Third, Communicating Friendship is what Little calls 'the pure type ... It is about knowing and being known, about communicating singular identities.'[15] However, sometimes this type of friendship is not real. Sometimes it is the creation of our imagination: we create our friend in the image of our ideal self.

(k)   Peter Nardi has explored the meaning of friendship for lesbian and gay people: 'Friendship is typically seen as a voluntary, egalitarian relationship, involving personal choice and providing individuals with a variety of psychological, social, and material support.'[16] Nardi discovered that many lesbian and gay people, finding themselves rejected or disapproved of by their natural family, regarded their friends as their real family. Their friends provide them with the emotional, social, physical and psychological support that it is usually supposed will be provided by the natural family. However, the boundaries of the constructed family are often much wider than those of the natural family:

an emerging global connection has developed, as gay
subcultures, political and social, appear in many countries and
cities around the world. Interconnected by a network of customs
(clothing styles, for example), social institutions (such as bars
and AIDS organisations), and even language (the word 'gay' is
used in many languages), the globalisation of gay subculture has
resulted in an international family of friends who provide
travellers with places to stay, eat, and socialise. It's as if one is
visiting members of the family from the 'old world' or who have
moved away.[17]

Nardi and others discovered that many gay men and lesbians
are very aware of the sexual dimension of their friendships,
with 79 per cent of men and 77 per cent of women in a survey of
lesbian and gay people acknowledging that they had been
sexually attracted to the person they would now regard as their
best friend (partners were not included in this category). 59 per
cent of the men and 59 per cent of the women had had sex at
least once with their best friend, and 20 per cent of the men and
19 per cent of the women were currently involved in a sexual
relationship with their best friend. Lesbian and gay friendship
also had a strong political dimension, 'since at the core of the
concept of friendship is the idea of "being oneself" in a cultural
context that may not approve of that self ... The friendships
formed by a shared marginal identity, thus take on powerful
political dimensions as they organise around a stigmatised
status to confront the dominant culture in solidarity.'[18] Nardi
concludes that gay and lesbian people have 'elevated friendship
to an importance perhaps not matched by any other group'.[19]

(1) Women have been friends for millennia. Women have been
    each other's best friends, relatives, stable companions,
    emotional and economic supporters, and faithful lovers. But
    this tradition of female friendship, like much else in women's
    lives, has been distorted, dismantled, destroyed—in summary,
    to use Mary Daly's term, *dismembered*. The dismembering of
    female friendship is initially the dismembering of the woman-
    identified Self.[20]

Janice Raymond has helped to break the silence on women's

friendship, a silence engineered by patriarchy or, as she describes it, 'hetero-reality', which refuses to allow women to exist for anyone except men. As the authors of the oldest creation narrative in Genesis put it, 'your desire shall be for your husband, and he shall rule over you' (Genesis 3.16). Under patriarchy, friendships between women are discouraged, trivialized or dismissed as 'lesbian'. This is the ultimate threat to hetero-reality: the fear of women existing without men, and so the lesbian has been made into the 'terrible taboo', as Mary Daly put it. Yet in the midst of hetero-reality women have found each other, broken the terrible taboo and formed friendships. Raymond does not believe that female friendship is something that is natural or essential to women, but that 'it is formed in the cultural commitments that women have made to their Selves and each other in the face of repeated assaults of hetero-reality to be "essentially" and "by nature" for men'.[21] She sets out to re-member (to recover and rebuild) female friendship without idealizing it. Raymond believes that female friendship has always been and will always be the saving of women, for it is only in relationship with other women that women can exist for themselves and can become aware of their possibilities; as such, female friendship has 'revelatory power'. She pays particular attention to the history of friendship among women in religious orders and among Chinese marriage resisters. Raymond isolates certain important conditions of female friendship: thoughtfulness, passion, worldliness and happiness. She points out that women have been socialized into almost robotic 'thoughtfulness', indiscriminate caring; this is not the kind of thoughtfulness that underpins female friendship. No, female friendship thrives on a thinking thoughtfulness. Thinking is conversation with one's real Self, it is through friendship that a woman discovers a Self with which she can talk, and through conversation with herself she is prepared for conversation with others. Aristotle confined friendship to men precisely because he linked capacity for friendship to ability to think which, in his view, women did not have. It is often through friendship that women re-member their capacity to think, but thinking is never divorced from action: 'thinking ... is materialised in the thoughtfulness of female friendship.'[22] Passion was also claimed as a characteristic of male friendships in classical times and was associated with thought. Raymond believes that it is essential to retain the thoughtful dimension of passion:

> A thoughtfully passionate relationship is passion at its most active. It keeps passion active and does not allow it to degenerate into its more passive modes. More concretely, it helps two women to become their own person ... Friendship that is characterised by thoughtful passion ensures that a friend does not lose her Self in the heightened awareness of and attachment to another woman.[23]

Passionate friendship, which can exist between friends who are also lovers and friends who are not lovers, stands in contrast to 'sentimental friendship', which Raymond characterizes as romantic, shallow and unthoughtful. A shared passion for women empowers women to live in a world created by men whilst recreating it as they wish it to be. This is why women's friendship is worldly. It enables a woman to be an 'inside outsider'. Happiness is something the feminist movement, like Marxism, has tended to postpone for later when liberation is achieved. Raymond defines happiness as 'the feeling that accompanies the activity of the whole self, or the feeling of self-realisation. Along with this, happiness means the harmonious life itself.'[24] Happiness is a process rather than a condition which one is in or not in. 'Female friendship gives women the context in which to be "life-glad".' It creates a private and public sphere where happiness can become a reality. It provides the encouragement and environment for the full use of one's powers. Female friendship strives for the full use of the friend's powers.[25] Because under patriarchy women have been defined only in terms of men, their happiness has been linked only to men. Women unattached to men have therefore been defined as unhappy: lesbians, nuns, spinsters are figures of fun and to be pitied. Female friendship breaks through this hetero-reality because it averts women's gaze from men and focuses it on each other.

(m) Mary Hunt, the lesbian feminist theologian, has broken the theological silence around women's friendships. She defines friendship as 'those voluntary human relationships that are entered into by people who intend one another's well-being and who intend that their love relationship is part of a justice-seeking community'.[26] Like Raymond she believes that women's friendships have a revelatory power. The subjects of this revelation are ourselves, the world and the divine. Friendship is an 'honest mirror', teaching us about the best and worst of ourselves and others. Hunt also recognizes the reality that friendship can be enjoyed with the non-human, which reveals something about the interconnectedness of all life and also teaches us something about the necessity of balancing friendships. Understanding the divine in terms of friendship

> is more realistic than claiming that the divine is a many-breasted goddess whose goodness fairly oozes forth. Rather, as in all women's friendships, the potential for nurture and nastiness, comfort and challenge resides in all divine–human relationships. So, too, the divine friend surprises with Her revelations at times, inspiring humans to the same serendipity.[27]

Hunt offers a new theological model based upon the experience and analysis of women's friendships. She argues against Aristotle that most women cannot afford the luxury of hierarchically organizing their friendship; their survival depends upon 'a horizontal reaching out to those who will help'.[28] Hunt draws attention to the influence of Aristotle's model upon Christianity's approach to all issues of sexuality—relationships are evaluated in terms of how much, how long, and how far—an approach to relationships which she believes is foreign to women. There are four elements present in friendship: love, power, embodiment and spirituality. For women, love 'is an orientation towards the world as if my friend and I were more united than separated, more at one among the many than separate and alone'.[29] Love is always generative in one way or another; something new is born out of it. Power is 'the ability to make choices for ourselves, for our dependent children, and with our community'.[30] We are all caught in networks of power—structural and personal—which affect our ability to make choices. We bring these into our friendships where they have to be confronted and dealt with if the friendship is to work. Embodiment refers to the fact that 'virtually everything we do and who we are is mediated by our bodies'.[31] Women friends defy centuries of body-hating Christian theology; 'Women touch, cuddle, embrace, kiss, comfort, massage, make love, pat, prod, and otherwise show feelings in a physical way without the degree of homophobic embarrassment that limits most men to distance or athletic, buddy-like behaviour.'[32] Friends accept each other's bodies as they are and therefore provide a refuge from the pressures of the 'ideal body' industry whose *modus operandi* is to make women feel ugly and inadequate. Spirituality is to do with 'making choices about the quality of life for oneself and for one's community'.[33] This very concrete understanding of spirituality contrasts strongly with the privatized, disembodied, rather vague picture that the word usually conjures up. When these four elements exist in harmony and balance between friends the friendship is real and generative: 'right relation' exists.

This model reveals several important facts about friendship. First it is available to everyone and can exist in all kinds of relationship. It is therefore a model of relationship, indeed the only model of relationship, which excludes no one from it on grounds of gender, sexual orientation, age, class, race, physical ability and so on. Second, friendships are ambiguous and fluid. Friendship can often be a matter of luck rather than judgement. Our experience of friendship is never uniform but it is never insignificant. Third, quality not quantity is what matters in friendship. Hunt argues that friendships need to be attended to, they need reverence and celebration. She therefore suggests that we learn to sacramentalize friendship. This means to hold it up as something which is holy, which mediates the divine.

Like Raymond, Hunt is clear that women's friendships have an inherently political dimension. One of the things that women's friendships create is a survival space in a patriarchal world, communities of resistance working for justice, communities of 'justice-seeking friends' as Hunt calls them. These communities of justice-seeking friends can sometimes bring into coalition women whose experience of power is very different. Differences have to confronted, shared and respected, not hidden under the duvet of 'sisterhood'. Women have to learn how to share power.

We also need to face the fact that friendships end. Hunt suggests that friendships are often lost when the balance of love, power, embodiment and spirituality is distorted. The most fragile aspect of friendship is the power relations. This experience of the loss of friendships reminds us of the importance of learning to befriend ourselves so that we can survive the inevitable waxing and waning of relationship. One has to learn to survive even the experience of the absence of the divine friend. Loss teaches us that nothing is permanent, no one belongs to us as our private property:

> This dimension of friendship provides a hint about the divine, that God is not changeless, the still point of an ever dynamic universe. Rather, the divine is mutable, affected by us as we by the divine. Our losses count in the scope of things ... No one knows why one person finds another and becomes friends, why some are at the right place at the right time to meet people and others miss the chance. I like to think that this is what the Christian tradition has meant by the presence of the Spirit—a force for unity, a movement towards wholeness.[34]

Of course, all talk about God is metaphorical, but unlike the image of God as parent, the image of God as friend can usually be trusted to throw up positive emotions in most people. It can also include the image of parent. God is the attentive friend, immanent in creation, co-operating with creation as it moves through history. God as friend is always generating, always creating, always ahead of us, always beside us, always among us drawing people into community. God is always justice-seeking, always on the side of the marginalized and oppressed. Our experience of friendship may require us to think hard about one important aspect of the nature of the divine: is it monotheistic or polytheistic? 'Just as friends do not exist in the singular, neither is it feasible to imagine that something as complex and comprehensive as divinity could be singular either. There may even be a hint of this insight in the Christian trinitarian theologies ... This polytheistic approach deserves more attention.'[35] The image of divine friend(s) does make some sense of the ambiguous experience of prayer because friends do turn to each other in times of need or happiness, and sometimes they are disappointed.

Hunt concludes:

> Women's friendships, fierce and tender, provide clues for reappropriating symbols for the divine, ethical norms with human beings, and appropriate codes of behaviour toward animals and the earth. Most of all they provide the impetus for communities of justice-seeking friends to engage in active reflection and reflective action to create a friendly world.[36]

These snapshots teach us a lot about friendship. They teach us that friendship has not always been the 'forgotten love', that in the ancient and medieval world it was indeed regarded as the highest form of love. When was it forgotten? The Reformation seems to have played an important part in the de-idealization of friendship and the glorification of the family. Once celibacy had been the highest state a Christian could aspire to; now marriage took its place. This seems to have had a particular effect on men. Friendship gradually ceased to become an essential ingredient of men's lives. They were expected to have all their emotional needs met by their wives. Friendship was no longer the purest of loves, but the word for relations with one's work or recreational colleague. The increasing visibility of homosexuality has also led to a societal suspicion of male friendships. Under modern systems of patriarchy, men are encouraged to be self-sufficient, independent, controlled. Friendship has lost the power and nobility it had in the ancient world.

Nowadays when we want to down play a particular relationship we talk about being 'just good friends'. Cyril Connolly believed that three things led to the demise of friendship in Western society as a whole: industrialization of the world; the totalitarian state; and the egotism of materialism:

> the first through speeding up the tempo of human communication to the point where no one is indispensable, the second by making such demands on the individual that comradeship can be practised between workers and colleagues only for the period of their co-operation, and the last by emphasising whatever is fundamentally selfish and nasty in people, so that we are unkind about our friends and resentful of their intimacy because of something which is rotting in ourselves.[37]

Almost all the theorizers of friendship sampled above agreed on one basic fact: that friendship is a relationship that can usually only exist between people who enjoy equal power relations. This raises important questions. Does this mean that friendship is impossible between men and women, black people and white people, gay and straight, adults and children, until power relations between these different groups are balanced? A good theoretical case could be made out to support this view. However, such a view ignores the fact that unlikely friendships between unlikely people do occur and that it is often these friendships that motivate the struggle against social inequality. People who are locked into structural inequality sometimes do manage to struggle towards equality in personal terms whilst never losing sight of the structural differences which need to be fought. This is the subversive power of friendship that Socrates drew our attention to. Friendship can break rank, and when this happens we are given a tantalizing foretaste of what life could be like. Aelred would no doubt put it differently: he would say that in friendship we are recovering creation as God created it to be, we are rediscovering our equality.

Several of the snapshots speak about friendship being the means by which we discover our true selves and learn to love ourselves. Again a subversive dimension is introduced here when friendship grows between people who have been deprived of a sense of self and who have been taught to despise themselves; women and gay men are prime examples. In friendship women and gay men experience mutuality. This is defined by Carter Heyward as:

> a way of being connected with one another in such a way that both, or all, of us are empowered—that is, spiritually called forth; emotionally *feel* able; politically *are* able to be ourselves at our best, as we can be when we are not blocked by structures and acts of violence and injustice or by attitudes and feelings of fear and hatred.[38]

(1) What is the meaning of friendship?

Amongst these women and gay people friendship creates a counter-culture and survival space. For others, however, friendship is anything except subversive: for Aristotle, Homer and others it is a relationship only possible for the intellectual male élite and cements them together in mutual admiration.

The dissection and ordering of friendship is a process we observed in Aristotle, Little and others. This desire to dissect, classify and order is made more interesting by the fact that it appears to be something alien to women's experience. We shall explore this further. We might also note that several of the men surveyed talked about the highest experience of friendship as being the experience of a merging of souls, an analogy not used by the women.

Is there an erotic dimension to friendship? The women and gay men in our sample are very clear that there is. Simmel acknowledges that there is, but it must not be expressed or friendship becomes something else. Simmel locates the importance of friendship in play. It is in the play and creativity of friendship that we take a break from the daily round and allow ourselves space to dream.

God does not appear much in literature about friendship. Kierkegaard's reminder to himself and his friend that in the end God's demands come before all others reflects a strong tradition within Christianity that regards all human relationships as distractions from the central purpose of human life, which is to worship God with all our hearts, minds and strength. This is the jealous God, who battles our friends for our love. Emily Dickinson sums up this theology in a pithy and caustic poem:

> God is indeed a jealous God—
> He cannot bear to see
> That we have rather not with Him
> But with each other play.[39]

This view contrasts dramatically with Aelred's belief that it is through friendship that one attains friendship with the God who is friendship and Hunt's imaging of God as attentive, generative, justice-seeking friend, with all the strengths and weaknesses of any friend. The traditional resistance to talking about God's love for us in terms of friendship has much to do with the understanding of friendship set out by philosophers such as Aristotle, that is, that at its finest, friendship is a selective relationship reserved for a few and centred on one's self rather than the other person.

Lesbian and gay friendship

All the understandings of friendship captured in the snapshots are still alive today. Can we say, however, that there is a distinctive approach among those travelling on the edge— among women and gay men?[40] In a political, social, cultural and religious context which devalues friendship, women and gay men stand out as people who value friendship extremely highly. They cry out against C. S. Lewis's claim that friendship is 'the least *natural* of loves; the least instinctive, organic, biological, gregarious and necessary . . . Friendship is unnecessary, like philosophy, like art, like the universe itself.' Rather it is one of those things that give value to survival.[41] The illusion that friendship is unnecessary is an illusion of the powerful and so is the illusion that it is unnatural. It assumes that friendship is noble precisely because it is a relationship unnecessary for our survival as a species. It stands against the base instinct for survival of the fittest. People pushed to the edge, marginalized and oppressed, the victims of the survival-of-the-fittest world-view, often appreciate that friendship is the only means to survive. One of the most moving accounts of friendship to appear in recent years is the story of the relationship that developed between John McCarthy and Brian Keenan as they were held hostage in Lebanon. Two men completely different from one another, flung together in appalling circumstances, developed a relationship that literally kept them both alive. Keenan, reflecting on this experience after it was all over, wrote:

> In the circumstances in which we found ourselves physically chained together we both realised an extraordinary capacity to unchain ourselves from what we had known and been—and to set free those trapped people and parts of ourselves. We came to understand that these trapped people included our own captors and we were able to incorporate them in our healing process. All these people that John and I discovered and shared in the deepest intimacy of our confinement spoke, I believe, of a world familiar to us all—a world laden with social, cultural, political and philosophical divisions which manifest themselves in their most extreme and confused forms on the streets of Belfast and Beirut. The extraordinary bond that developed between John and myself was a bonding not just of two separate human beings caught up in a mortal whirlwind. It was also the bonding of our innermost selves or 'people' in a manner which all of us perhaps deep down aspire to. This act of transformation and transcendence could be seen as a metaphor for the times we live in, an age that has seen the massive transformations in Eastern Europe and the Arab world and the West's own sea-changes. John and I discovered not only a love for each other which

transcended our divisions and backgrounds. We also discovered a renewed love for the world and its possibilities which, whilst nascent in us as children, had become buried by the accretions of the conscious worlds we had been brought up in.[42]

Through his friendship with McCarthy Keenan believes he discovered his humanity. This is a sentiment shared by George Santayana who said that 'one's friends are that part of the human race with which one can be human'. The friendship between McCarthy and Keenan became a mirror in which they could confront themselves and also what stood between them, and in confronting those barriers could transcend them. Understanding themselves and the barriers that had been erected between them helped them to understand something of the divisions of the wider world. Their ability to understand and break through the barriers in their own relationship gave them hope for a divided world. The friendship was anything but sentimental. Reading their accounts of their time together you become aware of how important humour and laughter are as weapons of despair. They would constantly throw abuse at one another, acting out and thereby holding up to ridicule the stereotypes, the history, that should divide them. It is laughter that brings them back from the edge of self destruction. They also shared dreams, visions about the future. Again, these dreams were anarchic; they subverted the ghastly hopelessness of the situation. When told of his impending release, Keenan finds himself struggling to decide whether to leave McCarthy: 'For how much freedom can there be for a man when he leaves one half of himself chained to the wall?'[43] He finds that great love has weakened him and discovers himself torn between love of his family and his friend. In the end the choice is made because of the effect the two men have had on one another, the strength they have given one another:

If in my defiance I walk back into that room and have myself chained, refusing to go home, I will have diminished him, for he is a bigger man than to succumb to the needs that isolation

breeds. I cannot do this, I cannot belittle him. I know that in
going free I will free him. He will not surrender, he has gone
beyond it.[44]

Brian and John could presumably have chosen not to be
friends but they probably would not have survived intact. For
them, as for any marginalized, oppressed people, friendship is
about survival. The forgotten love is nurtured among forgotten
people. Here it is the socially subversive force binding people
together who should be kept apart, and when they are together
they dream their subversive dreams of freedom as McCarthy
and Keenan did. Proverbs tells us that 'where there is no vision
the people perish' (29.18)—visions are the art of friendship. I
think C. S. Lewis was wrong to suggest that friendship is
unnecessary for survival, but even if he was right about
humanity in general, he failed to appreciate its life-sustaining,
life-changing potential among some groups of people.

Friendship for those of us who are lesbian or gay emerges as a
relationship which, as it grows between people, results in mutual and equal acceptance, respect and delight. It is an embodied relationship with social and political repercussions. It is
not an inherently rare relationship nor is it a relationship that
can only be achieved with one or two people at a time. As Pope
wrote to his friend Swift, who believed that as far as friendship
goes 'he cannot give to one without Robbing another', 'My
Friendships are increas'd by new ones, yet no part of the
warmth I felt for the old is diminish'd'.[45] For lesbian and gay
people friends often offer the kind of physical and emotional
support that society expects of families. Friendship has a social
and political dimension, and is always subversive in a social and
political climate which devalues friendship and promotes other
relationships. Desire is to a large extent socially constructed; we
are taught what to desire in others. To give but one simple
example, in the West men are encouraged to desire women
who are thin, whilst in some Eastern cultures rounded women
are considered the more beautiful. The one advantage to living
in a context in which friendship is not held up as the ideal is that

more effort is put into 'policing' other relationships, with the result that friendship can become a sacred space in which people encounter one another, freed from the conscious and unconscious assumptions, prejudices and expectations that we are taught and bring into other relationships. We are not taught how to be friends, we are not taught what to expect of friendship—except perhaps if our parents once told us that a friend or friends 'were not suitable': this makes friendship a dangerous place of discovery, a country without roads or maps.

Keenan, in his reflection upon his relationship with McCarthy, felt that they had experienced something that most people yearned for. Kierkegaard summoned up a wonderful image when reflecting upon his friendship with Boesen; he talked about being able to 'jump about stark naked' before him. McCarthy and Keenan achieved that complete vulnerability before each other. I suspect that we all yearn for this radical vulnerability, to be accepted as we are. But for lesbian and gay people who receive constant messages about their unacceptability, the yearning to be loved as they are is perhaps more conscious than in other people. Friendship provides a context in which it is safe to dance naked. Here mutuality is vital, for, as Christopher Rowland has noted, 'There cannot be intimacy when one person is naked and the other clothed, one open and the other closed. That involves a distortion in the relations and *prevents* intimacy.'[46]

One of the interesting things lacking in the last three snapshots of friendship was talk about friendship involving the merging of selves or souls. It is a beautiful image but only works if you have a self/soul/heart to merge with that of another. The problem for gay men and most women is that we often do not have a self/soul/heart to merge. It is hard to be ourselves, since we are often defined in the terms of others or taught to hate ourselves by the hatred of others. We are already broken, and Christianity continues to preach that salvation is to be found through sacrifice of the self, for pride and selfishness is the root of all sin. We are asked to give up even that which we do not have. Since any sense of self, any sense of being a valid,

valuable, lovable person comes about through our relationships with others, and that is the very thing we as lesbian and
gay people are asked to sacrifice, the psychological consequences are enormous. We are taught to be ashamed, to hide
our relational character, and this affects our relationships with
everyone.

In the many years I have spent being alongside people who
are locked into a prison of self-hatred because of their sexual
orientation I have noticed that this self-hatred is powerfully
expressed in the body. Touching people in this situation is very
like touching a corpse. For a start there is often a reluctance to
engage in any physical contact: bodies are often hunched,
closed against the world, eyes are cast down, the voice is
reluctant and weak. The skin is cold, clammy, with no life in it,
no response, just the shadow of death. To ask such people to
sacrifice their selves is as absurd as asking a corpse to die. The
difference is that the corpse cannot hear the ridiculous request
and so could not even make an attempt to do so; the living-dead
can and often do. We are faced with the appalling spectacle of
men and women already bruised, bleeding and dying trying to
crucify themselves and there are plenty of people around to
encourage and help them in this task. I have also had the
privilege of being alongside people as they emerge out of
self-hatred, and once again this is manifest in their body. The
body opens up like a flower: the head is lifted up, the voice
becomes stronger, the flesh becomes warmer. I witness resurrection. This resurrection only occurs because someone has
rolled the stone away, someone has loved the person into life.
Sometimes the lover may not even be aware of doing so—my
own journey from death to life began with a befriending
through the pages of a book. Gaining a heart/soul/self is salvation for many of us; to lose it or give it up would be as
ungracious as pushing the risen Christ back into the tomb. So
the merging of selves is not a popular image among those of us
who have been deprived of a sense of self. The language is also
problematic because it assumes that there is a self/soul/heart
which is separate from the body, an assumption which, as we

shall see, is challenged by the experience of women and gay men. No one would want to deny that we are the product of our relationships. Who I am today is because of who was around me yesterday; our selves are in continual flux as relationships change, develop, are born or die. What happens in a friendship is that two people meet and, rather than thinking of this in terms of merging, we might say that they impress their image on each other, so that both are changed, both are made into something new and the impact of this encounter shakes the world around them. We are like pieces of wet clay, every encounter changes us. This impact is not a one-off but a continual process, and of course the impact is not restricted to one person. So we are continually being created, renewed and changed by our relationships. We carry all our encounters around with us in the shape of our personalities. Audre Lorde wrote: 'Every woman I have ever loved has left her print upon me, where I have loved some invaluable piece of myself apart from me—so different that I had to stretch and grow to recognize her. And in that growing we came to separation, that place where work begins.'[47]

Sometimes the impact will be destructive and tear us apart, sucking life from us. Sometimes the impact will be healing and inject us with life; this is what happens when friendships are formed. Our selves are not merged but created in our friendships. Because we are shaped by our encounters, our personalities are very different and often of unequal force. Smothering or endeavouring to form another person in our own image is a temptation for some of us, but friendship also involves the negotiation of equality and mutuality in terms of strength of encounter.

Lesbian and gay people are prepared to recognize an erotic dimension to their friendships. The words of one lesbian woman would, I think, be typical:

I am attracted to a lot of my women friends on some level. There aren't any lines or definitions. It is kind of nice, but kind of scary too. Being heterosexual is easier that way because the roles are so much more defined—the boundaries are clearer. Things are just not that way with lesbians.[48]

In my experience most women who would identify themselves as heterosexual are also prepared to acknowledge an erotic element to their friendships once they have got over the shock that such a suggestion causes. However, most heterosexual and some homosexual men still wrestling with internalized homophobia find such an idea completely alien. I once gave a one-day retreat to a group of naval chaplains, all of whom were men. They coped very well with all the feminist theology I introduced them to but when we got to friendship, and in particular the erotic in friendship, they became physically and emotionally very uncomfortable indeed and could not understand or relate to the concept. This experience has been repeated again and again among groups of heterosexual men who, it seems, do compartmentalize and order their love.

In the ancient Hellenistic world there were several words used for loves: *agapē*, *philia*, *erōs*, *epithymia* and *storgē* being the most often cited. *Agapē* was considered to be self-giving love, total dedication to another regardless of cost. *Erōs* was the love that drove a person towards others in the quest for self-fulfilment. *Epithymia* was sexual desire/lust. *Philia* was friendship, the purpose of which was growth in virtue. *Storgē* was domestic love, affection. Despite this classification system, in actual use there seems to have been considerable overlap between terms.[49] C. S. Lewis, whose book *The Four Loves* popularized the notion that the Greeks drew hard and fast distinctions between different kinds of love and certainly hierarchically ordered them, said of the difference between *erōs* and *philia*: 'Lovers are normally face to face, absorbed in each other; Friends, side by side, absorbed in some common interest.'[50] Christian theologians like Lewis have arranged these loves into a hierarchy, always with *agapē* at the top. At one time friendship would have appeared directly underneath it—these two were regarded as the purest forms of love because they were believed to be the least physical. It is common to blame the Greeks for introducing body-hating ways into Christianity, but I think this is unfair. There are certainly at least seeds of this kind of thing in some parts of Judaism.

The Holiness Code of Leviticus 17 – 26 reflects an increasing association of uncleanness with the bodily functions, particularly in women, which came to obsess certain Jews during and after the Babylonian exile. By the first century CE some parts of Judaism were making a distinction between a sacred, spiritual realm and the profane world of the physical and the bodily, between a person's body and their spirit. Undoubtedly, however, it was Greek philosophy, particularly forms of Platonism, which developed a thorough-going dualistic understanding of the human person which most of Christianity absorbed. Human beings were thought to be made up of two parts: the body and the soul/spirit/mind. The former is finite, fallen, prone to sin, whilst the latter is eternal and of God, in continual battle with the body in which it is encased at the moment but from which it will hopefully be set free to return to God. The body was associated with the uncontrollable—passion, desire, emotion—whilst the soul is associated with the rational, will and control. Women were perceived as being more bodily than men, unable to transcend their bodiliness and hence subject to passion, emotion, irrationality. Just as the body had to be tamed for the good of the soul, so women had to be tamed for the good of their own souls and the good of the men who might be tempted by them. Nature was associated with the bodily and also had to be tamed and transcended by men. The earthy, the bodily, were what we needed redeeming from by a God who is all spirit. As Luce Irigaray has put it, 'the earth becomes a great deportation camp, where men await celestial redemption'.[51]

The Newtonian understanding of matter as dense, dead stuff served to reinforce the image of souls imprisoned in flesh. Religion became associated with that private realm inside a person. When this happened a reverse dualism took place. Women, mistresses of the private realm, became identified with the spiritual and were elevated from daughters of Eve to angels of light. Men now became associated with the non-spiritual at a time when religion in the industrialized West was on the wane. This dualistic way of viewing the person has profoundly affected the way that Western people have understood reality and constructed their lives and institutions. We have learnt to think and live in terms of opposites: male/female, heaven/earth, living/dead, adult/child, young/old, gay/straight, science/arts, leader/followers, socialism/capitalism, black/white, employed/unemployed, and so on. Each of these pairings carries value judgements, with one side of the opposite often defining the other. (Lesbian and gay people are often told, particularly by church leaders, that there is a distinction between their sexual orientation and practice.) The psychologist Carl Gustav Jung believed that this was the way all human beings thought, and claimed that we each inherit a psyche in which opposite symbols exist. Structuralists like Levi-Strauss also argued that human thought and reality consisted and worked according to a system of binary opposites. It should be pointed out that Eastern Orthodox Christianity managed to hold to a much more positive attitude to nature and sexuality than Western Christianity, whilst not being immune from dualism itself.

Hatred of the body still persists in Western society, however secularized it appears to have become. When I was a teenager I went to hear a famous American evangelical preacher. The only thing I can remember from his address was a passing remark he made about bodies. It went something like this: 'Scripture teaches us that the body is the temple of the Holy Spirit and God does not want to live in a fat temple.' I remember going home and ransacking my Bible looking for God's instructions on ideal body weight. The journalist Jo Ind has explored how a woman is taught to hate her body, and she has described the destruction such hatred unleashed upon her own life.[52] These days almost every magazine, paper, TV or radio show bellows out the message that, as far as bodies are concerned, the less of them the better. Whilst most people would find the ancient monastic practices of self-discipline rather revolting, I see strong parallels between these practices and the modern obsession with diet and fitness. The body in both is seen as something that needs to be kept under strict control by the mind or will. Inflicting pain, fasting and confession were then as now the ways to do this (for confession read 'diet clubs'). The old aim was spiritual health, the new is physical health. All this is particularly true of women's bodies. The less space women take up the better; the smaller, more delicate, more vulnerable, the better. Andrea Dworkin has noted:

> Standards of beauty describe in precise terms the relationship that an individual will have to her own body. They prescribe her mobility, spontaneity, posture, gait, the uses to which she can put her body. *They define precisely the dimensions of her physical freedom.* And of course, the relationship between physical freedom and psychological development, intellectual possibility, and creative potential is an umbilical one. In our culture, not one part of a woman's body is left untouched, unaltered. No feature or extremity is spared the art, or pain, of improvement.[53]

Behind the ideal of slim waif also lies a fear of female sexuality, as Elaine Graham has pointed out, for the waif stands for a 'vision of beauty that refuses pleasure ... women are not to regard themselves as big and powerful, and being fat is associated with a loss of self-control that is in some way obscene, carrying traces of a reprehensible sexual appetite as well as a gastronomic indulgence.'[54] Some of those who have suffered from this dualistic classification system have managed to break out from it and challenge it.

Certainly the tendency of Western scholars to read into other societies what they want to see has been exposed. As Lucy Goodison has pointed out, in the West life and death may appear to be clear opposites but this does not hold true in societies where belief in reincarnation or continued access to the dead is strong.[55] And the same holds true for many other of the binary opposites that Jung and others held to be inherent

Why has love + friendship been taught to hate one another?

and universal. It would be wrong to dismiss dualism completely. Its continuing appeal to many people lies in the truth it does encapsulate, namely that human beings are not merely flesh and blood, every aspect of our lives explainable in material terms. Monism (the opposite of dualism) is unable satisfactorily to explain consciousness. The philosopher P. F. Strawson developed a theory of person which managed to transcend both dualism and monism whilst retaining the truth of both. He asserted against the dualists that a person is one thing which cannot be dissected, as dualists claim, but it cannot be satisfactorily explained simply by reducing it to mere materiality, as the monists do. A person is so complicated that to explain it requires two perspectives or 'double-aspects'. It requires two levels of description to understand a person adequately.[56] So abandoning dualism does not necessitate the reduction of humanity to mere bone, blood and tissue. If we were to remove our dualistic spectacles how would it change our understandings of our world?

Re-membering love

Eros of course was the Greek god of love:

> the most beautiful of all the gods and the most powerful, for by the love which he inspires in all living things, he defeats wisdom and carefully laid plans ... In this way Eros often brings suffering and destruction upon human lives ... On the other hand Eros, who is often called the oldest of the gods, has from the beginning joined in love both gods and men, and so by his agency new life comes into being. Moreover love, the gift of Eros, can bring men more happiness than anything else on earth.[57]

Eros emerges from Greek mythology as the chief intermediary between the divine and human worlds. He was, of course, the force behind sexual attraction but also seems to have been regarded by some as the creator of all attraction between humans. Plato believed he inspired desire for wisdom, beauty and goodness.[58] Apuleius offered a story of Cupid (the Roman equivalent of Eros) and Psyche. Cupid saves Psyche from the jealous wrath of Venus but will not allow her to look on him:

> 'Why should you wish to behold me?', he said. 'Have you any doubt of my love? Have you any wish ungratified? If you saw me, perhaps you would fear me, perhaps adore me, but all I ask of you is to love me. I would rather you love me as an equal than adore me as a god.'[59]

Psyche cannot resist and so Cupid leaves her, remarking that 'Love cannot dwell with suspicion',[60] but it all works out well in the end.

This understanding of *erōs* is very different to the image that the word 'erotic' usually conjures up. The black lesbian feminist Audre Lorde was among the first to reclaim *erōs* from the hands of men where it has been made into 'the confused, the trivial, the psychotic, the plasticized sensation', and remembered it as deep knowledge of a capacity for joy, for satisfaction, a drive towards self-fulfilment. It is that which reveals what is possible, what ecstatic pleasure is available to us.[61] It is not a rational knowledge but a deep bodily knowledge:

> The considered phrase, 'It feels right to me', acknowledges the strength of the erotic into a true knowledge, for what that means and feels is the first and most powerful guiding light toward any understanding. And understanding is a handmaiden that can only wait upon, or clarify, that knowledge, deeply born. The erotic is the nurturer or nursemaid of all our deepest knowledge.[62]

The problem I have with Lorde's description of the erotic is that she seems to assume that this power, this knowledge, is inherent in every woman waiting to be uncovered. I think that women, who have been victims of the idea of inherent, biological differences between men and women, have to be very wary of making any claims to inherent forms of knowledge. I would accept Carol Gilligan's thesis that men and women understand themselves in relation to the world very differently, but I would want to argue with her that this is not due to inherent biological

differences between men and women but is the result of the
history of the different power relations that exist between men
and women. This is not in any way to down-play the radical
differences between men and women and how they relate, for,
as Ceila Hahn has noted, the problem with dismissing differences between women and men as 'only cultural' is that it
presumes that humanity is in essence not cultural, which would
be foolish.[63] What I am trying to say is that if women do enjoy
this creative source of knowledge identified by Lorde, then it is
not because they have discovered it deep inside themselves, like
long-forgotten treasure, but because it is a power, force, way of
knowing that has been created in the interaction between
persons. We love because we are first loved. Those who love us
first, before we are able to love, spin powerful threads between
us. It is through their love that we learn to love ourselves: we
learn that we survive through connection with others, through
interdependence, that it is in relationship with others that we
become persons, that we grow and change and develop. We
also learn the physicality of all this. If we are very lucky indeed
we learn this in our early years. The exceptionally lucky learn it
through and from their parents, others from a sibling or aunt or
uncle, perhaps a grandparent.

However, for a great many people the early years are years of
learning how not to love, often in the name of love. Physicality
is associated with pain and they learn to hate bodies. Survival is
dependent on independence, on avoiding relationship, on severing connection. Often even those who have been lucky in
the early years go through some kind of traumatic experience
which leaves them profoundly broken, so that they have to
begin recreating themselves, relearning love. This explains why
we have such ambiguous attitudes to our bodies and physical
expression; for many of us our bodies and physicality have
always equalled pain, invasion and diminishment. Boys are
forced to unlearn the lessons of love if they have been lucky
enough to receive them in their earliest years, for they are
taught that to become men they must sever their attachment to
their mother. This explains why Gilligan found that men think

of themselves as isolated, independent selves in competition with others and they find intimacy threatening, whilst women think of themselves in relation to others and find the thought of aloneness threatening.[64] Rita Nakashima Brock uses the metaphor of the heart for the human self and describes most of us as 'broken-hearted', our hearts broken by our earliest relationships, by patriarchy, by racism or classism, by rejection and abuse in our later relationships.

Only love can heal us. Only by being loved can we learn to love again or for the first time. Of course, sometimes people have been so badly damaged that they will not allow another person to get too close to them. People open themselves to love in a number of ways. Animals are often the friends who break through the barbed wire we erect around our broken selves. I have known innumerable people learn to love for the first time or again through the friendship of people who write books. In particular I think of one book which has transformed several women of my acquaintance living through the trauma of abuse or rape. Love mediated through the pages of a book is a particularly gentle and tender and discreet form of friendship for those who at that time cannot bear too much presence. In the book I am thinking about the author simply told of her experience of abuse: she had taken part of her clay and moulded it into the ink and paper; incarnate in a different form she met her readers and befriended them. Art functions in a similar way.

Through being loved we learn how to love and we learn that our survival, our happiness, our self-fulfilment lies in connection, in interdependence with others. This is erotic knowledge, the power of *erōs* that propels us out towards others, to build up right relationship in the world. An important aspect of *erōs* is anger. Anger or rage is a deep physical reaction to the disconnection, injustice, violence and wrong relationship in our world. It is the pain of disconnection when we have known connection. It is the rocket fuel of *erōs*. Beverly Harrison has defined it as:

a feeling-signal that all is not well in our relation to other persons or groups or to the world around us. Anger is a mode of connectedness to others and it is always a vivid form of caring. To put the point another way: anger is—and it always is—a sign of some resistance in ourselves to the moral quality of the social relations in which we are immersed. Extreme or intense anger signals a deep reaction to the action upon us or toward others to whom we are related ... Where anger rises, there the energy to act is present.[65]

Anger is an expression of love, hatred is an expression of absence of love. Hatred is the pain of disconnection when we have not known connection. Where there is only disconnection, connection is to be feared, the 'other' becomes a threat, one's own self becomes a threat, one fears being engulfed, being out of control, being taken over. When we are loved we learn to be angry; when we are broken we learn hatred of ourselves and others. Hatred is something to be overcome through the binding up of the broken-hearted; anger is something to welcome and own, for it is our motivation to change the world. Mary Daly has put it well: 'Rage is not a stage. It is not something to be gotten over. It is a transformative, focusing force.'[66]

Erōs reminds us of the embodiment of love. Studies have shown that infants deprived of touch are much more prone to death than those who are held, cuddled and generally warmly touched.[67] I will never forget the pictures of the children in Romanian orphanages, pictures that were beamed into our homes after the fall of the Ceauşescu régime. These children had been deprived of touch for years and they were barely recognizable as human beings, but as journalists, TV crews and others began to pick them up and cuddle and talk to them their physical appearance began to change; they became more and more recognizable as human beings. Generations of children in the United States and Europe were brought up with child manuals which discouraged parents from touching children. Morton and Barbara Kelsey believed that 'one of the reasons that sexual problems are so prevalent in much of Western society is the lack of warmth, affection and touch that we have received and that our parents and grandparents have received before us'.[68] The welcome exposure of the extent of child sexual abuse has, however, escalated into a panic, to the point that we are in danger of making adults so frightened of touching children for fear of being accused of assault that the only touch some children will experience is the touch of pain and violation. *Erōs* is a feeling which reminds us of our physicality because it is experienced physically. In the gospels a word often translated as 'moved with pity' or 'moved with compassion', or sometimes 'moved with anger', when referring to Jesus, literally refers to a person's bowels or entrails turning over. This is what we experience with *erōs*—a connection deep within our bodies which propels us out towards other bodies. However, as Beverly Harrison points out, we have been taught to devalue our bodies and bodily knowledge so much that we do not really live in them; we live in our heads with the result that we no longer feel any connection—positive or negative—with other beings so we treat others as 'objects', as 'its'.[69]

Another element of *erōs* is play. Western culture does not value play for adults. The capitalist work ethic teaches us that everything we do must produce some kind of good or it is suspect, indulgent, 'wicked'. Play, if it is for anything, is for children. They are allowed to do things just for the fun of it, to experiment, fantasize, pretend, imagine. Most of us were never as creative as when we were children, never as curious, never as open to different possibilities, never as connected with the rest of creation. Suddenly we are expected to grow out of all this. The power of the erotic is the power of play, of taking delight in doing and enjoying things in their own right, of letting the imagination roam, of enjoying the being of another. W. H. Auden noted that 'as a rule it was the pleasure-haters who became unjust'. Play values people, animals, nature for what they are, not for what use they are. Play widens the imagination and allows us to think the unthinkable. Rita Nakashima Brock says of the child deprived of play: 'Marginalized from intimacy with the world, such selves seek to assert control over the world or to give in as victims of it. Causality begins to be seen as direct and narrow, as deterministic.'[70]

Ann Ulanov defines *erōs* as 'the psychic urge to relate, to join, to be in the midst of, to reach out to, to value, to get in touch with, to get involved with concrete feelings, things, and people, rather than to abstract or theorize'.[71] I would add that it is a power awakened or brought to birth in us by the experience of being loved. It is deep body knowledge of our interconnectedness and interdependence, our own self-worth and worth of all life. It appears as righteous anger, playfulness, creativity, loving touch. Love breeds love. Once touched by the power of *erōs* we cannot contain it, we want to touch the world with it. We might say, using the imagery of Hildegard of Bingen, that *erōs* is that power that keeps us as moist clay, able to interact with others without being smashed or smashing them, able to change and help change.

Notes

1 See M. R. Loner, 'Permanent partner priorities: gay and straight' in J. P. DeCecco, *Gay Relationships* (New York: Harrington Park, 1988); Peter Nardi, 'That's what friends are for: friends as family in the gay and lesbian community' in Ken Plummer, *Modern Homosexualities: Fragments of Lesbian and Gay Experience* (London: Routledge, 1992), pp. 108–20; Barbara Ponse, *Identities in the Lesbian World: The Social Construction of Self* (Westport: Greenwood Press, 1978); Donner M. Tanner, *The Lesbian Couple* (Lexington, MA: D. C. Heath, 1978).

2 Aelred of Rievaulx, *Spiritual Friendship*, 1.54–55 (Kalamazoo: Cistercian Publications, 1974), pp. 62–3.

3 Aelred of Rievaulx, *Spiritual Friendship*, 1.69–70, pp. 65–6.

4 Aelred of Rievaulx, *Spiritual Friendship*, 2.21–23, 26, pp. 74–6.

5 Aelred of Rievaulx, *The Mirror of Charity*, 3.109–110, cited in John Boswell, *Christianity, Social Tolerance and Homosexuality: Gay People in Western Europe from the Beginning of the Christian Era to the Fourteenth Century* (Chicago: University of Chicago Press, 1980), pp. 225–6.

6 Aelred of Rievaulx, *The Mirror of Charity*, 3, cited in Kenneth C. Russell, 'Aelred, the gay Abbot of Rievaulx', *Studia Mystica*, vol. 5, part 4 (Winter 1982), p. 57.

7 Aelred of Rievaulx, *The Mirror of Charity*, 3.109–110, cited in Boswell, *Christianity, Social Tolerance and Homosexuality*, pp. 225–6.

8 Graham Little, *Friendship: Being Ourselves with Others* (Melbourne: The Text Publishing Company, 1993), pp. 23–4.
9 Little, *Friendship*, p. 31.
10 Little, *Friendship*, p. 33.
11 Little, *Friendship*, p. 54.
12 Little, *Friendship*, p. 53.
13 Little, *Friendship*, p. 14.
14 Little, *Friendship*, p. 14.
15 Little, *Friendship*, p. 14.
16 Nardi, 'That's what friends are for', p. 108.
17 Nardi, 'That's what friends are for', p. 112.
18 Nardi, 'That's what friends are for', pp. 115–16.
19 Nardi, 'That's what friends are for', p. 120.
20 Janice Raymond, *A Passion for Friends: Towards a Philosophy of Female Affection* (London: The Women's Press, 1986), p. 4.
21 Raymond, *A Passion for Friends*, p. 21.
22 Raymond, *A Passion for Friends*, p. 223.
23 Raymond, *A Passion for Friends*, p. 225.
24 Raymond, *A Passion for Friends*, p. 238.
25 Raymond, *A Passion for Friends*, p. 238.
26 Mary Hunt, *Fierce Tenderness: A Feminist Theology of Friendship* (New York: Crossroad, 1991), p. 29.
27 Hunt, *Fierce Tenderness*, p. 84.
28 Hunt, *Fierce Tenderness*, p. 95.
29 Hunt, *Fierce Tenderness*, p. 100.
30 Hunt, *Fierce Tenderness*, p. 101.
31 Hunt, *Fierce Tenderness*, p. 102.
32 Hunt, *Fierce Tenderness*, p. 104.
33 Hunt, *Fierce Tenderness*, p. 105.
34 Hunt, *Fierce Tenderness*, p. 133.
35 Hunt, *Fierce Tenderness*, p. 167.
36 Hunt, *Fierce Tenderness*, pp. 175–6.
37 Cyril Connolly, *The Unquiet Grave* (London: Hamish Hamilton, 1944), cited in D. J. Enright and David Rawlinson, *The Oxford Book of Friendship* (Oxford: Oxford University Press, 1991), p. 19.
38 Carter Heyward, *When Boundaries Betray Us: Beyond Illusions of What Is Ethical in Therapy and Life* (HarperSanFrancisco, 1993), p. 69.
39 Thomas H. Johnson, *The Poems of Emily Dickinson* (Cambridge, MA: Harvard University Press, 1951).
40 I am including 'straight' women here. Differences between lesbians and straight women are often not as great as between lesbians and gay men. Lesbians and straight and bisexual women share the common experience of being women under patriarchy, although sexuality, class, race all modify that common experience.

41 C. S. Lewis, *The Four Loves* (London: Collins, 1960), pp. 56, 67.
42 Brian Keenan, *An Evil Cradling* (London: Vintage, 1992). p. xvi.
43 Keenan, *An Evil Cradling*, pp. 291–2.
44 Keenan, *An Evil Cradling*, p. 292.
45 Alexander Pope, letter to Swift, August 1723, in Enright and Rawlinson, *The Oxford Book of Friendship*, p. 11.
46 Christopher Rowland, 'Jesus, the gospels and intimacy', *Christian Action Journal* (Summer 1993), p. 7.
47 Audre Lorde cited in Mary Hunt, *Fierce Tenderness*, p. 165.
48 Cited in Suzanna Rose, Debra Zand and Marie A. Cini, 'Lesbian courtship scripts' in Esther D. Rothblum and Kathleen A. Brehony, *Boston Marriages: Romantic but Asexual Relationships Among Contemporary Lesbians* (Amherst: University of Massachusetts Press, 1993), pp. 73–4.
49 Boswell, *Christianity, Social Tolerance, and Homosexuality*, p. 46, and *Same-Sex Unions in Premodern Europe* (New York: Villard Books, 1994), pp. 4–8.
50 Lewis, *The Four Loves*, p. 58.
51 Luce Irigaray, *Marine Lover of Friedrich Nietzsche* (New York: Columbia University Press, 1991), p. 174.
52 Jo Ind, *Fat Is a Spiritual Issue: My Journey* (London: Mowbray, 1993).
53 Andrea Dworkin, *Woman-Hating* (New York: Dutton, 1974), pp. 113–14.
54 Elaine Graham, 'Towards a theology of desire', *Theology and Sexuality*, vol. 1 (September 1994), p. 27.
55 Lucy Goodison, *Moving Heaven and Earth: Sexuality, Spirituality and Social Change* (London: The Women's Press, 1990).
56 For a highly creative use of Strawson's theory in developing a Christology, see Adrian Thatcher, *Truly a Person, Truly God: A Post-Mythical View of Jesus* (London: SPCK, 1990).
57 *Collins Concise Encyclopedia of Greek and Roman Mythology* (Glasgow: Collins, 1965), p. 103.
58 Sandra Friedman and Alec Irwin, 'Christian feminism, eros, and power in right relation', *Cross Currents*, vol. 40 (Fall 1990), pp. 387–405.
59 *Bulfinch's Mythology* (London: Spring Books, 1963), p. 62.
60 *Bulfinch's Mythology*, p. 63.
61 Audre Lorde, 'Uses of the erotic: the erotic as power' in James B. Nelson and Sandra P. Longfellow, *Sexuality and the Sacred: Sources for Theological Reflection* (London: Mowbray, 1994), pp. 75–9.
62 Lorde, 'Uses of the erotic', p. 77.
63 Celia Allison Hahn, *Sexual Paradox: Creative Tensions in Our Lives and in Our Congregation* (New York: The Pilgrim Press, 1991), p. 5.
64 Carol Gilligan, *In a Different Voice? Psychological Theory and Women's Development* (Cambridge, MA: Harvard University Press, 1982).

65 Beverly Wildung Harrison, 'The power of anger in the work of love: Christian ethics for women and other strangers' in Ann Loades, *Feminist Theology: A Reader* (London: SPCK, 1990), p. 206.

66 Mary Daly, *Pure Lust: Elemental Feminist Philosophy* (Boston: Beacon Press, 1984), p. 375.

67 Morton Kelsey and Barbara Kelsey, *Sacrament of Sexuality: The Spirituality and Psychology of Sex* (Warwick: Amity House, 1986), p. 37.

68 Kelsey and Kelsey, *Sacrament of Sexuality*, p. 37.

69 Harrison, 'The power of anger in the work of love', p. 205.

70 Rita Nakashima Brock, *Journeys by Heart* (New York: Crossroad, 1991), p. 36.

71 Ann Belford Ulanov, *The Feminine in Jungian Psychology and in Christian Theology* (Evanston: North Western University Publishers, 1971), p. 155.

3 Sex and friends

I can imagine that many heterosexual men reading the definition of the erotic offered in the previous chapter would be happy to acknowledge this dimension in their friendships. They may think I have been rather sneaky in the use of the word 'erotic', because as it is used in common parlance it is associated with specifically sexual desire—perhaps more approximate to *epithymia* in Greek. This is what so many cannot countenance, the idea that sexual desire might be an element in their friendships. 'I do not nor have I ever wanted to sleep with my best friend', many might be thinking. Freud is often caricatured as declaring that all relationships are sexual, in the sense that underneath all our relating is the desire to have sex with one another. This is not what he meant. In fact, Freud made a distinction between genital functions and sexuality in the wider sense. I want to follow Freud in making this distinction.

Foucault pointed out that something extraordinary happened in the post-Enlightenment period: the homosexual person was invented. By this he meant that during this time a person's sexual identity came to be understood as the defining aspect of that person; everything that person did was influenced by his or her sexuality: 'Homosexuality appeared as one of the forms of sexuality when it was transposed from the practice of sodomy onto a kind of inner androgyny, a hermaphrodism of the soul. The sodomite had been a temporary aberration; the homosexual was now a species.'[1] Those of us who identify as lesbian or gay or bisexual are therefore now socialized into defining our whole person in terms of our sexuality; our sexuality becomes the most dominant factor in our lives. Perhaps, then, we are more aware than people who would be defined as heterosexual of the part that sexuality plays in all our relationships. In fact heterosexual people are not defined by their sexuality, they are only so defined in contrast to gay, lesbian and bisexual people.

What is 'sexuality'? *The Concise Oxford Dictionary* provides no separate definition of the word but refers to it under 'sexual', which it defines as 'of or relating to sex, or to the sexes or the relations between them'. This reflects a common belief that sexuality is about who you have sex with. However, in my experience, lesbian, gay and bisexual people have a much wider understanding of sexuality. Bernard Lynch, a gay Roman Catholic priest, often defines sexuality as 'the seat of our relationality'. James Nelson comes very close to the lesbian and gay understanding of sexuality:

> It is our way of being in the world as gendered persons, having male or female biological structures and socially internalized self-understandings of those meanings to us. Sexuality means having feelings and attitudes about being 'body-selves.' It means having affectional orientations toward the opposite sex, the same sex, or quite possibly toward both. It means having the capacity for sensuousness. Above all, sexuality is the desire for intimacy and communion, both emotionally and physically. It is the physiological and psychological grounding of our capacity to love. At its undistorted best, our sexuality is that basic *eros* of our humanness—urging, pulling, luring, driving us out of loneliness into communion, out of stagnation into creativity.[2]

Our sexuality is, then, as Nelson makes clear, the *erōs* that we identified earlier, the deep bodily knowledge that is awakened in us by love. It is as active, as Audre Lorde noted, in 'dancing, building a bookcase, writing a poem, examining an idea' as it is in having sex with someone. This explains some behaviour which may look a bit odd to many heterosexual people. When engaging in a study of lesbian and gay teenagers in Chicago, Gilbert Herdt and Andrew Boxer sat in on a support group for teenagers at the very earliest stage of coming out, that is, publicly acknowledging themselves as gay or lesbian:

> The advisor asked if being gay was only about having sex? The group resoundingly responded 'No!' Most of the youth perceived being gay as a 'way of life.' To some of the kids, being gay or lesbian has made them 'different' beyond their 'sexual preference.' Tiffany said that it influenced 'all areas of her life'—how she dressed, what she read, where she went.[3]

Men and women who are vowed celibates will often identify themselves as gay or lesbian or bisexual. I remember the startled incomprehension of many colleagues when the *Times Higher Education Supplement* ran an article which revealed that some women refuse the label 'heterosexual' even though they do not sleep with women. Of course it could be said that we have been socialized by the sexologists to believe that our sexual desires say something about our intrinsic being, so that, even if we are vowed celibates, the fact that we are sexually attracted to the same sex rather than the opposite sex or to both sexes labels us gay/lesbian or bisexual. No doubt there is an element of truth in this.

I think that, on the whole, the sexologists of the nineteenth century did more harm than good. Havelock Ellis was the best-known and influential sexologist in the late nineteenth–early twentieth century in Britain. It was his theories about homosexuality that underpinned Radclyffe Hall's novel about lesbian love, *The Well of Loneliness*, which, both when it was published in 1928—and banned as obscene—and for decades afterwards became *the* piece of literature for the woman struggling with her sexual idenitity. The tragic heroine of the story is a woman named Stephen Gordon. She is given this name because her father wanted a son. He brings her up as his son and heir who must learn to manage the family estate. She is born an 'invert', part of a 'third sex': inside her woman's body a man's mind is trapped. Her body is 'mannish', her God-given destiny to suffer in a world which cannot understand her. As Alison Hennegan has pointed out, it is no accident that Hall names her heroine after the first Christian martyr and brings her into the world on 26 December, St Stephen's day.[4] Exiled from home and country (although the country is glad of her services when war breaks out), Stephen finds that she can only fall in love with 'real' women, with inevitably tragic consequences. In the closing pages Stephen, having sacrificed her love, hears and sees inverts known and unknown to her:

> They possessed her. Her barren womb became fruitful—it ached with its fearful and sterile burden. It ached with the fierce yet helpless children who would clamour in vain for their right to salvation. They would turn first to God, and then to the world, and then to her. They would cry out accusing: 'We have asked for bread; will you give us a stone? Answer us: will you give us a stone? You, God, in Whom we, the outcast, believe; you, world, into which we are pitilessly born; you, Stephen, who have drained our cup to the dregs—we have asked for bread; will you give us a stone?' ... 'God,' she gasped, 'we believe; we have told You we believe ... We have not denied You, then rise up and defend us. Acknowledge us, oh God, before the whole world, Give us also the right to our existence!'[5]

There were in fact two types of female invert: the 'congenital' invert which Stephen represents, who embodies all the 'masculine' traits of physical and intellectual prowess: leadership qualities, assertiveness, practical skills and so on! The other type of invert was one who can be 'converted' to inversion by a relationship with an invert: these women in their dress and abilities mirrored 'normal' women. The creation of the sad, third sex had a profound effect not only upon the way that society began to view those who had sexual relations with the same sex but also upon the way that all same-sex friendships were viewed. Carroll Smith-Rosenberg, in a ground-breaking work which examined women's friendships in the nineteenth century, noted how towards the end of the century a new class of women emerged. Dubbed 'new women', these were those women who were taking advantage of the increased educational and career opportunities for women. They formed intense friendships—'passionate friendships' is the term usually used—with other women as they supported each other in the journey into the brave new world of college, profession and social action. They often became social reformers.[6] The sexologists, however, regarded these new women as inverts, and the fear of being classified as one of these unhappy lepers drove many women into marriage and put the fog of suspicion around all friendships. As far as most physicians of the nineteenth century were concerned, a man was ruled by his head, a woman by her reproductive organs, and if either one of these attempted to live out of anything except these parts of their bodies they would soon fall sick and begin to turn into the opposite gender. Vera Brittain, a contemporary of Hall's who enjoyed her own passionate friendship, could not identify with Hall's inverts and she also recognized that Ellis's theory depended on assumed gender characteristics to which she did not assent. Stephen was not a sad congenital accident but a normal young girl

> who happens to possess more vitality and intelligence than her
> fellows ... If one of the results of women's education in the
> eighteen-nineties was to attach the ugly label 'pervert' to a
> human being whose chief desire was for a wider expression of
> her humanity than contemporary convention permitted, then
> that education was an evil thing indeed.[7]

The idea of the congenital invert whose relationships were based on masculine and feminine 'role-play' became orthodoxy very quickly, both among sexologists and same-sex lovers themselves. Feminism exposed and challenged the patriarchal assumptions behind it, for example, that women who were assertive, intellectual and strong were not 'real' women but men inside; that no woman would love another woman unless there was something inherently perverted about her; that women can only be sexual by imitating men. 'Masculinity' and femininity' were shown to have nothing to do with biological determinism, but were socially contructed fallacies designed to keep men free and women slaves. Anyone with even a passing acquaintance with drag queens or transvestites soon learns that 'femininity' has little to do with being a woman. Men are often so much better at achieving it!

In some parts of late-twentieth-century feminism the term 'lesbian' was adopted, not just by women who had sexual relations with women but also by women who wished to step outside the 'hetero-reality' which they came to regard as the servant of patriarchy. For in 'hetero-reality' women are defined and controlled by men. Adrienne Rich famously argued that the term 'lesbian' includes all those women who love women and who choose to live and relate primarily to other women. Rich suggested that there was a 'lesbian continuum' which includes:

> a range—through each woman's life and throughout history—of woman-identified experience, not simply the fact that a woman has had or consciously desired genital sexual experience with another woman. If we expand it to embrace many more forms of primary intensity between and among women, including the sharing of a rich inner life, the bonding against male tyrant, the giving and receiving of practical and political support ... we begin to grasp the breadths of female history and psychology which have lain out of reach as a consequence of limited, mostly clinical definitions of *lesbianism*.[8]

Monique Wittig has noted that the terms 'man' and 'woman' exist in binary opposition. In this construction, woman functions as a subordinate inferior. A lesbian, Wittig declares, is not a woman. Wittig is not simply returning to a Hallesque third sex. What she is pointing out is that a lesbian, by refusing to play the role assigned to women in a patriarchal context, exposes the patriarchal understanding of women to be a social construct, and thereby subverts it.[9] And so we can begin to understand why some women who would not be defined as 'lesbian' by a society which thinks of a lesbian as 'a homosexual woman', and regards homosexuality as 'feeling or involving sexual attraction only to persons of the same sex',[10] would choose to identify as lesbian, or steadfastly refuse the label 'heterosexual', as a personal political statement.[11] Feminism also attempted to blow apart the idea that sexuality was biologically determined:

> In the seventies lesbian feminists, myself included, wore badges saying 'Any woman can be a lesbian' and we believed it. We believed it not just on good political grounds such as our resistance to biological theories of gender or sexual behaviour, but because for many of us it was our experience. Thousands of women who had not knowingly considered lesbianism as a possibility, left men and committed all their emotional and sexual energies to women, and are still so committed today.[12]

I think that the sexology that underpins *The Well of Loneliness* and that still holds some currency today is wrong; it depends upon some virulently misogynistic assumptions. However, it did hit on something important which has been confirmed by those who ditched most of its theory: sexuality involves something more than desire for 'genital contact' and has an effect upon the whole of a person's relating. So women who claim the name 'lesbian' or even 'bisexual', but who do not sleep with or desire to sleep with women, are saying something about the most important people in their lives: their nurturers and supporters, their friends. Many women would, of course, not claim the name lesbian but would still be woman-identified in many ways. Being lesbian, gay or bisexual in a context which regards such people as abnormal, sick, perverted and dangerous obviously has an effect upon your whole life and all your relationships, but it is not just a context of marginalization and/or oppression which involves your sexuality in every aspect of your life; it may be that the context of marginalization/oppression enables you to see what part sexuality plays in everyone's life. Sister Charles, a vowed celibate, when asked if she would still regard herself as sexual, replied:

> Oh yes, I have no doubts that I am sexual. I do not engage in sexual intercourse, but the sexuality that I live is like a pulse that goes right through me. There is an erotic part of who I am that is lived out in deep relationships of love.[13]

Perhaps the matter will become clearer if we ask the question 'what is it that we do when we make love to someone?' The answer to this is that it depends on the context. A man and woman having penetrative sex may be engaging in a mutually pleasurable act which conveys their love for each other, or the man may be raping the woman. The man may think the act is consummating and expressing the beginning of a long-term commitment to each other; the woman may think it is just a one-night stand, a bit of fun. The point is that the act of sex has no inherent meaning, 'rather in the course of interactions and over the course of time, individuals and societies spin webs of significance around the realm designated as "sexual"'.[14] For example, in Western societies we would describe two men engaging in mutual masturbation as engaging in a homosexual act, and we would assume these men to be 'gay'. However, in Turkey the same act would not be interpreted in these terms. In Turkish society sex is defined in terms of 'active' and 'passive' roles; the male role in a sex act is to be active, the woman's to be passive. Men should not play the role of women. So whereas Turkish society would certainly regard penetrative intercourse between two men as a homosexual act because one is playing the role of a woman, they would not interpret mutual masturbation in these terms since 'it does not jeopardize the value of the phallus at all',[15] and the men involved would not be labelled homosexual. Indeed, it is only the participant who is penetrated in penetrative sex who is so labelled. Few people realize that in British law 'sex' is defined as vaginal intercourse, so that unless a woman has been penetrated by a man's penis she is still technically a virgin. In most countries rape is defined as unlawful sexual *intercourse*, which means a penis must have penetrated a vagina; any other form of sexual violence (although Britain has recently recognized the crime of male rape), the insertion of other objects into the vagina or anus, oral sex or anal intercourse is regarded as sexual assault, which is a lesser crime.[16]

I am sure this is one of the reasons why the Churches have such difficulty in dealing with issues of sexuality—they ignore the fact that sexual acts take on different meanings in different

① Sets out problems with theology
② Attempts to re-define meaning + love

circumstances. The Christian compulsion seems to have been to establish one universal meaning for sex. The result has been a failure to recognize mutuality, justice and beauty in some sexual relationships which do not embrace the universal meaning, and a perhaps more unforgivable failure to recognize exploitation, violence and abuse in relationships that were supposed naturally to embody the universal meaning. So Christianity eventually came to the conclusion that the chief purpose of sex was to reproduce, using arguments from 'nature' to justify this conclusion. Aquinas argued forcefully that God, as the creator, has arranged everything for the good of his creation so we must follow the 'natural' law that is written into creation. Things like sweat, urine, faeces have no purpose and so they are expelled from the body:

> But semen is needed to be emitted for the purpose of generation, to which coitus is ordered. From which it is obvious that every emission of semen in such a way that generation cannot follow is against the good of man. And if this is done on purpose, it must be a sin ... But if generation cannot follow an emission of seed *per accidens*, it is not therefore against nature, nor a sin—as when the woman happens to be sterile.[17]

Every sexual act which is not open to reproduction (with the inconsistent exception of intercourse between a man and a sterile woman, even if they know she is sterile) is therefore sinful; it is 'disordered', a sin against nature. This search for a universal meaning and purpose for sex led to the argument that homosexual sexual acts were more sinful than a rape of a woman because, even though the latter is sinful (originally because a man, whether her father, husband or guardian, was dishonoured in the process), it is still a 'natural act' whilst the former is not. The Roman Catholic Church still holds to the belief that every act of sexual intercourse has the same meaning and purpose. In recent years the nature of this meaning has been elaborated upon. Pope John Paul II regards sex as a language:

> Sexuality, by means of which man and woman give themselves

[handwritten: B) Transforms the idea of sexuality]

to one another through the acts which are proper and exclusive to spouses, is by no means something purely biological, but concerns the innermost being of the human person as such. It is realised in a truly human way only if it is an integral part of the love by which a man and a woman commit themselves totally to one another until death. *The total physical self-giving would be a lie if it were not the sign and fruit of a total personal self-giving, in which the whole person, including the temporal dimension, is present: if the person were to withhold something or reserve the possibility of deciding otherwise in the future, by this very fact he or she would not be giving totally.* [my emphasis][18]

Sexual intercourse is an act of total self-giving; therefore, if two people engage in sexual activity outside the context of a relationship based upon a commitment to mutual total self-giving, that sexual activity is a lie.

The Congregation for the Doctrine of Faith in a letter to Catholic bishops about homosexuality argue that the meaning of sex has something to do with divinely ordered complementarity:

God, in his infinite wisdom and love, brings into existence all of reality as a reflection of his goodness. He fashions mankind, male and female, in his own image and likeness. Human beings, therefore, are nothing less than the work of God himself; and in the complementarity of the sexes, they are called to reflect the inner unity of the Creator. They do this in a striking way in their co-operation with him in the transmission of life by a mutual donation of the self to the other ... To choose someone of the same sex for one's sexual activity is to annul the rich symbolism and meaning, not to mention the goals, of the Creator's sexual design. Homosexual activity is not a complementary union, able to transmit life; and so thwarts the call to a life of that form of self-giving which the Gospel says is the essence of Christian living.[19]

All these arguments for a universal meaning to sexual activity have received devastating criticism from the Roman Catholic theologian Gareth Moore. He exposes the fact that natural law is nothing of the kind, but a reading into nature of already held beliefs for the purpose of social control. In dealing with John Paul's argument about sexual language he points out that gestures or activities do not have the character of a language. Bodily gestures are not substitutes for words, they are another form of communication altogether:

> If it is a mistake to think of our actions as ways of literally saying something, it is similarly wrong to think that actions can be true or false, that we can lie with our actions, except metaphorically. It is sentences, what we say, that can be true or false, not our actions ... We certainly can mislead others with our actions, give them a false impression ... If Andrew does not love Jane, he can deceive her into thinking that he does by taking her to bed. If his sex with her is deceitful, however, it will likely be only one element in a wider context, in a pattern of deception. He will probably deceive her in other ways as well—take her out to dinner, buy her expensive presents; principally, he may have to lie to her by saying: 'I love you.' But that he will also lie to her does not make his deceitful sex with her into a lie. Just as our possibilities of expression are not confined to speaking, so the ways in which we deceive are wider than lying.[20]

Moore also points out that to lie a person must know what they say is false and must have the intention to deceive. Are people who intend to have casual sex with each other just for the sake of mutual pleasure and who know they will part for ever afterwards deceiving each other? The answer is obviously not. Their sexual activity is not a total mutual self-giving at all. Similarly the concept of complementarity relies upon a failure to face up to reality, to the fact that there are people who do not fit into the categories of male and female. It is often based upon understandings of 'maleness' and 'femaleness' which bristle with patriarchal stereotyping made very popular by Jung. It claims for itself an understanding of Genesis 1.26–27 which has no history in the Christian tradition and is not a natural meaning of the text, which assumes that the only way to mirror God's creativity is through the production of children, again an assumption not found in Christian tradition and scripture. This is sometimes accompanied by an argument that penis and vagina were obviously made for each other and therefore for no other use. Janice Raymond has also asked a devastating question of those who advance the notion of complementarity:

> If the complementarity of male–female organs and the complementary reproductive capacity of both sexes are the main biological arguments for the maintenance and support of hetero-relations, the question must be asked why so many physically abusive actions have been necessary to enforce the 'natural' state of hetero-relations. Something that is so natural should never have to be coerced for so many women.[21]

The Vatican cannot really believe that human beings are only 'half' of what God intended us to be until we attach ourselves to a member of the opposite sex. If it did, it would not hold celibacy in such esteem. The Pope, priests and members of religious orders would be locked for ever by their vow of celibacy in a state of truncated development.

Failing to start with reality, with people's experience, has led Christianity to develop a theology of sexuality which not only excludes and bruises many but also rests on embarrassingly weak arguments which can easily be dismantled.

Having made the point that it is ridiculous and dangerous to create and impose a universal understanding of the meaning of sex, can we make any statements about sex between consenting adults? Well, most obviously, when two people have sex together they are relating to one another in an explicitly physical way. We cannot ignore the fact of our embodiment when we are enjoying sex! We touch, kiss, rub, lick, stroke, smell and gaze at another human body and this gives us pleasure, because we are enjoying doing these things. Our embodiedness is our connection with the rest of life around us; it is also the source of our solidarity with life around us, which is why hatred of the body has produced alienation from the world around us, and unjust actions towards it. When does sex begin? This is an important question and one that has exercised moral theologians and conscience-ridden Christians for a long time. The title of David Lodge's famous novel *How Far Can You Go?* has been the cry of many us solemnly taught that sex must be confined to marriage. When helping to run study days for 16 to 18-year-olds I have been surprised by how many of them believe that lesbians cannot 'have sex', so closely is sex associated in their minds with penis in vagina. Yet survey after survey has shown that a majority of women do not enjoy penetrative sex.[22] Composers of church statements on sexuality, mindful of the anarchic possibilities of defining sex so narrowly, tend to talk in terms of 'genital acts'. But would the Church Fathers then approve of two women or two men giving each other a naked massage to the point of orgasm even if they studiously avoided the genital region? The fact that they haven't even considered the possibility demonstrates once again the blindness of patriarchy for, as Luce Irigaray has noted, 'Woman has sex organs just about everywhere. The geography of her pleasure is much more diversified, more multiple in its differences, more subtle, more complex than is imagined.'[23] Even focusing on mutual orgasm as somehow central in defining sex is problematic from a feminist perspective because once again it makes sex a goal-oriented process. Carter Heyward can write of orgasm:

> Sexual orgasm can be literally a high point, a climax in our capacity to know, ecstatically for a moment, the coming together of self and other; sexuality and other dimensions of our lives; a desire for control and an equally strong desire to let go; a sense of self and other as both revealed and concealed; the simultaneity of clarity and confusion about who we are; and tension between the immediacy of vitality and pleasure and a pervasive awareness, even in moments of erotic ecstasy, that the basis of our connection is the ongoing movement—that is, the friendship—that brings us into this excitement and releases us into the rest of our lives, including the rest of this particular friendship.[24]

But many women do not experience orgasm in such a positive and meaningful way. Although the 'discovery' of the female orgasm was claimed as an advance for the women's movement, Sally Cline and Dale Spender discovered that in fact orgasms came to be seen as the compulsory purpose of sex, not primarily in order to give pleasure to women but to bolster the male ego: 'We discovered orgasms were seen as obligatory, and were a form of manipulated emotional labour which women worked at in order to reflect men and to maintain male values.'[25] This explains why a large number of women feel it necessary to fake orgasms and why the language of pathology is employed to deal with those women who will not or cannot 'play the game'.[26] They are labelled 'frigid'. This is all part of what Cline calls 'the genital myth', the belief associated with Freud that sexual (i.e. heterosexual) genital activity is essential for health, happiness and the common good. The defining of sex as 'foreplay', followed by 'intercourse', and finally 'orgasm', betrays all the patriarchal tendencies of dissection and hierarchical ordering that we earlier noticed in connection with friendship.

> Sex would be more nourishing. Self to self, self to others—lots of warmth and involvement and love and touching on all possible levels as a natural expression of body and emotions. Babies, children, pets, old, young, everyone would be cuddled and fondled, touched and encouraged to do so to and for each other and themselves. There would be public rejoicing in the pleasure of affection and the human body.[27]

These are the words of a woman taking part in a Hite survey answering the question 'In the best possible of all worlds, what would sexuality be like?' Many of the women who responded to Hite spoke about their ideal vision of 'sex' in terms that would not normally be recognized as 'sex', as close bodily and emotional contact, with the emphasis on touch and very little emphasis on the genitals or on orgasm.[28] A number of women said that their favourite kind of touching involved face-to-face body pressing. The whole language of sex and sexuality is a relatively recent invention (the term 'sexual intercourse' first appeared in *The Oxford English Dictionary* in 1779) and was developed in the context of the medicalization of human nature. The very word 'sex' (deriving from the Latin verb *secare* which means 'to cut, or divide') first referred to the differences between men and women, and the act of reproduction. In view of its origins it is perhaps not surprising that the language of sex is inadequate to express much of women's experience. As Claudia Card notes: 'When one tries to abandon a phallocentric conception of sex, it is no longer clear what counts as sexual and what does not.'[29] In which case, the dualism between sexual orientation and practice becomes a nonsense. This is an extremely important point. It will be my contention that the experience of gay men and women in general, but perhaps particularly of lesbians, demonstrates the all-pervasiveness of sexual desire and releases it from its patriarchal prison of genital activity.

Perhaps we could say that what happens when two adults, who know each other well, enjoy each other's bodies through various types of touch is that they enjoy each other in an intimate way; they enjoy being enjoyed as embodied persons because of the wider relationship they share. Particular acts of bodily intimacy express the nature of the relationship as a whole. And if we were also to remind ourselves of the definition of friendship that emerged out of the experience of women and gay men—'a relationship which, as it grows between people, results in mutual and equal acceptance, respect and delight ... an embodied relationship with social and political repercussions' (p. 48)— the close connection between friendship and sexual activity becomes clear. They are both based upon mutual acceptance, respect and delight. The pleasure of both is of being able to enjoy mutual intimacy with someone you know and like, and of being enjoyed by another, not just anybody but someone you know, respect, admire and like. Mutual attentiveness, enjoyment, excitement are what make both a pleasurable and playful experience. Remember too that we recognized the presence of the erotic in our friendships as '"the psychic urge to relate, to join, to be in the midst of, to reach out to, to value, to get in touch with, to get involved with concrete feelings, things, and people, rather than to abstract or theorize" [Ulanov] ... a power awakened or brought to birth in us by the experience of being loved. It is deep body knowledge of our interconnectedness and interdependence, our own self-worth and worth of all life' (p. 62). The erotic has always been recognized in sexual activity; it is now beginning to be owned in friendship. The erotic force which constitutes our sexuality and propels us out towards others to connect with them, to engage with them bodily in friendship, is the same force which propels us into 'sexual' activity. In fact, it may be impossible to draw a distinction between 'sexual' and 'non-sexual' activity. This I think is one of the great insights that lesbian, gay and bisexual people have to offer and it is an insight that many, but perhaps particularly heterosexual men, are afraid of. C. S. Lewis was particularly panicked by this thought. He takes great trouble in *The Four Loves* to demolish any idea of an inherent connection between *philia* and *erōs*:

> Those who cannot conceive Friendship as a substantive love but only as a disguise or elaboration of Eros betray the fact that they have never had a Friend. The rest of us know that though we can have erotic love and friendship for the same person yet in some ways nothing is less like a Friendship than a love-affair. Lovers are always talking to one another about their love; Friends hardly ever about their Friendship. Lovers are normally face to face, absorbed in each other; Friends side by side, absorbed in some common interest. Above all, Eros (while it lasts) is necessarily between two only. But two, far from being the necessary number for Friendship, is not even the best.[30]

James Nelson has noted that one of the reasons why heterosexual men have problems making friends is their homophobia. Their homophobia arises out of Western man's alienation from his body, caused by the dualism which still runs through our culture. The body and its messages are to be ignored or tamed. This is particularly true of certain deep erotic feelings:

> As a male predestined to either/or dichotomies in understanding sexual orientation, as one programmed by religion and society to believe that heterosexuality is normative, I still get some same-sex feelings. But because of my conditioning, I find them intolerable. So I project my rejection outward onto those visible symbols, gay males, punishing them for what I feel in myself but cannot tolerate.[31]

Nelson also believes that jealousy lies behind much male homophobia. Gay men are defined by their sexuality and in our
culture sexuality is largely interpreted in terms of genital sexual
activity. In a context where to be a sexual success a man must be
potent, and impotence is interpreted in terms of a failure to be a
'real man', the stereotyped promiscuous gay man actually
threatens the masculinity of many straight men. In addition,
gay men have for centuries been seen to undermine male power
by 'playing the role of the woman' in sex. This threatens a
system of power when the powerful take on the role of the
oppressed, the superior the role of the inferior. So in Western
society most men become caught in a trap. Homophobia flour-
ishes because most straight men do not have the experience of
close male friendship, but it is homophobia that prevents
friendships forming even between fathers and sons.[32]

Nelson also notices that male acquaintances have a
'shoulder-to-shoulder' relationship rather than a face-to-face
one, an understanding of friendship conveyed in Lewis's
remarks about the differences between *erōs* and friendship:
they come together to do something rather than actually enjoy
each other. Lewis makes the claim:

> We do not want to know our Friend's affairs at all. Friendship,
> unlike Eros, is uninquisitive. You become a man's Friend
> without knowing or caring whether he is married or single or
> how he earns his living ... We meet like sovereign princes of
> independent states, abroad, on neutral ground, freed from our
> contexts. This love (essentially) ignores not only our physical
> bodies but that whole embodiment which consists of our family,
> job, past and connections.[33]

I find that statement extraordinary and deeply sad because of
the fear of intimacy and bodiliness that inspired it. Note the
contrast between Lewis's understanding of friendship and that
of Aristotle, Socrates, Aelred, Kierkegaard, Hunt, Nardi and
Raymond—all of whom would, I think, argue that friendship
does involve facing each other: there is no point 'dancing

naked' in a line! Listen to some girls talking about their best friends for *The Hite Report on the Family*:

> She has velvet eyes, and a very sensual voice. She is honest and fair. When we get together we sit and talk, laugh, and drink coffee. We have an intense friendship.

> Dancing in the house and hugging. We get together and put on the music, and laugh, sing, talk and cry. When we are together, we show our souls to each other.

> My friend is a magnificent woman: warm, emotional and ambitious. We write letters, phone for hours, talk all night long, go on holidays, and cuddle. I feel relaxed, happy and content when I am with her.[34]

You cannot fail to recognize the presence of the erotic as I have defined it in the descriptions of these relationships. There is simply no equivalent voice from boys—except those boys who identified as gay! There is plenty about joining the 'male club' and male groups, but nothing about friendship. The comments of some fathers on their relationship with their son/s do, however, make interesting reading:

> I have five sons, between two and eleven, and God should strike me dead if I ever touch them. I would prefer them dead, that would guarantee them heterosexuality.

> I like a certain amount of snuggling with our two sons, but like most men, I wanted them to be all boy, as I was, so I cut it off.

> Recently my eight-year-old son asked if we could get into bed together naked and cuddle, so we did. It was really fine. We both had erections, but that just seemed a natural thing to happen. There was no sexual activity, it was just a warm and happy time.[35]

Behind all the homophobia, behind the fear of sexuality, *erōs*, embodiment, lies a truth, a truth happily acknowledged by many women and gay men, that we cannot dissect and order love, we cannot disembody our love. Our bodies will remind us of this fact even if we try to avoid it. And the very fear of erotic feelings reveals their existence. Listen to another father:

I am the father of a five-year-old and live alone with him. I would like to mention areas that have caused concern for me. When playing with a child in situations where both I and the child were nude, my erection has worried me. If the child played with it, I would feel guilty even though I might enjoy it. If I told the child not to play with it I would be making an issue out of it and somehow reinforce the idea that there was something wrong with an erection.[36]

Fortunately this father discussed these feelings with a friend and decided that it would be unjust of him to involve a child in a sexual situation 'any more than I would permit him access to a knife'. Failing to be honest about the sexual dimension in all our relationships has two disastrous consequences: on the one hand it keeps people apart from each other, prevents friendship and leaves people isolated and lonely; on the other hand it can lead to irresponsible and unjust behaviour because the perpetrators are not encouraged to face their feelings and deal with them. Anger, shame, confusion are then taken out on the children. One father wisely noted that 'adults want children to suppress their sexuality because otherwise they, the adults, would have to deal with their own repressed feelings'.[37]

I do not underestimate the resistance to the idea that there is an erotic dimension to friendship and that our sexuality is also in play in our friendships, but I believe that it is a truth that can be ultimately liberating for all, including straight men. Any bogus claims that real friendship is impossible for heterosexual men are exploded by the examples of deep friendship between men throughout history and in our own time. I think that the friendship that developed between John McCarthy and Brian Keenan in the twilight world of Beirut demonstrates the possibilities for male friendship. Their friendship contradicts almost every word of Lewis's distinctions between *erōs* and friendship. They were intensely interested in every aspect of each other's lives—past, present and future. They kept watch over each other, nursed each other, lifted each other out of depression and were physically tender towards each other. Now one could argue that they *had* to behave in this way to survive, but the relations between other hostages undermines this assumption. After a considerable period of time with only each other for company Keenan and McCarthy found themselves sharing a cell with three American hostages:

> It took quite a while to put the Americans in proper perspective. They argued a lot, with Tom and Frank finally erecting an invisible wall between them. They hardly spoke more than a couple of words in six months. Terry was still talking to Frank, but Frank ridiculed everything he said to the point where they, too, hardly spoke. Terry and Tom argued as well, and there often seemed to be far more serious undercurrents than a simple difference of opinion.[38]

McCarthy and Keenan were able to transcend all the false barriers erected between them, barriers of class, nationality and maleness. They did this by recognizing the barriers, and pounding them down through discussion and humour. These two men, apparently contentedly heterosexual, unselfconsciously using the language of love of each other, embody erotic friendship: 'There was no room in this place for any distance between us. We lay or sat side by side all day, every day. Like lovers in bed. There was little that could be withheld for long.'[39]

Casual sex

What are we to say about people who engage in genital activity with people whom they do not know at all or only slightly? There is, in fact, a distinction drawn in the gay community between 'casual' sex and 'anonymous' or 'impersonal' sex . Impersonal or anonymous sex takes place between people who use each other purely for the purpose of sexual behaviour. It 'avoids intimate person exchanges (e.g., conversation is minimal or non-existent) and total bodily interaction (e.g., elaborate and affectionate foreplay)'.[40] Casual sex, on the other hand may occur between acquaintances who may have sex with each other more than once. Casual sex is normally more intimate than impersonal sex and the relationship between the participants is more than simply utilitarian. The experience of

using + building blocks of

these men and women is usually ignored by those who attempt to develop a theology of sexuality and by official Church documents, or dismissed judgementally as being deliberately sinful, or categorized patronizingly as really being on a sad, lonely quest for a permanent relationship. Some of my friends and acquaintances who fall into this category are looking for a permanent relationship and do hope one day to come across 'the one', but many of them are not. The pleasure of such encounters comes from the excitement of the stranger, the possible risk and the lack of commitment, the enjoyment without much responsibility except for safe sex and if necessary appropriate contraception. If we accept that there is no universal meaning to 'sex', but touch only takes on meaning in a context, that in a context of friendship, touching takes on the meaning of friendship, and that genital contact is not 'the ultimate' expression of closeness or affection, then the phenomenon of casual sex becomes less of a problem. Genital activity, as long as it takes place, as all relationships should, in a context of honesty and justice, is not inherently more intimate than rubbing sun screen on a person's back. I will return to this issue later when questions about monogamy will have to be faced.

Language

Often when I have discussed the subjects of this chapter with groups, people have been ready to recognize and confirm the truth of what I have said, that any friendship has an erotic dimension and that our sexuality is concerned with much more than who we want to sleep with. However, there have nearly always been some who have argued that we should construct a new language to convey this. They argue that the words 'erotic' and 'sexuality' have become too closely and narrowly identified with genital heterosexual activity and, therefore, using them actually acts as a barrier to recognizing and articulating the truth. Marilyn Frye the philosopher has expressed this problem from a lesbian perspective:

We shall use

In situations of male dominance, women are for the most part excluded from the formulation and validation of meaning and thereby denied the means to express themselves. Men's meanings, and not women's meanings, are encoded in what is presumed to be the whole population's language. (In many cases, both the men and the women assume it is everyone's language.) ... women's meanings are not encoded in the dominant languages and ... this keeps our experience from being fully formed and articulate ...[41]

Perhaps invoking Eros, the oldest of the male gods, was bound to have a rather ambiguous result for lesbian feminists, and Frye believes that the adoption of such language has not rescued lesbians from phallocentric concepts but may have seduced them into adopting them in their own lives. Perhaps the problem is even more complex than that, as Asian feminist theologian Kwok Pui-Lan explains:

[But] strangely enough, the language of the erotic is noticeably missing in the theological construction of Afro-American women, and feminist theologians from other parts of the world also find it difficult to speak about the power of female sexuality ... Asian women find it embarrassing to talk about sex and the erotic not only because decent women are not supposed to raise those issues in public, but also because many of our sisters are working as prostitutes in the hotels, night-clubs, bars, disco joints, and cocktail lounges in the big cities like Manila, Bangkok, Taipei, Hong King, and Seoul ... The magnitude of the international flesh trade and the courageous action of these women's groups challenge us to rethink the connection between the language of the erotic, the control of the female body, and power over women in its naked and symbolic forms.[42]

We simply cannot ignore the fact that the language of the erotic is the language of 'sex' and that 'sex' for many women is experienced as part of unequal power relationship between women and men. Catharine MacKinnon has argued that gender and sex are social constructions and both are systems of male domination over women. Dominance and submission are eroticized and women experience domination primarily through 'sex', that is, through rape, abuse, sexual harassment, fear of being out at night or alone, and pornography.[43] So to ask women to reclaim the language associated with violence and exploitation is perhaps to ask too much. Mary Daly has tackled this problem head on, producing a whole new language for women, rescuing the original meaning of ancient words and creating new ones to express women's experience: a dip into her *Wickedary* is always a hilarious and informative experience. Neither 'sex' nor *erōs* or their derivatives appear in Daly's book, but she does offer some words which express the understanding of *erōs* and 'sexuality' which I have arrived at:

> E-motion *n* [derived fr. L *exmovere,* to move out, move away— *Webster's*]: Elemental Passion which moves women out/away from the fixed/framed State of Stagnation; Pyrogenetic Passion that fires deep knowing and willing, stirring Metamemory, propelling Wild Women on the Otherworld Journey.

> Pure Lust [*lust* 'VIGOR, FERTILITY ... and intense longing: CRAVING ... EAGERNESS, ENTHUSIASM'—*Webster's*]: the high humour, hope, and cosmic accord/harmony of those women who choose to escape, to follow our hearts' deepest desire and bound out of the State of Bondage ... pure Passion: unadulterated, absolute, simple, sheer striving for abundance of be-ing; unlimited, unlimiting desire/fire.

> Physical Ultimacy: actualization of relations that are fired/inspired by Pure Lust; Realisation of connections with Others as well as with one's Self that are far-reaching, demanding the stretching of physical, imaginative, psychic powers beyond 'normal' limitations; mode of connection among Elemental Women, the rhythms of whose bodies/minds are— like those of the tides—in harmony with the moon, the sun, and the farthest stars.[44]

There is a lot about Mary Daly's philosophy which I cannot swallow. In particular I think she fosters a dangerous dualism, both in her understanding of the human person and in her desire to call women into an 'Otherworld'. She also has a tendency to ignore differences between women (for which she has been consistently criticized by black women). I think that language is extremely important, it shapes as well as expresses our thought. Inclusive language matters. However, I am unsure of the effect of imposing a whole new language system upon people. I do not think it works. So I am not convinced that if we substituted E-motion, Pure Lust and Physical Ultimacy for the words *erōs* and 'sexuality' it would have the desired effect, except perhaps for those who are conversant with Daly and agree with her approach (and they are unlikely to be interested in my enterprise since they have abandoned Christianity as irredeemably patriarchal). However, there is a word that reappears in Daly's definitions which may be of help to us and that is 'passion'. Passion is defined in the *OED* as 'strong barely controllable emotion ... an outburst of anger ... intense sexual love ... a strong enthusiasm ... the suffering of Christ during his last days'. 'Passion' is one of the rare words which we use in love-talk which has not been reduced to genital activity. It encompasses within its widely accepted meanings a strong force driving a person outwards, anger, enthusiasm, pain and violence (which we will later see is vitally important), as well as sexual love in the narrowest sense of that term—all elements of the 'erotic' as Lorde conceived it. It is also a particularly appropriate term because it has already been coupled with friendship.

Passionate friends

In the eighteenth century, relationships that were labelled 'romantic' or 'passionate' friendships between women came to be extolled and written about in Europe. Emma Donoghue has undertaken a detailed study of these relationships. She notes that in literature then and now the assumptions about these friendships were that they were non-sexual and limited to the upper class. Indeed, many men believed that these friendships cultivated in women the qualities of faithfulness, devotion and sensibility which would be invaluable when transferred to their husbands. However, the women themselves talked in terms of being 'in love', 'dazzled', and of their 'deep affection' and 'sincere and tender passion'.[45] In novels by women which dealt with this subject the ideal outcome involved the friends achieving economic independence and retiring to live together. See, for example, Sarah Scott's *A Description of Millenium Hall* (1762), which became a classic on the subject. Many works extolled the value of women's love for each other, comparing it favourably with the love between men and women. Anne Hughes, who published *Henry and Isabella* in 1788, describes passionate friendships between women as:

> more sweet, interesting, and to complete all, lasting, than any other which we can ever hope to possess; and where a just account of anxiety and satisfaction were to be made out, would, it is possible, in the eye of rational estimation, far exceed the so-much boasted pleasure of love.

Many of these passionate friendships co-existed with marriage, but Donoghue has noted that there were also a significant body of women who furiously resisted marriage.

One of these was Mary Astell who wrote two works on the subject. She asked the subversive question: 'If Marriage be such a blessed State, how comes it, may you say, that there are so few happy Marriages?' She concluded that a woman 'has no reason to be fond of being a Wife, or to reckon it a piece of Preferment when she is taken to be a Man's Upper Servant'.[46] Equality was regarded as being an essential of such friendships. Queen Anne could not bear it when her friend Sarah Churchill, who had been a close companion since childhood, was expected to treat her as a superior; she proposed that they write to each other as equals under false names, so they became Mrs Morley and Mrs Freeman. This relationship was passionate not only in its intensity but also in its stormy character, and it eventually ended in a morass of bitterness.[47] It seems that these relationships were generally not assumed to be 'Sapphist' and Lillian Faderman argued that this assumption was broadly correct, although she saw late twentieth-century lesbian-feminism as an 'analogue' of romantic friendships, arguing that 'had the romantic friends of other eras lived today, many of them would have been lesbian-feminists; and had the lesbian-feminists of our day lived in other eras, most of them would have been romantic friends'.[48]

Donoghue has questioned the assumption that a 'Sapphic' element did not exist. The famous case of the 'Ladies of Llangollen'—Lady Eleanor Butler and Sarah Ponsonby, who eloped together in 1778, settling in Wales where they became celebrities receiving the likes of the Duke of Wellington, Wordsworth and Walter Scott—is often cited as an example in which there was no Sapphic element, because one of Sarah's relatives mused that there was no serious impropriety because the elopement was with a woman rather than a man. However, a friend of both women described them as 'damned Sapphists' and alleged that other women were frightened to stay with them unless chaperoned by a man.[49] Donoghue draws attention to the work of the poet Anne Finch who was Countess of Winchilsea, particularly to her poem 'The white mouses petition to Lamira the Right Honble the Lady Ann Tufton now Countess of Salisbury'. In this extraordinary poem the author assumes the form of a mouse, which was the traditional symbol of female lust, a mouse which runs all over her friend's body:

> I sue to wear Lamira's fetters
> And live the envy of my betters
> When I receive her soft caresses
> And creeping near her lovely tresses
> Their glossy brown from my reflection
> Shall gain more lustre and perfection
> And to her bosom is admitted
> My colour there will be so fitted
> That no distinction cou'd discover
> My station to a jealous Lover.

As Donoghue points out, it is the sameness of colour (i.e. the sameness of gender) that allows the mouse to wander unnoticed, and this protects it from the jealousy of male admirers of the Countess. Only very recently have the diaries of Anne Lister (1791–1840) been decoded to reveal that she had sexual relationships with women. She was ambiguous about her

Extols the value of female friendship, sexual or otherwise?

attraction for women, internalizing the general fear and suspicion of lesbianism. She tried to draw a distinction between her own feelings which she felt were not chosen and those of 'Sapphists' who chose their behaviour. Faderman and Donoghue have shown that passionate friendships between women were a vitally important phenomenon in the eighteenth century, indeed they were the context in which some women expected and found the best and most satisfying form of love. Some of these relationships were undoubtedly 'sexual' in the usual sense of that term, some were not, but they were all passionate. Katherine Philips, a seventeenth-century poet who extolled the virtues of female friendship, wrote to a friend: 'I gasp for you with an impatience that is not to be imagined by any soul wound up to a less concern in friendship than yours is, and therefore I cannot hope to make others sensible of my vast desires to enjoy you.'[50] She uses the language of what we would call 'sexual' love in her poetry and letters, but her principal aim seems to be to 'speak of our Love'. The American novelist Charles Brockden Brown in an unpublished work on female friendship has one of the characters say to the other: 'I want you so much. I long for you. Nay, I cannot do without you; so, at all events, you must come ... You shall dine, sup, and sleep with me alone. I will have you all to myself.'[51] The pair, Jessica and Sophia, vow never to marry and dream of retiring to the country together. Jessica, reminiscing about a night spent together, declares: 'Ever since that night I have been a new creature; to be locked in your arms; to share your pillow with you, gave new force, new existence to the love which before united us.'[52] Faderman discovered that 'it was virtually impossible to study the correspondence of any nineteenth-century woman ... and not uncover a passionate commitment to another woman at some time in her life'.[53]

The term 'Boston marriage' was coined in late nineteenth-century New England to describe a long-term, committed relationship between two unmarried, financially independent and usually feminist women who often made notable contributions to the arts and/or to local society through 'social' work.

Henry James and Louisa May Alcott were among several nov-
elists to write about the Boston marriage, Alcott making the
point in her 1883 novel *An Old Fashioned Girl* that even the
most well-intentioned and liberal of husbands could never give
a woman the necessary freedom and support she needs in order
to realize her potential in the world. Donoghue has done much
to undermine the popular notion that people in the seventeenth
and eighteenth centuries had no notion that women could or
would want to have sex with each other. She also shows that
there were some suspicions around women's romantic friendship during this period. Faderman has shown that as long as
women continued to behave and dress in 'feminine' ways their
relationships were tolerated. It was when they defied these
conventions that they became a threat to the social order
and became objects of intense suspicion and often hate. The
'Ladies of Llangollen' probably owed their tolerance, affection
and admiration from the establishment to their high social
position and their intensely conservative outlook on politics.
The sexologists sounded the death knell for societal acceptance
of and encouragement of passionate friendships between
women. Richard von Krafft-Ebing and Havelock Ellis, building upon the eighteenth-century belief in the female hermaphr-
odite, the woman with the enlarged clitoris who sought out
members of her sex, invented the congenital invert, the third
sex:

> Love between women was metamorphosed into a freakishness,
> and it was claimed that only those who had such an abnormality
> would want to change their subordinate status in any way.
> Hence, the sexologists' theories frightened, or attempted to
> frighten, women away from feminism and from loving other
> women by demonstrating that both were abnormal and were
> generally linked together.[54]

It is important to understand that much of the nineteenth-
century obsession with classifying and ordering sexuality was
linked with the eugenics movement and the poor were often
blamed for causing inversion and threatening the survival and
dominance of the white race. One American doctor claimed

that inverts were born to degenerate parents who themselves lacked the strong characteristics of their sex.[55] Freud on the other hand blamed the 'perversion' not on nature but on nurture, on something going wrong in childhood, thus offering an implicit assurance that the condition was 'curable'—creating a whole new psychological industry to which men and women who could not bear the weight of freakishness flocked.

Faderman notes that, whereas there is little evidence in the form of diaries etc. that working-class women enjoyed passionate friendships, what little evidence there is suggests that such relationships did flourish among prostitutes and in penal institutions where the overtly sexual element of the friendships was more apparent. Certainly by the end of the nineteenth century, when working-class women were beginning to enjoy more independence, such friendships flourished when women were thrown together in shared rooms. Faderman also argues that the phenomenon of women passing as men was more common among working-class women simply because it was often the only way that they could gain any kind of social or economic independence.[56] The association of passionate female friendship with lesbianism, and lesbianism with feminism, and lesbianism with sick, unhappy, sordid lives was a masterstroke of anti-feminist propaganda at a time when more women were challenging male constructions of womanhood and beginning steadily to rock the boat of the social order. This association is still alive and was used to great effect in Britain to undermine the message of the women who in the 1980s camped on Greenham Common in protest against the nuclear weapons in the US air base there. Faderman has noted that in the United States of America these passionate friendships between women were still possible in the early twentieth century but, as Freud became the hero of the nation, the phenomenon died out. She cites an interesting experiment conducted by two women friends at a high school in California in 1973:

> For three weeks the girls behaved on campus as all romantic friends did in the previous century: they held hands often on

campus walks, they sat with their arms around each other, and they exchanged kisses on the cheek when classes ended. They expressly did not intend to give the impression that their feelings were sexual. They touched each other only as close, affectionate friends would. But despite their intentions, their peers interpreted their relationship as lesbian and ostracized them. Interestingly, the boys limited their hostility to calling them names. The girls, who perhaps felt more anxiety and guilt about what such behaviour reflected on their own impulses, threatened to beat them up.[57]

Faderman also tells the story of the distressed teenage girl who discovered that her deeply meaningful relationships with other women at high school were in fact 'sick' and 'perverted' from reading a book about teenage love which recommended she get counselling.[58] A similar reaction took place among passionate friends when the sexologists and psychologists began to publish their works. Many passionate friends could not recognize themselves in the scientists' mirrors. Mary Casal in her autobiography, published in 1930, in which she described her passionate friendship with a woman called Juno, felt it necessary to draw a distinction between the love they enjoyed and that of the 'real inverts': 'While we did indulge in our sexual intercourse, that was never the thought uppermost in our minds . . . But we had seen evidences of over indulgence on the part of some of those with whom we came in contact, in loss of vitality and weakened health, ending in consumption.'[59] Faderman cites cases of women who, even though they enjoyed passionate friendships, sought to prevent other women, often under their care, from falling into the dangerous sickness of lesbianism. However, many women, like Hall, welcomed the sexologists as providing them with a discourse upon which to build a case for societal toleration and, as Esther Newton has pointed out, the theory very importantly allowed women a full sexuality outside the bounds of marriage and procreation and provided them with a discourse to articulate it.[60] Regarded as a man in a woman's body, the lesbian was allowed male sexual freedom and assertiveness. Passionate friendship between

women was not purely a European/North American phenomenon—parallels can be found among women in religious
institutions all over the world, among the Chinese marriage-
resisters of the late nineteenth–early twentieth century and
amongst women in India and Africa.

Passionate friendship between men also existed and was
written about, sometimes in a self-consciously sexual way,
most often not. Alfred Lord Tennyson, the poet laureate of
England, wrote one of the greatest celebrations of male friendship in *In Memoriam*:

> Tears of the widower, when he sees
> A late-lost form that sleep reveals,
> And moves his doubtful arms, and feels
> Her place is empty, fall like these;
>
> Which weep a loss for ever new,
> A void where heart on heart reposed;
> And, where warm hands have prest and closed,
> Silence, till I be silent too... (13)
>
> My love involves the love before;
> My love is vaster passion now;
> Though mixed with God and Nature thou,
> I seem to love thee more and more. (80)

In the United States the poet Walt Whitman was the most
eloquent exponent of male love:

> O tan-faced prairie-boy,
> Before you came to camp came many a welcome gift,
> Praises and presents came and nourishing food, till at last
>   among the recruits,
> You came, taciturn, with nothing to give—we but look'd
>   on each other,
> When lo! more than all the gifts of the world you gave me.

Novels also exhorted the nobility of male friendship, sometimes as a preparation for marriage, sometimes as an alternative
to marriage.[61] The sexologists had an equally ambiguous effect
upon male friendship.

Despite all the restraints put upon it, passionate friendship still does exist. In the 1987 Hite Report on *Women and Love*, a staggering 87 per cent of married women and 95 per cent of single women claimed that they had their deepest emotional relationship with a woman friend.[62] The language of eighteenth- or nineteenth-century women talking about their love for one another is not very far removed from the voices of the girls in the *Hite Report on the Family* or indeed from the deeply moving testament to friendship embodied and told by Brian Keenan and John McCarthy. Nor are the voices of those passionate friends who were not 'lovers' in the usual use of that term so different from the language of passion between lovers. In fact, as both Faderman and Donoghue point out, we simply cannot tell, with most of the friends whose letters and poems survive from the seventeenth, eighteenth and nineteenth centuries, whether the relationships were genitally expressed or not. They were certainly physical: touching, kissing, stroking, hugging were perfectly acceptable, as was admiration of the other's physical appearance as well as her intellectual qualities. The degree of passion was at least equivalent to, at most far greater than, that experienced between those women and their husbands if they had them. The point is that in passionate or romantic friendships of the past we learn that the dissection and ordering of love is not a universal, eternal experience. Passion can be as real in friendship as in 'sexual' relationships. Relegated into a separate world from men, to the extent that they were often referred to as a separate race or species, women of the Renaissance, Enlightenment and Victorian periods found in friendship with each other love, affirmation and freedom to be themselves and courage to face and often challenge the injustice meted out on themselves and others. Relegated to a world of cells, chains and darkness Keenan and McCarthy found the same, and relegated to the margins of society gay men and lesbian women have also discovered the importance and passion of friendship. It is a passion that is obvious too in the extraordinary writings of St Aelred of Rievaulx who, like the romantic women friends, used erotic language to talk of friendship, even friendship between Christ and the beloved disciple and Christ and the believer. I do not think it a coincidence that this medieval monk wrestled with feelings which we would today label 'homosexual'. He too internalized the fears of his age but not to a neurotic extent. In one book he launched a scathing attack upon some religious houses: 'Some effeminate young men parade about with their buttocks half exposed like prostitutes. Of those responsible for this Scripture remarks: "And they have assigned boys to a brothel." '[63] He warned his sister against the temptations of the flesh by citing the example of two elderly monks who slept in each other's arms thinking that because they were impotent such affection was harmless. Yet his biographer Walter Daniel tells us that Aelred encouraged his monks to form close friendships and allowed them to hold hands.[64] Aelred does not seem to have surrendered his own experience of love through friendship to the body-fearing suspicious climate of the Church of his day. As Russell concludes: 'He became a saint and a spiritual master not by repressing his sensitivity but by trying to respond to its appeal.'[65] It is for this reason that he has been adopted as patron saint by many lesbian and gay Christian groups in Britain and the United States.

The passion of friendship is the same passion that lies behind our 'sexual' relationships. We are not talking about different types of love but different expressions of love. Mary Daly, writing about friendship between women, noted that 'female identified erotic love is not dichotomized from radical female friendship, but rather is one important expression/manifestation of friendship'.[66] All talk about sex and sexuality (including the Church's) has become so genitally focused that few bother to draw breath long enough to ask whether this reflects people's real experience. Surveys of lesbian couples reflect what I would risk guessing was the experience of most people—gay, straight, bisexual—in committed relationships: that genital acts are not the rock upon which the relationship is based but the expression and celebration, along with many other 'acts', of the relationship. Again and again it is passionate friendship that is seen as the rock, not sex. What would happen

Contextual

if we took all this experience seriously and tried to build a Christian theology of sexuality on the basis of friendship? //

- Need to question
- What is the aim of this book!

Notes

1 Michel Foucault, 'The perverse implantation' in Edward Stein, *Forms of Desire: Sexual Orientation and the Social Constructionist Controversy* (London: Routledge, 1990), p. 18.

2 James Nelson, *The Intimate Connection: Male Sexuality, Masculine Spirituality* (London: SPCK, 1992), p. 2.

3 Gilbert Herdt and Andrew Boxer, *Children of Horizons: How Gay and Lesbian Teens Are Leading a New Way Out of the Closet* (Boston: Beacon Press, 1993), p. 118.

4 Alison Hennegan in the Introduction to Radclyffe Hall, *The Well of Loneliness* (London: Virago, 1982), p. x.

5 Hall, *The Well of Loneliness*, pp. 446–7.

6 Carroll Smith-Rosenberg, *Disorderly Conduct: Visions of Gender in Victorian America* (New York: Alfred A. Knopf, 1985).

7 Vera Brittain, *Radclyffe Hall: A Case of Obscenity?* (London: Femina Books, 1968), p. 51.

8 Adrienne Rich, 'Compulsory heterosexuality and lesbian existence' in *Blood, Bread and Poetry: Selected Prose 1979–1985* (London: Virago, 1987), pp. 51–2.

9 Monique Wittig, *The Straight Mind and Other Essays* (Hemel Hempstead: Harvester Wheatsheaf, 1992).

10 Definitions from *The Concise Oxford Dictionary* (Oxford: Clarendon Press, 8th edn, 1990).

11 See Sue Wilkinson and Celia Kitzinger, *Heterosexuality: A Feminism and Psychology Reader* (London: Sage Publications, 1993) where many women whom others would label 'heterosexual' discuss their dislike of that term.

12 Sheila Jeffreys, *The Lesbian Heresy: A Feminist Perspective on the Lesbian Sexual Revolution* (London: The Women's Press, 1994), p. 77.

13 Sally Cline, *Women, Celibacy and Passion* (London: André Deutsch, 1993), p. 129.

14 Stephen Epstein, 'Gay politics, ethnic identiy: the limits of social constructionism' in Stein, *Forms of Desire*, p. 247.

15 Huseyin Tapinc, 'Masculinity, femininity, and Turkish male homosexuality' in Ken Plummer, *Modern Homosexualities: Fragments of Lesbian and Gay Experience* (London: Routledge, 1992), p. 40.

16 Diane Richardson, 'Constructing lesbian sexualities' in Plummer, *Modern Homosexualities*, pp. 188–90.

17 Aquinas, *Contra Gentiles*, 3.122, cited in Gareth Moore, *The Body in Context: Sex and Catholicism* (London: SCM, 1992), p. 75.
18 Pope John Paul II, *Familiaris Consortio* (London: Catholic Truth Society, 1981), para. 11.
19 Congregation for the Doctrine of Faith, *Letter to the Bishops of the Catholic Church on the Pastoral Care of Homosexual Persons* (London: Catholic Truth Society, 1986), paras 6–7.
20 Moore, *The Body in Context*, p. 106.
21 Janice Raymond, *A Passion for Friends: Towards a Philosophy of Female Affection* (London: The Women's Press, 1986), p. 58.
22 Cline, *Women, Celibacy and Passion*, pp. 149–50.
23 Cited in Arlene Stein, *Sisters, Sexperts, Queers: Beyond the Lesbian Nation* (New York: Plume, 1993), p. 13.
24 Carter Heyward, *Touching Our Strength: The Erotic as Power and the Love of God* (San Francisco: Harper and Row, 1989), p. 33.
25 Cline, *Women, Celibacy and Passion*, p. 150.
26 Cline, *Women, Celibacy and Passion*, p. 150.
27 Shere Hite, *Women as Revolutionary Agents of Change: The Hite Reports: Sexuality, Love and Emotion* (London: Sceptre Books, 1994), p. 111.
28 Hite, *Women as Revolutionary Agents of Change*, pp. 108–12.
29 Cited in Sarah Lucia Hoagland, 'From lesbian ethics: desire and political perception' in Judith Barrington, *An Intimate Wilderness: Lesbian Writers on Sexuality* (Portland, OR: The Eighth Mountain Press, 1991), p. 166.
30 C. S. Lewis, *The Four Loves* (London: Collins, 1960), p. 58.
31 Nelson, *The Intimate Connection*, p. 61.
32 Nelson, *The Intimate Connection*, pp. 59–64.
33 Lewis, *The Four Loves*, pp. 66–7.
34 Shere Hite, *The Hite Report on the Family: Growing Up Under Patriarchy* (London: Bloomsbury, 1994), pp. 131–2.
35 Hite, *The Hite Report on the Family*, pp. 329–32.
36 Hite, *The Hite Report on the Family*, p. 329.
37 Hite, *The Hite Report on the Family*, p. 221.
38 John McCarthy and Jill Morrell, *Some Other Rainbow* (London: Corgi Books, 1994), pp. 309–10.
39 Brian Keenan, *An Evil Cradling* (London: Vintage, 1992), p. 124.
40 Wayne R. Dynes, *Encyclopedia of Homosexuality*, vol. I (London: St James Press, 1990), p. 578.
41 Marilyn Frye, 'Lesbian "sex"' in Barrington, *An Intimate Wilderness*, p. 6.
42 Kwok Pui-Lan, 'The future of feminist theology: an Asian perspective', *The Auburn News* (Fall, 1992).
43 Catharine MacKinnon, *Only Words* (Cambridge, MA: Harvard University Press, 1991).

44 Mary Daly and Jane Caputi, *Websters' First New Intergalactic Wickedary of the English Language* (London: The Women's Press, 1988), pp. 74, 88–9.

45 Emma Donoghue, *Passions Between Women: British Lesbian Culture 1668–1801* (London: Scarlet Press, 1993), p. 112.

46 Donoghue, *Passions Between Women*, p. 123.

47 Donoghue, *Passions Between Women*, pp. 158–64.

48 Lillian Faderman, *Surpassing the Love of Men: Romantic Friendship and Love Between Women from the Renaissance to the Present* (London: The Women's Press, 1985), p. 20.

49 Donoghue, *Passions Between Women*, pp. 149–50.

50 Faderman, *Surpassing the Love of Men*, p. 69.

51 Faderman, *Surpassing the Love of Men*, p. 110.

52 Faderman, *Surpassing the Love of Men*, p. 111.

53 Faderman, *Surpassing the Love of Men*, p. 15–16.

54 Faderman, *Surpassing the Love of Men*, p. 240.

55 Lillian Faderman, *Odd Girls and Twilight Lovers: A History of Lesbian Life in Twentieth-Century America* (London: Penguin, 1992), p. 40.

56 Faderman, *Odd Girls and Twilight Lovers*, pp. 37–9, 43.

57 Faderman, *Surpassing the Love of Men*, p. 312.

58 Faderman, *Surpassing the Love of Men*, p. 311.

59 Faderman, *Odd Girls and Twilight Lovers*, p. 54.

60 Esther Newton, 'The mythic mannish lesbian: Radclyffe Hall and the New Woman' in Martin Bauml Duberman, Martha Vicinus and George Chauncey, Jr, *Hidden from History: Reclaiming the Gay and Lesbian Past* (London: Penguin, 1991), pp. 281–93.

61 Robert K. Martin, 'Knights-errant and gothic seducers: the representation of male friendship in mid-nineteenth-century America' in Duberman et al., *Hidden from History*, pp. 169–82.

62 Hite, *Women as Revolutionary Agents of Change*, p. 318.

63 Aelred of Rievaulx, *Mirror of Charity*, 3.26, n. 64, cited in Kenneth C. Russell, 'Aelred the gay Abbot of Rievaulx', *Studia Mystica*, vol. 5, part 4 (Winter 1982), p. 58.

64 Russell, 'Aelred the gay Abbot of Rievaulx', pp. 56–8.

65 Russell, 'Aelred the gay Abbot of Rievaulx', p. 60.

66 Mary Daly, 'Sparking: the fire of female friendship', *Chrysalis: A Magazine of Women's Culture*, vol. 6 (1978), pp. 27–35.

4 The idolatry of the ideal

Lesbian and gay marriages?

Why is it that many lesbian and gay people do not define their relationships in terms of marriage? It would be dishonest of me not to acknowledge that some do. The gay theologian Robert Williams has made out a strong case for incorporating lesbian and gay relationships into the Christian institution of marriage. He squashes the fallacy that lesbian and gay people are incapable of maintaining committed monogamous relationships by citing a random survey that was made of gay male couples in 1984. In that survey of 156 couples, 95 had been together more than five years and 20 had been together for more than 20 years, showing a slightly better 'survival rate' than heterosexual couples.[1] This evidence is supported by the experience of the Episcopalian diocese of Rochester in New York where same-sex relationships have been blessed for over 20 years and shown to have a higher success rate than heterosexual marriages. Williams also establishes a precedent for the Church recognizing and celebrating marriages which lack the sanction of the state. The early Church recognized the relationship between a slave and free citizen as marriage and the Anglican Church in the USA often blessed the marriages of slaves and inter-racial couples when they were illegal. He argues that as soon as reformers of the sixteenth century began to redeem marriage from its status as 'second best' to the ideal of celibacy, and in the process widened its purposes from being narrowly focused on procreation, and 'a remedy against sin, and to avoid fornication', as the Book of Common Prayer states it, so as to include 'mutual society, help, and comfort' (which Martin Bucer argued were more important than procreation), the door was opened for the eventual inclusion of lesbian and gay people. He argues that the only purpose of marriage which lesbian and gay people cannot fulfil is procreation, and in that respect they are in the same position as heterosexual couples unable to procreate (although both gay/lesbian and heterosexual couples may, if the law allows, adopt children or bring up children conceived through artificial insemination or care for children from previous heterosexual marriages). Willliams offers a new inclusive definition of marriage which remains close to that found in present Episcopalian canon law but which is worded in such a way as to include same-sex couples:

> A lifelong union of two persons in heart, body, and mind, as set forth in liturgical forms authorized by this Church, for the purpose of mutual joy, for the help and comfort given one another in prosperity and adversity; sometimes also for the procreation and/or rearing of children, and their physical and spiritual nurture.[2]

Williams attacks those who would argue that lesbian and gay relationships cannot be marriages because marriage is in essence a relationship between a man and a woman. He compares their arguments to those used against the ordination of women which stated that a woman could not be ordained because ordination is by definition a state only open to men. A similar line has been taken by another theologian, Adrian Thatcher. Although not gay himself, Thatcher mounts a powerful and impassioned critique of the Christian Church's response to homosexuality. He is one of the few heterosexual male theologians who attempts to take lesbian and gay experience seriously and his work deserves to be better known. Thatcher also takes modern ecclesiastical definitions of marriage and notes how they can be easily applied to same-sex unions. The Second Vatican Council spoke about married love in the following terms:

Married love is an eminently human love because it is an affection between two persons rooted in the will and it embraces the good of the whole person; it can enrich the sentiments of the spirit and their physical expression with a unique dignity and ennoble them as the special elements and signs of the friendship proper to marriage. The Lord, wishing to bestow special gifts of grace and divine love on it, has restored, perfected, and elevated it. A love like that, bringing together the human and the divine, leads the partners to a free and mutual giving of the self, experienced in tenderness and action, and permeates their whole lives; besides, this love is actually developed and increased by the exercise of it .... Married love is uniquely expressed and perfected by the exercise of the acts proper to marriage. Hence the acts in marriage by which the intimate and chaste union of the spouses takes place are noble and honourable; the truly human performance of these acts fosters the self-giving they signify and enriches the spouses in joy and gratitude. Endorsed by mutual fidelity and, above all, consecrated by Christ's sacrament, this love abides faithfully in mind and body in prosperity and adversity and hence excludes both adultery and divorce. The unity of marriage, distinctly recognised by our Lord, is made clear in the equal personal dignity which must be accorded to man and wife in mutual and unreserved affection.[3]

The document goes on to make clear that children are the supreme gift of marriage and that married love is 'by nature ordered to the procreation and education of children'.[4] But Thatcher argues that gay and lesbian couples are as capable of 'a free and mutual giving of the self, experienced in tenderness and action' as childless heterosexual couples. His argument founders on the insistence of the Vatican that sexual acts are always open to the transmission of life, so that a childless heterosexual couple would still be required to make love in such a way that there is a possibility (even if that requires a miracle) that conception can occur. Of course it could be argued that, if we are bringing the miraculous into it, condoms, pills, imaginative positions and the lack of the necessary genital equipment are no obstacles to the divine (remember the virgin birth)! But the Vatican does not look at it that way. Thatcher is on stronger ground when he examines the understandings of marriage in the Church of England. The Book of Common Prayer declares a threefold purpose of marriage:

> First, It was ordained for the procreation of children, to be brought up in the fear and nurture of the Lord, and to the praise of his holy Name.
> Secondly, It was ordained for a remedy against sin, and to avoid fornication; that such persons as have not the gift of continency might marry, and keep themselves undefiled members of Christ's body.
> Thirdly, It was ordained for the mutual society, help, and comfort, that the one ought to have of the other, both in prosperity and adversity...

Examining the second purpose, Thatcher notes: 'Since homosexual people are just as randy as heterosexual people, this blunt concession is clearly applicable to them if it is applicable to anyone.'[5] He also points out that if that second purpose still stands it is wrong for the Church to deny marriage to gay and lesbian people because in doing so it is depriving them of the means to avoid fornication. In the Alternative Service Book that second purpose is dropped and replaced by something more positive:

> Marriage is given, that husband and wife may comfort and help each other, living faithfully together in need and in plenty, in sorrow and in joy. It is given, that with delight and tenderness they may know each other, in love, and, through the joy of their bodily union, may strengthen the union of their hearts and lives. It is given, that they may have children and be blessed in caring for them and bringing them up in accordance with God's will, to his praise and glory.

Once again Thatcher believes that that the first two purposes of marriage are capable of being realized by lesbian and gay people and they stand in the same position as childless heterosexual couples when it comes to the third. Just as the Church does not withhold marriage from those men and women who cannot have children so it cannot justify excluding lesbian and gay people from it. In fact it is not marriage itself that the Church is withholding but its recognition and solemnization of it:

> Those same-sex couples who have committed themselves to a faithful lifelong union before God, *are* married before God. That is because, as Aquinas says, 'the ministers of the sacrament of marriage are the bride and bridegroom themselves, and the form of the sacrament is their consent'. They are denied recognition, and so solemnization and blessing from the church, but God and the church are often on different sides ... But lesbian and gay couples will testify to the sacramental character of their unions: they may be even more conscious of it than their heterosexual counterparts since the discernment of God's grace has to be made out of much religious and social disapproval. That moving description in the Alternative Service Book of the married relationship fits the actual, lived experience of same-sex couples in the same way as the conventionally married.[6]

Thatcher is quite clear that it would be a mistake to call same-sex unions anything other than marriage:

> If same-sex unions are not marriages, then they are something else, and that something else is certain to be regarded as inferior, 'substandard' or 'abnormal'. The understanding and practice of marriage has changed historically, and a further change, which includes same-sex unions but without a change of name, is now appropriate.[7]

Thatcher has tried to grapple with the concept of friendship as the context and model for sexual relationships but has not quite grasped the theory and theology of friendship being developed by Hunt, Heyward, myself and others, since he seems to assume that the adoption of this model necessarily involves promiscuity or at least a less than strong commitment: 'Lifelong unions, not friendship, provide the most appropriate context for having children ... Sexual friendships may be particularly apt among the elderly ... Marriage is open to them. But they may be just friends.'[8] So although he tries to understand why many lesbian and gay people may not want to be incorporated into marriage and tries to appreciate the model of friendship, Thatcher ends up taking the view that marriage is a relationship superior to that of those who are 'just friends'.

So why is it that, despite such strong arguments, many lesbian and gay people reject the model of marriage for their relationships? A few quotations from a variety of feminists over a wide period of time speaking about marriage may give us a few clues:

> [It] is a labour relationship ... The marriage ceremony parallels with the signing of indentures, or even more with the selling of oneself into personal, domestic slavery when one can see no other way to support oneself adequately.[9]

> [It] is not a union of two souls or a partnership of equals. It is not a highly developed form of relationship but the most degraded.[10]

> [It] is an institution which robs a woman of her individuality and reduces her to the level of a prostitute.[11]

> Chief vehicle for the perpetuation of the oppression of women.[12]

> Someone coming from another planet and looking at a marriage contract and the semi-slavery it entails for the woman would think it insane that she should enter into it voluntarily.[13]

And of course we have already met Mary Astell and her strong seventeenth-century views on the subject: '[A woman] has no reason to be fond of being a Wife, or to reckon it a piece of Preferment when she is taken to be a Man's Upper Servant.'[14] Few would or could deny that, historically speaking, marriage has not been an ideal relationship for women and even today, despite lip-service being paid to equality, it is a lucky woman who finds it in marriage. Overall, the mental health of women deteriorates significantly when they get married, whilst the mental health of men improves.[15] And we are all surely aware of the scale of violence and abuse that can take place in marriage. In Britain 25 per cent of all violent crime is wife assault. Researchers in the United States found that 75 per cent of victims of domestic violence are wives.[16] The purposes of marriage as set out in the ASB are not being fulfilled for a large number of people. As a headline in a British national newspaper put it, 'Lovely idea—shame about the reality'. Despite dramatically declining figures for those over 16 marrying for the first time (in 1990 the rate was 39.6 per thousand, in 1981 the figure was 51.7 and in 1971 82.3), nine out of ten people marry before they are 30 and two-thirds of all marriages are between those who are marrying for the first time. In Britain one in three marriages ends in divorce; in the United States the failure rate is worse. The average span of what is supposedly a lifelong relationship is nine years. 9.5 per cent of marriages in Britain end in divorce in the first two years of marriage. Shere Hite discovered that 70 per cent of women married for five years or more are not faithful to their husbands. 72 per cent of men married for two years were not faithful to their wives.[17] The success rate of marriages entered into after divorce is poor; men are much more likely to remarry than women and do so with much more haste than women who remarry.[18] Psychiatrist Julian Hafner has noted: 'Although divorce for many women with young children means near-poverty, women's post-divorce emotional adjustment is superior to that of men. This underlines the extent to which marriage sustains men's emotional well-being.'[19] There is considerable evidence, then, to suggest that marriage simply does not measure up to the vision of the ASB, particularly, but not exclusively, as far as women are concerned. And yet politicians, Church and society still push marriage as the ideal relationship; if anything goes wrong it is not the institution's fault but human frailty and sin. David Oliphant has drawn attention to the way in which Church and state collude with the extremely lucrative 'wedding industry' to obscure the reality of marriage. He has some extremely harsh words to say about 'marriage propaganda' produced by Church, state and wedding industry, particularly about its unique suitability as the context for bearing and rearing children:

I am not sure that marriage and family as we have known and produced it produced the goods in these terms. At best it produced men and women who could continue the traditional social roles, and this on balance gave society a centre and a stability. At worst it produced badly damaged people ... Any attempt by the Church or any other organisation to hang on to old idealism about marriage has got to face and give account of this terrible reality. The depth of woundedness in our society from abuse in families is appalling. At this level traditional marriage has failed to produce reasonably whole and separate adults.[20]

Yet there are few signs that that Church or state is willing to face reality. Marriage itself seems to be above criticism. It has become an idol. We are all supposed to offer ourselves up to it and those who will not or cannot (like lesbian and gay people) are expected either to remain celibate[21] or acknowledge that our relationships could never live up to the ideal.[22] Feminists have learnt to be highly suspicious of ideals of any sort, since they can be used, and often are, as weapons to disempower and subjugate. The ideals of womanhood embodied in the Virgin Mary and the Page 3 girl in the tabloid press are obvious examples. The ideal of marriage disempowers and subjugates many women who enter into it and also disempowers and subjugates those not part of it.

We have such short memories. It is only because we have no sense of the history of marriage that others are able to sell us the ideal of marriage with such persuasiveness. The idea that people should marry for love and mutual happiness is (for the Church at least) an embarrassingly late one. Speculation about the origins of patriarchy is rife. Some suggest that things began to get rough for women when the connection between sexual intercourse and childbirth was recognized. Before this connection was made women were revered and respected for their apparently magical powers of fertility and this was reflected in an array of female figures, found particularly in tombs, which are thought to represent female deities. After c. 8000–7000 BCE these deities began to disappear, to be replaced by male counterparts, and the webs of patriarchy began to be spun. However, there is little evidence to suggest that these figures did represent deities and even if they did we cannot be sure that they reflect a woman-affirming context. The concept of a lost paradise has strong roots in the Jewish and Christian traditions and ecofeminist and creation-centred theologians have created their own version of this tradition: the lost matriarchal order focused on the immanent goddess in which peace, equality and ecological justice reigned.[23] Usually connected with areas in and around Greece or Turkey, it is believed by some that this idyllic existence was destroyed by invading forces from the north. Rosemary Radford Ruether, on the other hand, suggests that hunter-gatherer societies were matrifocal, with women responsible for the growing of vegetable food which constituted most of the diet. Since women had control over this vital food supply they had a great deal of power and prestige, but where edible plants were scarce the male hunting role became dominant and patrifocal and patrilineal social patterns developed. Tribal groups began to develop concepts of ownership which were applied to animals and to women. Of course, not all human societies followed this pattern. In some societies the decline in wildlife led to an expanded role for woman as plant-gatherer. In others, there was a movement from plant-gathering to agriculture, accompanied by a reverence for woman's fecundity and also fear of her control over life and death.

> Although actual hunting receded as a food source, the weapons of hunting remained identified with males. As humans became sedentary, population expanded and differences of accumulated wealth appeared. Social stratification within settlements, conflicts with rival settlements, and challenges from migrating nomads increased. The weapons of hunting were at hand to become the weapons of war, owned and controlled by males.[24]

When plough agriculture developed, men were able to define land and products as 'belonging' to them and plant-gathering became a male rather than female occupation. Urbanization was a response to competition for resources from without and within groups. Elites began to develop. Priests controlled sacred knowledge; warriors fought off competition from other groups. As a class hierarchy emerged, the relations between men and women were also redefined in terms of this hierarchy. Ruether believes it is a dangerous mistake to idealize matricentric societies:

> The psychological weakness of matricentric society lies in its difficulty in drawing in the contribution of the grown male without either conceding to this male a dominating role over women, or else producing a demoralised male deeply resentful of women ... The societies that have achieved gender parity in Sanday's study[25] were societies that either had elaborately structured mutual acknowledgement of male and female prestige and power, where women conceded power roles to men and men acknowledged that they received these from women, or else societies of considerable gender-role fluidity.[26]

Whatever the theory of how the webs of patriarchy began to be spun, most of the theorists agree that one of these webs was monogamy.

> Once the idea of maintaining power and influence *through male children* became established, it became necessary to *control female fertility*. How could a man be sure that the children borne by his official wife or wives were his own? How could he be sure that it was *his* eldest son who would inherit his power and status? How could the followers of a powerful chief be sure that it was truly *his* son who would succeed him as their leader? Unless all this could be guaranteed, the whole patriarchal social system would fall apart.[27]

And in societies where life after death was not an option, the only way to survive death in any form was through your children. And so marriage (if we can use that term of formalised, permanent bonding) was born to ensure a woman's faithfulness to her man. Engels imagined a similar process in his speculations on the origins of the family:

> The first class antagonism which appears in history coincides

with the development of the antagonism between man and woman in monogamous marriage, and the first class oppression with that of the female sex by the male. Monogamy was a great historical advance, but at the same time it inaugurated, along with slavery and private wealth, that epoch, lasting until today, in which every advance is likewise a relative regression, in which the well-being and development of one group are attained by the misery and repression of the other ... It was the first form of the family based not on natural but on economic conditions.[28]

Despite various attempts by Christian theologians to define marriage in other terms (they will be examined shortly), it remained little more than a social contract between men (one man, usually the father, handing over his daughter to another man) for most of its history. Not only did a marriage involve the coming together of two people, but also and usually more importantly the coming together of two families, and two sets of economic assets. Marriage ceremonies and contracts were devised to formalize these arrangements. In ancient Judaism the act of sexual intercourse was the principal ceremonial enactment of marriage. In some parts of the late Roman Empire an understanding of marriage emerged which did not view the woman as the property of her husband, but emphasized the necessity of her consent for the marriage to be valid and restricted the husband's right to female and male concubines.[29] Consummation of the marriage (i.e. 'sexual intercourse') was not considered essential to Roman marriage—consent and mutual affection were the components of validity—nor was procreation thought to be essential. Christianity took over the concept of Roman marriage with little difficulty; its lack of emphasis on 'carnality' suited the growing distaste for the body. Boswell believes that a later campaign led by Roman officials to encourage the dwindling upper classes to reproduce, which included penalties for the childless and rewards for those that were not, coupled with moral persuasion, 'doubtless influenced—even if subconsciously—educated Christian leaders such as Ambrose, Jerome, and Augustine' who were seeking to understand the divine purpose behind sexual desire.[30] For its first thousand years the Church in the West took very little part in marriage, offering blessings only to priests and well-to-do lay people. (In the East where Church and state were intimately entwined earlier, the practice of the well-to-do being blessed by a priest was required by the emperor in the sixth century CE, but such a ceremony was not essential for validity.) But even by the early nineteenth century only about half of the adult population was formally married.[31] It was only a matter of concern for those who sought to retain their social standing and avoid the dreaded state of poverty. The Western Church became particularly interested in the process of marriage in the twelfth century when a variety of royal marriage scandals raised questions about what was necessary for a marriage to be valid.[32] This interest was further excited by the Albigensian heresy which took hold in southern France in the late twelfth and early thirteenth centuries. These people held to an absolute, dualistic view of the world, regarding all matter as evil and rejecting the sacraments and the resurrection of the body. They did, however, believe that casual sex and homosexual acts were less pernicious than marriage, for the latter perpetuated matter through procreation. (The word 'buggery' comes from the French word *bougre* meaning 'heretic' and was first applied to this heresy.) The controversy around their views was long and difficult. Many of the popes would have liked to insist that vows be made before a priest but could not because of the implications for the validity of those marriages which had not been contracted in that manner. The Fourth Lateran Council (1251) ordered banns to be read and weddings to be held in public but did not insist on ecclesiastical benediction. The whole matter was eventually officially resolved in the Roman Catholic Church at the Council of Trent, when it was decided that a marriage must take place in the context of a public Christian ceremony and marriage came to be regarded as a sacrament. Therefore public Christian ceremony combined with the much-debated consent and consummation as the basis of validity.

The idea that love might be an essential element in this

process took a very long time to emerge. The romantic poetry of the medieval troubadours reminds us of the fact that love and passion were things often only experienced outside marriage and in any case rarely realizable:

> The seasons come and go in varied play,
> Days, months and years, in ever changing race.
> But I, alas, do not know what to say,
> For my desire is ever in one place.
> It stands without remove,
> For I have but one love,
> And have not known the joy of her embrace.[33]

The reason why this love was by necessity adulterous is explained by Countess Marie of Champagne:

> We declare and we hold as firmly established that love cannot exert its powers between two people who are married to each other. For lovers give each other everything freely, under no compulsion of necessity, but married people are in duty bound to give in to each other's desires and deny themselves to each other in nothing.[34]

The rise of courtly love can be attributed in part to the fact that under feudal law a woman could inherit wealth, property and title from her father and this gave her greater freedom and made her a powerful force and attractive proposition to men of her rank. And as Marina Warner has noted, courtly love is associated with adultery: 'Matriliny greatly diminishes the social disruptiveness of a wife's adultery, while patrilinity requires first and foremost the chastity of a wife, for otherwise she could deceive her spouse with heirs that are not his flesh and blood.'[35] Colin Morris has said of the troubadours:

> The love of which they spoke was a physical one, directed to the body of their lady and not to her beauties of character, which they rarely mentioned. The evidence supports the opinion that 'fin'amors is a hidden love, adulterous and dominated by physical desire.' It is distinguished from common-or-garden adultery by the requirement of sincerity and by certain

conventions of elegance: 'the ambition not to love like everybody else, like the general run of people. The sphere of courtly love is an ideal world, which is excluded from the comprehension and approach of the ignoble.'[36]

There is no shame in the adultery and many of the poems include prayers to Jesus to help the lover achieve his adulterous goal. It was in this celebration of extra-marital desire that what Marina Warner calls 'the quarrel between body and soul' which had rumbled through a millennium of Christianity came to a truce:

> Passion and reason were not bitter enemies, but could be reconciled in the camp of civilisation, by directing desire and love at an object of sublime moral and physical beauty; the body and soul were not locked in mortal combat, for the ability to love in this way at all was the distinguishing human mark, defining man's superiority to the animal, which cannot shape its instincts and desires in an ideal mould. A man or woman in love was not a brute in prey to lusts, or a creature of God invaded, like saints Antony and Jerome, by demons in enticing human form.[37]

But the truce was short-lived and by the early thirteenth century the troubadours were regarded with disgust. Love became tainted with sin once again and the language of the troubadours was reapplied to the Virgin Mary. Where courtly love had made its home—in Provence and Languedoc—the new dualistic heresy flourished. As Morris has shown, the emergence of courtly love took place within the wider context of the emergence of the concept of the individual and a sense of self-consciousness. Eventually and very slowly the development of this concept would lead in the West to marriage being quasi-redefined as a free union of two people in love with one another; not any two people but each person with the one ideal person destined for them. This is not to argue that love between married persons was unknown before this period—the Bible, for example, contains a number of very moving descriptions of married love[38]—but it was not the essential ingredient it was to become. Susan Dowell draws attention to the *quasi* dimension of the free, love-based union in her analysis of the effects of romantic love upon marriage:

> The debased romanticism which our culture loads on to marriage has been a primary means of taming women ... Romantic love rang the death knell of any sense of marriage as a communal interest, a social contract. It yields the same result as the arranged marriages it subverted in its early days: domesticity (you start by sinking into his arms and end up with your arms in his sink); but a domesticity accompanied by the dangerous delusion of 'choice' and a destructive guilt and grief when the magic wears off. 'Falling in love' operates a psychic tripwire placed across liberated sexuality.[39]

The privatization of marriage has put it beyond most forms of justice. Police are notoriously reluctant to become involved in what are euphemistically called 'domestic disputes'. The legal concept of marital rape is extremely new. The whole concept of choice is a dubious one. Most people in Europe or the United States look with pity on those in our midst who undergo 'arranged marriages', whether they ask for our pity or not. But, as William Williamson has pointed out, in doing so we ignore the fact that our parents educate us, train us and send us to certain places to groom us to meet a certain type of person.[40] We also ignore the pressure that our society puts upon us to marry and the economic pressures women in particular are put under if they do not marry. Mary Crawford, discussing 'heterosexual privilege', notes:

> Mundane life is *easier* for me. No one discounts my feminist analysis of social problems by calling me a man-hater ... No one hassles me at my child's school, at the doctor's office or at work. No one tells me I'm an unfit mother. Because I am legally married, my job provides health care benefits for my partner and family ... Wills and mortgages, taxes and auto insurance, retirement pensions and social enrollment for the children—all the ways that individuals ordinarily interface with social structures—are designed to fit people like me and my partner.[41]

Part of the problem is that we have burdened marriage with

too much. We have taken an institution which began as an economic contract, a union of two sets of assets in a male-dominated society, in which love's place was not defined, and in the space of but a few hundred years we have redefined it so that now we see it, in our culture at least, as a lifelong commitment of love where the people involved, motivated by romantic love, are supposed to fulfil the other's emotional needs in a relationship based upon equality. A feminist would want to ask: can an institution conceived on the premiss of unequal power relations ever fulfil the purposes of marriage outlined in the ASB? The evidence is not convincingly positive and that is why many lesbian and gay people ask whether they should be looking to marriage as a model for structuring and understanding their relationships.

However, it would be foolish and dishonest to ignore the fact that many heterosexual marriages do work and do fulfil the purposes of marriage as set down in the ASB. Commitment, hard work and a great deal of struggle can produce relationships which clearly manifest the presence of God within them. This private commitment has to be made in a public context which does not expect, respect or encourage mutuality in relationships between men and women. Now, the obvious question is: if marriage as an institution does not automatically guarantee this kind of relationship, is there a relationship which is in operation among those couples who do have successful marriages? In my experience if you ask a happily married couple the secret of their relationship, nine times out of ten the answer will run along the lines of 'we are friends first and foremost', or 'she/he is my best friend'.

Sacred texts and sacred models

So we are back to where we began—with friendship. But before we go any further we must go back again, this time to the arguments of those gay people (I have yet to find a lesbian who has argued this) who want to define their relationships in terms of marriage. Although British Anglican priest Jeffrey John thinks that it 'would be a mistake to apply the term "marriage" to same-sex partnership, because, at the physical level, at least, it is clearly not the same thing', he does think it is quite wrong to define our relationships in terms of friendships.[42] I have left considering his arguments until now because, whilst in general they are very similar to those articulated by Thatcher and Williams, John does develop his arguments in direct confrontation and opposition to mine as they were first outlined in my book *Daring to Speak Love's Name*.[43] I quote him at length because it is important to identify and deal with his powerful arguments against this model:

VERY IMPORTANT CRITICISM.

But in Christian doctrine a marriage, even considered apart from procreation, is far more than friendship, and the term friendship is wholly inadequate to cover what marriage and sexual commitment imply theologically. There is no warrant at all in scripture or tradition for making friendship the theological model for a sexual relationship. Stuart cites the example of Hosea in her discussion of the theology of friendship, but the instance proves my point. Hosea's marriage was, precisely, a marriage, and as such a symbol of the passionate, covenanted, exclusive love of God for his people. In Hosea we are at the root of Paul's concept of marriage as the sacrament of Christ and the Church: The Bible's insistence that human sexual love is, or should be, a reflection of God's image in us. God is a faithful, covenanting God; and our sexuality is meant to express faithful, covenanted commitment to one partner … Friendship in any normal use of the word does not imply sexual activity, still less does it in any theological use, and it is an abuse to try and force it to do so. Stuart calls on Aelred of Rievaulx in her support, but Aelred is perfectly clear that, though limited physical demonstrations of affection between monastic friends could be countenanced, sex could not. It is equally misleading to cite Ruth and Naomi, David and Jonathan, Jesus and the Beloved Disciple, because there is no reason to suppose that any of these friendships, deep as they were, were sexually expressed. Friendship and a relationship of sexual commitment are qualitatively different. One may have many friends; one may not, within any moral framework which remotely links with Christian teaching, have many sexual partners.[44]

John's response to my theology of friendship exposes very clearly the different theological approaches distinguished by James Nelson. He begins with scripture and tradition and endeavours to construct a theology of lesbian and gay relationship from that basis. I want to begin from lesbian and gay experience and bring scripture and tradition into dialogue with it.

My first response to John's criticism would be to note some of the language he uses. He talks of marriage being 'more' than friendship, of the term 'friendship' not implying any sexual activity. He seems to have bought into the dissection and rigid hierarchical ordering of relationships that was discussed earlier, not to mention the reduction of sexuality to genitalization. The experience of many lesbian and gay people defies both of these assumptions but I want to suggest that, even if we adopt John's methodology and try to begin with the biblical narratives, we will end up defying those assumptions.

John maintains that 'there is no warrant at all in scripture or tradition for making friendship the theological model of a sexual relationship'. He believes that the only model offered is that of marriage. Let us explore this claim. In a fascinating book that traces the understanding of *erōs* in ancient and modern Judaism David Biale has noted:

> Sexuality was a central issue in Israel's self-conception, with adultery and fidelity the dominant metaphors both for Israel's relationship to God and for national identity. The prophet Ezekiel combines the two explicitly in his accusation that Israel is whoring with her neighbours, the 'well-endowed Egyptians' (16.26); Israel's depravity, he explains, derives from her origins: 'You are daughters of a Hittite mother and an Amorite father' (16:45). Sexual anxiety is thus at the very heart of the struggle with this ambiguous identity.[45]

Ezekiel is not the only Hebrew prophet to portray God as the wronged and jealous husband; all the major prophets employ

the metaphor at some point, but it is the book of Hosea which
has caught most of the attention of those interested in sexuality.
Whereas in Ezekiel the emphasis is upon judgement and re-
venge, in Hosea the emphasis is upon the return of the wander-
ing wife. Hosea's imagery may well be inspired by the very
Canaanite fertility cult that he rails against (according to which
every year the goddess Anat and her brother Baal came
together and by their union set the forces of nature in motion).
There is plenty of evidence to suggest that, well into the seventh
century BCE at least, a sizeable number of ancient Israelites
worshipped the Canaanite goddess Asherah or Anat as consort
to Yahweh. She may or may not be identified with the 'Queen
of Heaven' who seems to have been the object of exclusively
female devotion (Jeremiah 44.15–19). We also know from the
antagonism of the prophets that cultic prostitutes were used in
ancient Israel: 'The outstanding importance of the praxis was
in terms of sexuality, the union of the human with the divine,
which itself represented such communion.'[46] First the prophets and then the priests sought to rid Israel of all this.
Yahweh, Asherah and the El, another Canaanite goddess, were
amalgamated into El Shaddai (which may mean 'God with
breasts' or 'the God who suckles') but who was regarded as
male.[47] The process of monotheizing and monogamizing the
people of Israel seems to have gone hand in hand, with similarly
erratic and patchy results.

In the opening of his work the prophet Hosea is forced to take
part in a series of acted parables which portray Yahweh's
relationship to his people in terms of a husband saddled with an
habitually unfaithful wife. There is no question of divorce;
rather, the wronged husband lays various plans to get her back.
First he threatens:

> I will strip her naked
> and expose her as in the day she was born ...
> Upon her children also I will have no pity,
> because they are children of whoredom ...

(2.3–4)

Then he devises some cunning plans to disenchant her with her lovers:

> Therefore I will hedge up her way with thorns;
> and I will build a wall against her,
> so that she cannot find her paths.
> She shall pursue her lovers,
> but not overtake them;
> and she shall seek them,
> but shall not find them.
> Then she shall say, 'I will go
> and return to my first husband,
> for it was better with me then than now.'
> She did not know
> that it was I who gave her
> the grain, the wine, and the oil,
> and who lavished upon her silver
> and gold that they used for Baal.
> Therefore I will take back
> my grain in its time,
> and my wine in its season;
> and I will take away my wool and my flax,
> which were to cover her nakedness.
>
> (2.6–9)

Finally he considers seduction:

> Therefore, I will now allure her,
> and bring her into the wilderness,
> and speak tenderly to her...
> There she shall respond as in the days of her youth...
> I will make for you a covenant on the day with the wild animals,
> the birds of the air, and the creeping things of the ground; and I
> will abolish the bow, the sword, and war from the land; and I
> will make you lie down in safety. And I will take you for my wife
> forever; I will take you for my wife in righteousness and in
> justice, in steadfast love, and in mercy. I will take you for my
> wife in faithfulness; and you shall know the Lord.
>
> (2.14–15, 18–20)

I have used these passages, particularly the last one, many times to draw attention to, to applaud and use the image of a passionate God, a lover God. John uses it to draw attention to the faithful God who demands faithfulness not only to himself, but also between ourselves. But John and I, and many other commentators, have been so enamoured with the picture of 'the Lord' that we have ignored the voiceless wife. We may be dealing with a faithful, passionate husband but it is a husband who believes that he has the right to threaten, shame, starve, expose and seduce his wife to return to him. Her desires do not come into it, except that she must be punished for making the wrong choice of lover. Only one of the characters is acting, the other is completely passive: 'I will *make* you lie down in safety. And I will *take* you for my wife ... I will *take* you for my wife ... I will *take* you for my wife ... and you *shall* know the Lord' (my emphasis). There is no mutuality here. We do not know if Hosea's wife Gomer was merely a literary creation or a living part of an acted parable. A similar problem arises with Ezekiel's wife who becomes the symbol of Judah and dies suddenly whilst Ezekiel is under divine command not to mourn her (24.15–18). Whether fictional or not, 'from a feminist perspective, one thing is certain: the women and the children—the possessions and the powerless—are *used*'.[48]

Jeffrey John also refers to the writings of St Paul. Writing to the Christian community at Corinth which he had helped to form, Paul found himself having to address a community which was wracked with internal strife, largely focused upon issues of sexual morality (*plus ça change*). Some were saying that 'it is well for a man not to touch a woman' (1 Corinthians 7.1); others were choosing to interpret Paul's teaching about being liberated from the law as a licence to do anything they wished (6.12). Some may have been divorcing their non-Christian spouses (7.12); others may have been practising celibacy within marriage (7.3–6). Paul wades in to legislate on all this. He is quite clear that ideally it was better not to enter into marriage because time is short, Christ's return is nigh and it is appropriate to devote all time to the 'affairs of the Lord' (7.8, 25–36). However, if people cannot exercise self-control they should marry 'for it is better to marry than to be aflame with passion'(7.9).[49] Paul's belief that marriage saves some people from sexual immorality also lies behind his instruction that 'The husband should give to his wife her conjugal rights, and likewise the wife to her husband. For the wife does not have authority over her own body, but the husband does; likewise the husband does not have authority over his own body, but the wife does' (7.3–4). It is interesting to see Paul conforming to his Jewish roots and speaking about marriage primarily in terms of satisfaction of sexual desire (rather than procreation) and this passage has been interpreted by many as talking in terms of a mutuality between husband and wife. But is that a correct interpretation? This passage has to be read in the context of Paul's wider theology.

A great deal of Paul's theology revolves around notions of slavery; he tends to see salvation in terms of being transferred from one lordship (sin or the law) to another (Christ). Christ has indeed attained our freedom but it is a freedom to be again enslaved under him (7.22). Every time Paul uses the terms of authority (*exousia*) in his letters it is in the context of complete capitulation, divinely sanctioned, 'whoever resists authority resists what God has appointed' (Romans 13.2). To have authority over another's body is to have complete power over it. Even if this power is reciprocal, as Paul seems to suggest it is, we should not be beguiled into thinking that this theology guarantees an experience of mutuality. We are talking the language of power and rights rather than mutual love or respect. It would also be naïve and foolish to think that people can enjoy power relations in bed fundamentally different to those they experience beyond the blankets. Whilst men retain primary control over women's bodies in society at large, men and women are never going to have equal authority over each other's bodies. Indeed, reclaiming authority over our own bodies has been the first and most symbolic and controversial aim of the feminist movement. Paul may have genuinely believed that his theology did guarantee mutuality, but if he did he understood very little about the place of women in his society. His principal aim, however, seems to have been the containment of sexual desire. If men and women could not control their desire then they should marry, and marriage should therefore be conducted in such a way that sexual desire could be satisfied. It is pointless getting married only to find that your partner is unwilling to engage in sexual activity. We do not know if Paul wrote the letter to the Ephesians which has long been attributed to him, but it is to a passage in this letter that Jeffrey John refers, a passage which is often read at weddings:

> Wives, be subject to your husbands as you are to the Lord. For the husband is the head of the wife just as Christ is the head of the church, the body of which he is the Saviour. Just as the church is subject to Christ, so also wives ought to be, in everything, to their husbands. Husbands, love your wives, just as Christ loved the church and gave himself up for her ... In the same way, husbands should love their wives as they do their own bodies. He who loves his wife loves himself. For no one ever hates his own body, but he nourishes and tenderly cares for it, just as Christ does for the church, because we are members of his body. 'For this reason a man will leave his father and mother and be joined to his wife, and the two will become one flesh.' This is a great mystery, and I am applying it to Christ and the church. Each of you, however, should love his wife as himself, and a wife should respect her husband.
>
> (5.22–25, 28–33)

Once again we see the institution of marriage becoming a model and reflection of relations between humanity and the divine and once again we find a basically unjust relationship. Wives must 'submit to', 'be subject to', 'obey' (all meanings of *hypotassetai*) their husbands (in the same way that children and slaves are later instructed to obey their parents and masters), but husbands are just enjoined to 'love' their wives. Some have argued that the injunction to husbands to emulate Christ's love for his Church in their love for their wives implies a renunciation of power. Anthony Harvey, although acknowledging the difficulties of the passage, particularly for women, still latches on to the imitation-of-Christ motif, interpreting it as follows:

> It is by studying Christ that men can learn how to love their

wives ... This loving involved Christ in utter self-sacrifice,
giving himself to the church in such a way that she is cleansed,
purified and perfected. Real love of one's body means bringing
it to the best condition of which it is capable. Real love of one's
wife means the kind of sacrifice of oneself which will release her
full potential.[50]

But I fail to see how the passage even hints at such an interpretation. If it implies anything it is in terms of faithfulness. Husbands are enjoined to love their wives as their own bodies, as
part of themselves, they must love their wives not for their
wives' sake but for their own. The wives are to subject themselves to their husbands as they do to Christ—we are back to
images of slavery. The wife is part of the husband's property,
she belongs to him, as do his children and slaves. Adrian
Thatcher has noted: 'The theology of marriage is ... integrated
into the institutions of slavery and the hierarchical order of
social relations which slavery serves.'[51] Very similar teaching is
to be found in another letter which is probably not by Paul but
is written by someone in his school. In Colossians, we find the
following instructions: 'Wives, be subject to your husbands, as
is fitting in the Lord. Husbands, love your wives and never treat
them harshly. Children, obey your parents ... Slaves, obey
your earthly masters...' (3.18–20, 22). Jeffrey John is no doubt
right to draw attention to the frequent use of the marriage
metaphor in the Hebrew scriptures to describe the chosen
people's relationship to God and the Pauline use of it to describe Christ's relationship to the Church (though it is hardly a
central metaphor in the Christian scriptures as a whole), but I
for one cannot simply accept this model and metaphor
uncritically.

At the heart of the metaphor, both in the Hebrew and
Christian scriptures, is an understanding of marriage very close
to slavery. In Hosea the woman whom the jealous but faithful
husband passionately pursues is an object to be shamed,
humiliated, starved and seduced, reduced to proper passivity.
In Paul the language of mutual authority obscures notions of
ownership in which the wife will always be disadvantaged

because of the web of power relations she has to exist in, which cannot be conveniently unspun in a marriage bed. The marriage model/metaphor may well be an important one in the scriptures, and have become more important through the Church's development of it, but it is simply an unacceptable one to those who take the pain and struggle of women seriously. If that is the 'ideal' relationship, and the most significant clue as to what God is like, then it is no wonder that many women (straight, lesbian, bisexual) and gay and bisexual men have responded with a polite 'No thank you' and gone on their way.

However, the situation is much more complex than that. Both the Hebrew and Christian scriptures are a muddle of metaphors; they burst with a confusion of images and spill over in tangles of theology. Many of the texts arise out of a context of theological dispute, so it is little wonder that we find blatant contradictions between them. When we talk about 'dominant' ideas, metaphors, etc., we are nearly always imposing our own interpretative wishes upon the texts. I do not wish to argue that there are models of relationship which are more dominant than marriage, but I wish simply to draw attention to some texts which offer alternative insights.

It is impossible to read the history of the people of Israel as told in the Hebrew scriptures without noticing that sexual subversion is a consistent theme. Sometimes this is portrayed negatively, as we have observed in the marriage metaphor of the prophets. More often, the broken laws and taboos are crucial in ensuring the survival and prosperity of the people of Israel. In the book of Ruth, for example, Ruth the Moabite, a member of a country which according to Genesis 19.30–38 was the product of an incestuous relationship between Lot and one of his daughters and according to Deuteronomy 23.3–4 should not be allowed into the 'congregation of the Lord', manages to secure the birth of a baby, who will be King David's grandfather, by defying expected roles and customs; she transgresses the law by uncovering the 'feet' (a euphemism for genitals) of her father-in-law's relation Boaz, in conspiracy with her Israelite mother-in-law Naomi. The book can be read in a number of ways. On the one hand, the whole story revolves around an attempt to 'catch a husband' in order to ensure that the name of a man will continue to live. So the story serves to reinforce patriarchy. On the other hand, the story is about a group of powerless women (and childless widows were among the most powerless people in ancient Israel) whose passionate commitment to each other motivates them to take the future into their own hands. The passionate commitment between Ruth and Naomi is described significantly as *davkah bah* (Ruth 'clung to Naomi'), which echoes the words of Genesis 2.24, 'Therefore a man leaves his father and his mother and clings (*davak*) to his wife, and they become one flesh'. It is this relationship between the Israelite mother-in-law and her Moabite daughter-in-law that secures the male lineage that will result in the birth of the great king. Even the levirate law which Ruth was endeavouring to fulfil, the law which decreed that the brother of a man who dies childless should marry his widow in order to ensure the continuation of his brother's name, is a violation of the incest laws found in the book of Leviticus (18.16; 20.21). A similar story is found in Genesis 38 in the story of Tamar. When one of her deceased husband's brothers refuses to fulfil his obligation towards her, and the other is not forced to do so by his father despite his promise to ensure this, Tamar disguises herself as a prostitute and sleeps with her father-in-law. When she reveals herself, her father-in-law declares that 'She is more right than I, since I did not give her to my son Shelah' (Genesis 38.26). Tamar gives birth to twins, one of whom, Perez, becomes an ancestor of David. King Solomon is born out of the adulterous and murderous union between David and Bathsheba (2 Samuel 11 and 12). The Hebrew scriptures are littered with stories that demonstrate Yahweh's purposes being forwarded by deliberate floutings of sexual convention and law—law which it was believed had come from the deity. Biale, commenting on the many stories which involve incest, notes:

All of these stories no doubt preceded the Levitical incest laws by many centuries; what is therefore noteworthy is that they were included in the biblical text. The authors or editors who produced the text were surely aware of the flagrant contradictions between the laws and the narratives, but they must have seen those contradictions as serving an important cultural function. The creation of the Israelite nation was seen by these later authors as a result of the suspension of conventions, a sign, perhaps, of divine favour for a ragtag, ethically mixed people. Far from a disgrace to be hidden, sexual subversion, like the repeated preference for younger over older sons, hints at the unexpected character of God's covenant with Israel.[52]

Occasionally the prophets and sages will challenge presumably dominant assumptions about who is and who is not blessed:

> For thus says the Lord: To the eunuchs who keep my sabbaths, who choose the things that please me and hold fast my covenant, I will give, in my house and within my walls, a monument and a name better than sons and daughters; I will give them an everlasting name that shall not be cut off.
>
> (Isaiah 56:4–5)

> Better than this is childlessness with virtue, for in the memory of virtue is immortality, because it is known both by God and by mortals ... But the prolific brood of the ungodly will be of no use, and none of their illegitimate seedlings will strike a deep root or take a firm hold.
>
> (Wisdom of Solomon 4.1, 3)

What is particularly interesting about most of the stories that deal with sexual subversion in the Hebrew scriptures is that the deity is remarkably absent: 'It is as if God must step backstage in order to make space for human actors, and particularly women, to bend social custom and law ... God's absence implicitly sanctions these inversions and subversions.'[53] Nowhere is this absence more obvious than in the Song of Songs. This love poem, which is probably constructed out of a collection of various poems, dates in its final form to the post-exilic period. It takes the form of a dialogue between a man and a 'black and beautiful' woman. It was only thanks to the passionate pleading of Rabbi Akiva that the book made it into the canon. He is said to have declared that 'all the ages are not worth the day on which the Song of Songs was given to Israel; for all the writings are holy, but the Song of Songs is the Holy of Holies'.[54] The crux of his argument was that the Song was in fact an allegory of the love between Israel and her God. First Judaism and then Christianity, as if they did not know how to handle a sacred book which revolved around humanity and not God, and humanity in its bodily glory at that, allegorized it into a poetic description of Yahweh's relationship to Israel, Christ's to his Church, his consecrated virgin or the Virgin Mary. However, there is little scholarly doubt that the Song was not written as an allegory. The woman is the main speaker, although it is difficult at times to tell who is speaking and, contrary to popular assumption, there is 'no indication that the male–female relationship described in the book is marital'.[55] Some scholars regard the Song to be a deliberate subversion of the story of Eden:

> We are presented with a garden that is not closed and barred, that is not a realm of delights from which we are expelled and over which for ever watches a cherubim with flaming sword to guard the way to the tree of life. Rather, this garden is open . . . (4.16) . . . There is no expulsion here; no constraint or curse in the Song; no taint or shame. The nakedness is not covered although neither is it unaware. In this garden of desire the fall is not our inevitable ancient memory. The garden is still that place of almost unutterable beauty but we may walk within it.[56]

At Eden the man seeks out the woman, leaving his home to do so, far away from the sacred tree; in the Song the woman does the seeking and takes her beloved back to the tree beneath which he was born, and to her own mother's house. Indeed their relationship itself is described in terms of a garden and fruit tree. Their embodied passion is the tree and fruit of life. The fact that it is extremely difficult to tell whether the man or the woman is speaking in several places demonstrates how little the constraints of patriarchy impose themselves in this work.

Fertility is not a concern of the Song; instead it revolves around desire and the quest for its fulfilment. The woman sets out actively to seek her beloved although she recognizes in a dream sequence the dangers of her activity, for the sentinels who find her in the streets beat and strip her (5.7) and her brothers, angry with her subversive behaviour, make her keeper of the vineyards (1.6). The Song shudders with passionate imagery, glories in the beauty of the body, and the glory is mutual. Heather Walton argues that the subversiveness of the Song even undermines those who would hold it up as a legitimation of heterosexual relationships:

> The love is certainly heterosexual, there is no question of this, but not straight in a straightforward sort of way. The lovers are more than lovers, they are, or seek to be, brother and sister. They are, or seek to be, twins ... The paradigm in the Song is not a continued supposed complementarity of two binary opposite sexes but of an integration or even disintegration of gendered selves. The lovers frequently eat each other, pass into each other, echo each other and an illustration of this is the fact that scholars have disagreed over which lover is speaking when ... The binary opposite presuppositions of heterosexuality are not the rules of this game and when those binary opposites are so confounded heterosexuality becomes a redundant category.[57]

But the Song recognizes the threatening nature of this gloriously free female sexuality. The brothers and 'sentinels' cannot cope with it. They either put her to work or humiliate her, they punish her and even her beloved cannot always bear it: 'Turn away your eyes from me, for they overwhelm me!' (6.5). Like the ancient symbols of female power Kali and Isis, the woman in the Song is beautiful, black, terrible, suffering and seductive. The Song of Songs is the closest the Hebrew scriptures come to presenting us with a just, equal and mutual passionate relationship between a man and a woman. But not even this relationship can be used to bolster the institution of marriage in the way so many theologians would wish. As Walton so eloquently puts it, it is not 'straight in a straightforward sort of way'. The male lover may refer to his beloved as 'my bride' (always in conjunction with 'my sister'), but the woman never refers to him in complementary terms. The echoes of incestuous desire cannot be ignored and there may well be echoes of a desire to return to the pregendered state of the first earth creature *hā'ādām* (Genesis 2.7; 5.1–2).

Where is Yahweh in all this? There may be one tiny explicit reference to the deity which is easy to miss, particularly in English translation. It comes in 8.6. The New Revised Standard Version renders this verse as follows:

> Set me as a seal upon your heart,
> as a seal upon your arm;
> for love is strong as death,
> passion fierce as the grave.
> Its flashes are flashes of fire,
> a raging flame.

In ancient Israel death and sheol, 'the grave', were often personified as unrelenting, inescapable powers, so to compare love and passion to these powers is to convey something about their depth and intensity. In speaking of the fire-like qualities of love the Hebrew uses the term *šalhebetyā* which means 'a flame of *yah*' or 'Yahweh flame'. It is unclear whether the term is comparing the love to the fire of the deity or whether their love is regarded as being part of Yahweh's burning love, but Murphy seems to prefer the latter option.[58] If that is so, then God is everywhere in this poem, not as a overpowering puppet-master presence demanding central stage, but as pulsating, longing, desperate and dangerous passion that is summoned up between these people. We are back again to the understanding of God as Hochma/Sophia/Spirit who also 'inebriates mortals with her fruits' (Sirach 1.16), and who herself is often described in terms of a tree; whose creation story also contains no fall, no alienation, and who lives among us as the fiery Spirit who animates all things and binds them together. Hildegard of Bingen, in her first vision, heard the following:

> I, the highest and fiery power, have kindled every spark of life, and I emit nothing that is deadly ... I, the fiery life of divine

essence, am aflame beyond the beauty of the meadows, I gleam
in the waters, and I burn in the sun, moon and stars. With every
breeze, as with invisible life that contains everything, I awaken
everything to life ... And thus I remain hidden in every kind of
reality as a fiery power. Everything burns because of me in such
a way as our breath constantly moves us, like the wind-tossed
flame in a fire.[59]

She sees a human form who, she is told, signifies the love of
God. This is God as Hochma/Sophia/Spirit and it is God
present in the Song of Songs—everywhere and nowhere. It is as
if the ancient writers when telling their tales of sexuality knew
that the presence of God was of a different order in these cases,
hidden in the actions, words and relationships of the participants. The only direct intervention Yahweh ever seems to
make in the realm of human relationships is on the issue of
barrenness or fertility, otherwise his presence is only implicit in
the mess and muddle and ambiguity of the stories of
relationships.

'Yahweh is between you and me forever.' These words could
very well have been spoken by the lovers of the Song of Songs
but in fact they are spoken by one man about another (1
Samuel 20.23). The texts of 1 and 2 Samuel which tell the story
of the relationship between King Saul's son Jonathan and the
musician-turned-soldier David have become a wrestling ring in
which scholars who want to claim that David and Jonathan had
a homosexual relationship, and those who want to claim they
did not, lock each other in an unwinnable grip. It is unwinnable
because ultimately there is not enough explicit evidence to
support either contention. However, the story is still extremely
important. The impetuous warrior Jonathan is deeply impressed, we are told, by young David's precocious slaughter of
the Philistine Goliath:

> When David had finished speaking to Saul, the soul of Jonathan
> was bound to the soul of David, and Jonathan loved him as his
> own soul. Saul took him that day and would not let him return
> to his father's house. Then Jonathan made a covenant with
> David, because he loved him as his own soul. Jonathan stripped

himself of the robe that we was wearing, and gave it to David, and his armour, and even his sword and his bow and his belt.

(1 Samuel 18.1–4)

Throughout the ancient Near East covenants were made between vassals and lords or between the conquered and their conquerors. They were formal agreements to resolve wars or disputes, in which the person with power stipulated the conditions under which the relationship would continue. Even marriage covenants were made in this context of inequality. The language of love was sometimes used in these covenants but it was always one-sided and referred to respect and obedience: the vassal or conquered was commanded to 'love' the lord or conqueror. The covenant between David and Jonathan is obviously of a very different order. Whereas the English translation gives the impression that Jonathan (the more powerful) initiated the covenant, the Hebrew is much more ambiguous and literally reads 'Jonathan and David, he made a covenant'. Scholars and translators have usually assumed that 'and' was meant to be 'with' as this would follow the usual expression found in covenant texts 'X made a covenant with Y'. However, Comstock suggests that the awkwardness of the Hebrew may be deliberate, 'because conventional covenant making served the superior–inferior relationship of parties brought into an agreement, the usual formula and terms did not suit the nature of Jonathan's and David's relationship and had to be modified, even if somewhat awkwardly'.[60] The exchange of clothing was probably made as a sign of the covenant and would probably have been mutual so that each carried around part of the other. There are no obligations to fulfil, no dispute to resolve. There is absolutely no evidence to support the theory that the covenant involved Jonathan abdicating his succession to the throne in favour of David.

What we seem to have in the story of David and Jonathan is the story of two friends whose friendship defied social rank, expressing their passionate commitment to one another using a model, form and language of commitment familiar to them both, whilst adapting it to their particular needs. Notice again how Yahweh is not directly involved in this story but his presence noted and affirmed as the bond that exists between both men. Once again we are dealing with a story which secures against the odds the succession of David. The passionate nature of the relationship between David and Jonathan is expressed not only in their declarations of love to one another and the trouble they both take to sustain their relationship in a situation which tried to structure them as enemies, but also in the reactions of Jonathan's father to their relationship. As Jonathan constantly frustrates Saul's efforts to get rid of the young pretender, Saul explodes at his son: 'You son of a perverse, rebellious woman! Do I not know that you have chosen the son of Jesse to your own shame, and to the shame of your mother's nakedness? For as long as the son of Jesse lives upon the earth, neither you nor your kingdom shall be established' (1 Samuel 20.30–31). This is the exasperation of a man who cannot understand how friendship can be put above family loyalty. The outburst casts angry aspersions upon Jonathan's parentage and connects the shame of Jonathan's behaviour to the 'shame of your mother's nakedness', which we know is a phrase used with regard to sexual relationships. The word 'shame' is also often associated with sexual activity in the Hebrew scriptures. The precise meaning is unclear but it is obvious that Saul finds his son's relationship with David deeply disturbing— certainly because he feels it violates his right to his son's loyalty, but possibly because he sees in it some sexual transgression. There is a curious passage which describes a secret meeting between Jonathan and David in which Jonathan warns David of his father's plot to kill him. The New RSV's version of this passage is 'He bowed down three times, and they kissed each other, and wept with each other; David wept the more' (1 Samuel 20.41). There is some difficulty over the translation of the last phrase. Other versions talk about them weeping until David 'recovered' or 'exceeded' himself. The Hebrew verb used is *higdîl*. The verb seems to be derived from the adjective *gādôl* which means 'large'. The variant readings of the

Septuagint and of some of the Hebrew manuscripts suggest that the Hebrew should be *'ad hagdēl*, which is translated in Greek as *heōs tēs synteleias*, which means 'until the ejaculation'. The Hebrew then may refer to David 'growing large' with sexual excitement.[61] We cannot be certain if this is the correct interpretation, but it is a possibility. The passion between the two men reaches a climax in David's elegy for this dead friend, combined with an elegy for Saul the father whom Jonathan refused to abandon, just as he refused to abandon his friend:

> Jonathan lies slain upon your high places.
> I am distressed for you, my brother Jonathan:
> greatly beloved were you to me;
> your love to me was wonderful,
> passing the love of women.
>
> (2 Samuel 1.25-26)

That David the great womanizer should say these words is significant in conveying the depths of his feelings for Jonathan.

In the story of David and Jonathan we find an example of the passionate friendship that we have been seeking so far in vain in the models and metaphors of marriage in the Hebrew scriptures. This is a relationship in which two people of different social standing managed to transcend to some extent the barriers to their relating. On a wave of passion they achieve a remarkable equality in their own relating although they were ultimately separated. We find a mutual rejoicing in the other that expressed itself in a form of covenant, a relationship which changed their behaviour and conditioned how they acted not only to each other but also to others. It was undoubtedly a socially subversive relationship which threatened the very throne of Israel. David and Jonathan were not by any legitimate stretch of the imagination 'homosexual' or 'gay'. There are some parallels between what we know of the passionate friendship of these two married men and the passionate friendships of post-Enlightenment Europe and North America. And we are faced with the same question 'was their relationship sexual?' I would not even want to guess whether David and Jonathan had or were thought to have had homosexual sex, but I think their relationship as portrayed was undoubtedly sexual in that it was passionate, intense and physically expressed. We must not fall into the very modern trap of using sibling language to make rigid distinctions between so called sexual and non-sexual relationships. In the ancient world the terms 'brother' and sister' were common terms of endearment between lovers, and, according to Boswell, were used to convey equality and mutuality as in the Song of Songs.[62] The Hebrew text bristles with ambiguity, perhaps deliberate ambiguity, to express the fact that here we are in the presence of a significant relationship for which there are no established means of description. Indeed, the Hebrew could be said to convey just enough to make it obvious that there was a sexual element and not enough to enable us to be sure about the exact nature of the relationship. Therefore, we have to focus on the passionate quality of the relationship and cannot be diverted into discussion about 'genital acts'.

Sexual ambiguity is virtually absent from the story of Ruth and Naomi. Yet again it is in the story of a friendship between two members of the same sex that we find evidence of mutuality, passion and justice. It is the story of women defying all kinds of social and religious convention to stick together and secure their future. Everything that should have kept them apart—different nationalities, different religions, different blood families—could not suffocate the affection between Ruth and Naomi. We have already noticed the parallel that is drawn between Ruth's relationship with Naomi and Adam's with his wife. Ruth's refusal to leave Naomi is one of the most beautiful expressions of passionate friendship between women, a friendship which later is acknowledged by the women in Bethlehem as being worth more than seven sons to Naomi:

> Do not press me to leave you
> or to turn back from following you!
> Where you go, I will go;

> Where you lodge, I will lodge;
> your people shall be my people,
> and your God my God.
> Where you die, I will die—
> there will I be buried.
> May the Lord do thus and so to me,
> and more as well,
> if even death parts me from you!
>
> (Ruth 1.16–17)

[handwritten marginal note: tries to show relationships btwn friends can be sexual!]

But once again, although they prove themselves far from powerless and able to flout convention to form their friendship, Ruth and Naomi cannot completely transcend their context. Their friendship cannot give either of them autonomy from men. Jeffrey John misunderstands me when he criticizes me for allegedly suggesting that David and Jonathan and Ruth and Naomi's friendships were sexually expressed. He assumes that I believe they had sex. This is not the point I am trying to make. I am trying to demonstrate that their relationships were passionate, bodily and therefore sexual in the wider sense of that term.

Sexual subversion lies at the heart of much of the Hebrew scriptural epic—the purposes of God are often furthered only by men and women breaking sexual conventions. These scriptures do not provide us with a model of passionate friendship within marriage. The nearest they get to presenting us with such a model is in the same-sex friendships of David and Jonathan and Ruth and Naomi and in the ambiguous relationship between the lovers of the Song of Songs. In the stories of the same-sex friendships it is made clear that such relationships, no matter how passionate and committed, are still pressurized by the social structures. Yahweh's presence in these stories is always understated within these relationships but still very real as the love that binds the friends together.

Notes

1 David P. McWhirter and Andrew M. Mattison, *The Male Couple: How Relationships Develop* (London: Prentice-Hall, 1984).

2 Robert Williams, 'Toward a theology of lesbian and gay marriage', *Anglican Theological Review*, vol. 72 (1990), p. 138.

3 *Gaudium et Spes: Pastoral Constitution on the Church in the Modern World* (7 December 1965), para. 49, in Austin Flannery OP, *Vatican Council II: The Conciliar and Post-Conciliar Documents* (Leominster: Fowler Wright, 1980), p. 952.

4 *Gaudium et Spes*, para. 50, in Flannery, *Vatican Council II*, p. 953.

5 Adrian Thatcher, *Liberating Sex: A Christian Sexual Theology* (London: SPCK, 1993), p. 145.

6 Thatcher, *Liberating Sex*, p. 146.

7 Thatcher, *Liberating Sex*, p. 147.

8 Thatcher, *Liberating Sex*, pp. 172–5.

9 Diana Leonard, *Sex and Generation: A Study of Courtship and Weddings* (London: Tavistock, 1982), p. 261.

10 Charlotte Perkins Gilman, *Women and Economics: The Economic Factor Between Men and Women as a Factor in Social Revolution* (Boston: Small Manyard, 1899), p. 5.

11 Mrs Flora Macdonald Denison in 1914, cited in Carol Lee Bacchi, *Liberation Deferred? The Ideas of the English-Canadian Suffragists 1877–1918* (Toronto: University of Toronto Press, 1983), p. 31.

12 Marlene Dixon, cited in Midge Lennert and Norma Wilson, *A Woman's New World Dictionary* (Lomita: 51% Publications, 1973), p. 7.

13 Sue Bruley, 'Women awake: the experience of consciousness-raising' in Feminist Anthology Collective, *No Turning Back: Writings from the Women's Liberation Movement 1975–1980* (London: The Women's Press, 1976), p. 64.

14 Emma Donoghue, *Passions Between Women: British Lesbian Culture 1668–1801* (London: Scarlet Press, 1993), p. 123.

15 Julian Hafner, *The End of Marriage: Why Monogamy Isn't Working* (London: Century, 1993), p. 7.

16 Anne Borrowdale, *Distorted Images: Christian Attitudes to Women, Men and Sex* (London: SPCK, 1991), p. 106.

17 Shere Hite, *Women as Revolutionary Agents of Change: The Hite Reports: Sexuality, Love and Emotion* (London: Sceptre Books, 1994), pp. 141, 366.

18 Hafner, *The End of Marriage*, p. 196.

19 Hafner, *The End of Marriage*, p. 197.

20 David Oliphant, 'Marriage—A union of equals? The 1991 Mary Body Memorial Lecture', *St Mark's Review* (Autumn 1992), p. 19.

21 This is, for example, the teaching of the Vatican.

22 This is the stance adopted by the House of Bishops of the General Synod of the Church of England in their report *Issues in Human Sexuality* (London: Church House Publishing, 1991).

23 See, for example: Carol Christ, *The Laughter of Aphrodite: Reflections on a Journey to the Goddess* (San Francisco: Harper and Row, 1987) and 'Rethinking theology and nature' in Carol Christ and Judith Plaskow, *Weaving the Visions: New Patterns in Feminist Spirituality* (San Francisco: Harper and Row, 1989), pp. 314–25; Mary Daly, *Gyn/Ecology: The Metaethics of Radical Feminism* (Boston: Beacon Press, 1978) and *Pure Lust: Elemental Feminist Philosophy* (Boston: Beacon Press, 1984); Matthew Fox, *Original Blessing: A Primer in Creation Spirituality* (Santa Fe: Bear and Co., 1983).

24 Rosemary Radford Ruether, *Gaia and God: An Ecofeminist Theology of Earth Healing* (London: SCM, 1992), p. 163.

25 Peggy Reeves Sanday, *Female Power and Male Dominance: On the Origins of Sexual Inequality* (Cambridge, UK: Cambridge University Press, 1981). Sanday studied 150 tribal societies and found that 32 per cent were characterized by gender equality, 28 per cent were male dominated and 40 per cent were conflictual in that although the men did not have complete control their aspiration to achieve it was expressed in all-male rituals and groups in which myths of male dominance were acted out.

26 Ruether, *Gaia and God*, p. 167. The Mbuti are an example of the first type of society, the Balinese are an example of the second. In the latter, every child was regarded as androgynous. In adolescence gender differentiation did occur but it was accompanied by fluidity of roles and cross-dressing. After marriage, androgyny returned. Such societies were usually to be found in mild climates with more than adequate resources, stable populations and no internal or external competition.

27 Hafner, *The End of Marriage*, p. 104.

28 Friedrich Engels, 'The origin and history of the family, private property and the state' in Karl Marx and Friedrich Engels, *Selected Works*, vol. 3 (Moscow: Progress Publishers, 1970), p. 233.

29 John Boswell, *Same-Sex Unions in Premodern Europe* (New York: Villard Books, 1994), pp. 48–50.

30 Boswell, *Same-Sex Unions in Premodern Europe*, p. 113.

31 Hafner, *The End of Marriage*, p. 186.

32 Janet Coleman, '*The Owl and the Nightingale* and papal theories of marriage', *Journal of Ecclesiastical History*, vol. 38, no. 4 (October 1987), pp. 517–68.

33 Bernard of Ventadour, whose poems date from *c.* 1145–75, cited in Colin Morris, *The Discovery of the Individual: 1050–1200* (London: Harper and Row, 1972), p. 115.

34 Cited in Vincent Brümmer, *The Model of Love* (Cambridge, UK: Cambridge University Press, 1993), p. 91.

35 Marina Warner, *Alone of All Her Sex: The Myth and the Cult of the Virgin Mary* (London: Picador, 1985), p. 142.

36 Morris, *The Discovery of the Individual*, p. 113.
37 Warner, *Alone of All Her Sex*, p. 136.
38 See for example the description of Jacob's love for Rachel in Genesis 29.20.
39 Susan Dowell, *They Two Shall be One: Monogamy in History and Religion* (London: Collins Flame, 1990), p. 190.
40 William Williamson, 'People we're stuck with', *The Christian Century*, vol. 107 (October 1990), pp. 924–5.
41 Mary Crawford, 'Identity, "passing" and subversion' in Sue Wilkinson and Celia Kitzinger, *Heterosexuality: A Feminism and Psychology Reader* (London: Sage Publications, 1993), p. 44.
42 Jeffrey John, *'Permanent, Stable, Faithful': Christian Same-Sex Partnerships* (London: Affirming Catholicism, 1993), p. 18.
43 Elizabeth Stuart, *Daring to Speak Love's Name: A Gay and Lesbian Prayer Book* (London: Hamish Hamilton, 1992).
44 John, *'Permanent, Stable, Faithful'*, p. 18.
45 David Biale, *Eros and the Jews: From Biblical Israel to Contemporary America* (New York: Basic Books, 1992), p. 12.
46 Asphodel P. Long, *In a Chariot Drawn by Lions: The Search for the Female in Deity* (London: The Women's Press, 1992), pp. 133–4.
47 Biale, *Eros and the Jews*, pp. 26–7.
48 Alice L. Laffey, *Wives, Harlots and Concubines: The Old Testament in Feminist Perspective* (London: SPCK, 1990), p. 169.
49 There is some dispute over the proper translation of this phrase. The language of burning may refer to the fire of judgement rather than passion, but the point is the same—better to marry than commit sexual sin.
50 A.E. Harvey, *Promise or Pretence? A Christian's Guide to Sexual Morals* (London: SCM, 1994), p. 47.
51 Thatcher, *Liberating Sex*, p. 16.
52 Biale, *Eros and the Jews*, p. 17.
53 Biale, *Eros and the Jews*, p. 31.
54 Mishnah, *Yadayim*, 3:5.
55 Laffey, *Wives, Harlots and Concubines*, p. 203.
56 Heather Walton, 'Theology of desire', *Theology and Sexuality*, vol. 1 (September 1994), p. 33.
57 Walton, 'Theology of desire', pp. 33–4.
58 Roland E. Murphy OCarm, 'Canticle of Canticles' in Raymond E. Brown SS, Joseph A. Fitzmyer SJ and Roland E. Murphy OCarm, *The New Jerome Biblical Commentary* (London: Geoffrey Chapman, 1991), p. 465.

59 Matthew Fox, *Hildegard of Bingen's Book of Divine Works with Letters and Songs* (Santa Fe: Bear and Co., 1987), pp. 9–10.
60 Gary David Comstock, *Gay Theology Without Apology* (Cleveland: Pilgrim Press, 1993), p. 85.
61 Wayne R. Dynes, *Encyclopedia of Homosexuality*, vol. 1 (London: St James Press, 1990), p. 298.
62 Boswell, *Same-Sex Unions in Premodern Europe*, p. 69.

5   No longer servants ... but friends

In a woodcut of the Holy Family dating to 1511, Hans Baldung Grien depicts Mary and her mother St Anne playing with the child Jesus whilst an adoring St Joseph looks on from behind a wall. Jesus' face is obscured as he reaches up to his mother's face. The focus of the piece is St Anne, who looks intensely at the child's genitals and plays with them with her fingers, her fingers being shown in the traditional shape of blessing. In a later painting by Veronese, *Holy Family with Saint Barbara and the Infant Saint John*, once again the face of the baby is barely visible; the focus of the painting is the boy John kissing the child's foot, but as your eye is lifted from the foot along the line of the chubby leg, there is the baby Jesus' hand resting on his genitals. This same pose is replicated in hundreds of Renaissance paintings and sculptures of the infant Jesus. It is also replicated in pictures of the dying or dead Christ. Maerten van Heemskerck produced a series of three paintings of the adult Christ as Man of Sorrows. In each of these pictures Christ is depicted with an erection. The art historian Leo Steinberg, who has undertaken a detailed study of such works, is quite clear that in the infancy paintings 'the evidence of Christ's sexual member serves as a pledge of God's humanation'.[1]

In the paintings of the dead or dying Christ the motif points to resurrection: 'If the truth of the Incarnation was proved in the mortification of the penis, would not the truth of the Anastasis, the resuscitation, be proved by its erection? Would not this be the body's best show of power?'[2] One of my students once remarked that when she thought about Jesus' body she could only imagine that beneath his loin cloth he was rather like 'Action Man': no genitals, just a smooth bit of plastic. The Renaissance artists used Jesus' genitals to draw attention to and celebrate his humanity. Augustine would have had a fit. Augustine had a problem with erections because they were beyond the control of the will, as was the lust that often accompanied them and took control of the body. For Augustine perfection was to be in complete control. He was endearingly and boyishly impressed by people who could at will wiggle their ears or distort their faces. He reasoned that the punishment for the fall was weak will, an abandonment to desire which turned humanity into brutish beasts.

> When the first man transgressed the law of God, he began to have another law in his members which was repugnant to his mind, and he felt the evil of his disobedience when he discovered himself most justly punished by the disobedience of his flesh ... For how is it that the eyes, lips, tongue, hands, feet, and the bending of back, and neck, and sides, are all placed in his power to be moved in ways suitable to perform their work ... but when it comes to children being generated, the members created for this purpose do not obey the will, but lust has to be waited for to set these members in motion, as having rights over them, and sometimes it will not act when the mind is willing, while sometimes it even acts against the mind's will! Does the freedom of the human will not blush at this, and through despising God when he commanded, it has lost all proper command even over its own members?[3]

For Augustine, then, to desire sexual pleasure was for desire to be out of control, to be overwhelmed body and soul, to become as an animal. Sexual pleasure was therefore sinful. For Augustine, Jesus, God made human, who came to redeem us from the effects of the fall, would not have been troubled by erections because he was sinless. Augustine's influence continues to haunt us so that any attempts in our day to do what the Renaissance artists did in theirs, and celebrate Christ's humanity by emphasizing his sexuality (just as the Renaissance artists emphasized his physicality), are met with howls of

protest. In the 1970s the British paper *Gay News* was pros-
ecuted and convicted for blasphemous libel when it published a
poem, 'The Love That Dares to Speak Its Name', because it
was essentially a gay love poem centred on the crucified Christ.
The film version of Nikos Kazantzakis' book *The Last Temptation of Christ* caused havoc on both sides of the Atlantic
because of its hallucinatory scene in which Jesus imagines
himself married with children and living in contentment with a
woman. Joan H. Timmerman puts it so well when she remarks
that the formula 'Jesus is like us in all things except sin' has in
fact been essentially understood to mean 'Jesus is like us in all
things except sex'.[4] Yet, because we have generally come to
accept the existence of 'sexuality' and its importance in human
nature, if we believe that Jesus was truly human (and whether
we believe he is uniquely God incarnate or simply hail him as a
revered ancestor in faith, a person whose Spirit-filled life is in
some way paradigmatic for our own), then we have to address
ourselves to questions concerning his sexuality—or rather,
since 'sexuality' was not a concept either he or those who wrote
about him would have recognized, his relationships, his
bodiliness.

Was Jesus married, was he celibate, may he even have been
gay? Scholars have embarrassed themselves by squabbling
over these questions for the last thirty years or so. The fact is
that there is not enough evidence to support convincingly any
of these theories. Although there is a little evidence to support
the first two—there were celibate and married rabbis, healers
and prophetic figures in Jesus' day—the third question is ana-
chronistic. These are the wrong questions.

Let us begin by looking at the way Jesus' attitude to the body
is presented to us:

> When the scribes of the Pharisees saw that he was eating with
> sinners and tax collectors, they said to his disciples, 'Why does
> he eat with tax collectors and sinners?' ... Now John's disciples
> and the Pharisees were fasting; and people came and said to
> him, 'Why do John's disciples and the disciples of the Pharisees
> fast, but your disciples do not fast?' Jesus said to them, 'The
> wedding guests cannot fast while the bridegroom is with them,

can they? As long as they have the bridegroom with them, they cannot fast.'

(Mark 2.16, 18–19)

One point of agreement among all the canonical gospels is that food and drink played an important part in Jesus' ministry. Eating and drinking with people—particularly the despised and distrusted—seems to have been central to his prophetic proclamation of the arrival of God's reign on earth. It is therefore highly appropriate that the primary means by which Christians have remembered Jesus and reminded themselves of their mission, as the incarnation of the same spirit that animated him, has been through a meal, albeit the rather emaciated meal it has developed into. At this meal bread and wine are declared to be his body and blood and we eat and drink it to remind ourselves that we are now his body. The author of John's gospel has Jesus declare himself to be the 'bread of life'. The ascetical images of Jesus, which we have become so used to, serve to disconnect us from this tradition. Stanley Spencer's image of a very rotund Christ balancing precariously on his knees whilst staring in awe at some flowers in a field is much nearer the mark. This is a man you can actually imagine causing offence by enjoying a raucous dinner with dubious friends, barging his bulky way through crowds and touching people. The Jesus portrayed in the gospels is a man passionately concerned about bodies: broken bodies, bodies that have become battle grounds for power, untouchable bodies, bodies pushed to the edge.

We must be very careful to avoid the trap of a subtle kind of anti-Semitism which makes Jesus appear radical only against the background of a repressive Judaism. It is now generally accepted amongst New Testament scholars that the evangelists do not accurately represent the Judaism of Jesus' day, which of course was as multi-faceted as modern-day Judaism, and they are particularly inaccurate in their presentation of the Pharisees. So all we can say is that the gospels portray Jesus as flouting purity laws and social and sexual convention to reach

out to bodies. However, some of his teaching has been con-
scripted for pro-dualist purposes:

> 'You have heard that it was said, "You shall not commit
> adultery." But I say to you that everyone who looks at a woman
> with lust has already committed adultery with her in his heart.'
>
> (Matthew 5.27)

> 'Do you not see that whatever goes into a person from outside
> cannot defile, since it enters, not the heart but the stomach, and
> goes out into the sewer?' (Thus he declared all foods clean.)
> And he said, 'It is what comes out of a person that defiles. For it
> is from within, from the human heart, that evil intentions come:
> fornication, theft, murder, adultery, avarice, wickedness, deceit,
> licentiousness, envy, slander, pride, folly. All these evil things
> come from within, and they defile a person.'
>
> (Mark 7.18–23)

These passages are among several in which Jesus is portrayed
as severing the link (which the Pharisees are portrayed as being
so keen to impose) between purity and access to God. He does
this in the synoptic gospels apparently by arguing that it is
purity of the heart that matters, not external purity. So it seems
that Jesus had a dualistic understanding of the human person,
with the inner person mattering more than the outer. However,
in reading the texts in this way we may well be reading back into
them centuries of dominant dualism. In dealing with the passage in Matthew 5, Gareth Moore has noted:

> The meaning of the verb *epithumeō* [which is translated as 'looks
> at a woman with lust' but which actually means 'covets'] has
> nothing to do with 'internal' thoughts as opposed to 'external'
> actions. It means seriously wanting something, setting desire on
> something and acting accordingly, if you can and if you have no
> stronger reason not to do so.[5]

In Hebrew, Greek and indeed in other languages, desire leads
to action unless something prevents it. In Matthew's Sermon
on the Mount Jesus is not talking about merely thinking or
fantasizing about someone with no intention of doing anything

about it, but about looking at someone and seeking to possess that person (in this case, in all probability, another man's wife). It is important to understand this because what Jesus is taking about here is not primarily sexual desire but infringement of another man's rights over his 'property', that is, his wife. This is most certainly not to say that thoughts and fantasies are not important—these will be considered later. It is just to point out that Jesus was not drawing a distinction between thought and action, or inner and outer person.

Now let us turn to those passages which appear to make a distinction between the 'heart' of a person and that person's external behaviour. A closer look at the Markan passage reveals the dualistic interpretation to be flawed: 'For it is from within, from the human heart, that evil intentions come: fornication, theft, murder, adultery, avarice, wickedness, deceit, licentious-ness, envy, slander, pride, folly. All these things come from within, and they defile a person' (Mark 7.21–23). The heart in Hebrew thought was the instrument of action—it is from the heart that this parade of sins proceeds. Heart and desire are intimately related: 'The heart is precisely the source of action. If it is in your heart to do it, then you do it, unless you are prevented from doing it. Likewise, if you are free to do it and yet do not do it, it is not in your heart to do it.'[6] When Jesus is portrayed as criticizing the legalism of the Pharisees his com-plaint is that, for all their apparent obedience to the law, their hearts are not in it and this is demonstrated in their inconsistent *behaviour*: 'For you tithe mint and rue and herbs of all kinds, and neglect justice and love of God; it is these you ought to have practiced, without neglecting the others' (Luke 11.42).

Some Christians also pick up on a sentence Jesus speaks in Luke's gospel:

> Once Jesus was asked by the Pharisees when the kingdom of God was coming, and he answered, 'The kingdom of God is not coming with things that can be observed; nor will they say, "Look, here is it!" or "There it is!" For, in fact, the kingdom of God is *entos humōn*.'

(17.21)

This Greek phrase has often been translated as 'within you', and on the basis of this one phrase alone, many have argued that the kingdom is all about changing individuals inside rather than transforming the external world. However, since nowhere else in the gospels does Jesus saying anything similar to this, and since he is unlikely to have said to those who are portrayed as his enemies that the kingdom is within them, this interpretation must be regarded as dubious. There are other possible and more probable interpretations. It is a rare phrase anyway but in recently discovered papyri which use common Greek of the first century it seems to mean 'within your reach' or 'it can be shared by you if you want it'. Stanton notes that this interpretation does make sense in this context.[7] Other scholars have suggested that the phrase should be translated as 'among you', which again makes some sense. So there are no grounds for attributing a dualistic understanding of the human person to Jesus on the basis of the teaching attributed to him. What matters to Jesus is where you put your body. Following him means literally getting up and walking off (Mark 1.16–20). It means standing with and among the non-persons; it means engaging in acted parables that draw attention to the presence and absence of God (e.g. the 'cleansing of the temple'); it means being prepared to be bodily tortured and killed for the sake of the vision.

One of the most moving stories in the gospels is a story in which Jesus himself becomes the object of sacramental touch:

> While he was at Bethany in the house of Simon the leper, as he sat at the table, a woman came with an alabaster jar of very costly ointment of nard, and she broke open the jar and poured the ointment on his head. But some were there who said to one another in anger, 'Why was the ointment wasted in this way? ...' But Jesus said, 'Let her alone; why do you trouble her? She has performed a good service for me ...'
>
> (Mark 14.3–4, 6)

In the gospels it is only women who ever recognize the needs of Jesus and attempt to respond to them. The other disciples could never accept Jesus as he was—they wanted a military saviour, a wonder-worker, an ordinary rabbi, anybody but the man who would not fit in with conventions and who knew that one day he would be killed. They carry on pretending he is someone else to the very end, but this anonymous woman recognizes the real Jesus. She does to him what he has done to so many: she reaches out to a frightened man and touches him with a touch that is sacramental, it communicates something of the love of God. She anoints him with oil, oil that was used for healing, to designate kings and priests as God's chosen, and to anoint the dead. All this symbolism comes together in this act. It is an act of recognition, and of extravagant passion (as the disciples note self-righteously, she has 'wasted' some very expensive nard). The story is paralleled in the other gospels. In Luke 7.36–50 the emphasis is slightly different and focuses on repentance. There are echoes of the Song of Solomon in both versions of the story:

> For your love is better than wine,
> your anointing oils are fragrant,
> your name is perfume poured out;
> therefore the maidens love you ...

> While the king was on his couch,
> my nard gave forth its fragrance.
> (1.2–3, 12)

The passionate dimension of the story is impossible to miss. Jesus is portrayed, particularly in the gospel of Mark but in the other gospels as well, as a man of passion. Jesus weeps, Jesus gets tetchy and Jesus despairs. In the light of this it becomes clear that the only appropriate and just vindication imaginable for a man so at home in and so in touch with (figuratively and literally speaking) bodies is resurrection. An explosion of re-embodiment which allowed him to eat and drink again and enjoy the company of his friends was the only possible happy outcome for Jesus of Nazareth. I particularly like the definition of resurrection provided by Patrick Kavanagh:

a laugh freed
for ever and for ever.[8]

This short description conveys both the joy and deep physicality of the event. As I have watched people I know die, whether from AIDS-related illness or from some other wasting disease, I have had exactly the same feelings as I have in reading the accounts of Jesus' life—only bodily resurrection is a good enough hope for these people. Nothing has taught me more about the unity of the human person than watching people slowly die, bodies and personalities diminishing together. *Long-time Companion* is an extremely moving film about the early days of the AIDS pandemic in the United States. The film closes with what I can only describe as a resurrection sequence. The surviving characters find themselves on the beach on a sunny day, greeting all their departed friends who have shed their emaciated, scarred bodies and stand tall, filled out, healthy, beautiful. They laugh together, hug each other, play together. If we believe in a God of justice, a God of love, a God of incarnation, this is the only possible ending: re-embodiment, re-incarnation. What form that might take I have no idea: whether it be in returning to and becoming again part of the body of the earth, or in the assumption of a different type of body in a different dimension, such as Paul imagined (1 Corinthians 15.35–55), or some other speculative theory which is not grounded in a dualistic understanding of the human person. I could not personally accept the venerable tradition of re-incarnation because it assumes like most theories of eternal life that it is possible to separate a human being, and indeed any being, like an egg: cook one half in an oven but keep the other half back to be blended with some other ingredients later. The periodic and almost ritualistic squabbles between Christians over the reality or mythic-quality of the stories of the empty tomb almost always miss the point that, whatever else the stories were meant to convey, they make clear that bodies are not dispensable cloaks or coatings but essential to the person and so taken up by and into God in this glorious act of vindication which symbolizes the beginning of the new age of God's reign.

In much the same way as the Hebrew scriptures and the Pauline corpus, the stories of Jesus of Nazareth present us with a confusion of images on some issues. The flouting of social and sexual convention exists alongside much that reinforces that convention. Liberal feminism has drawn attention to Jesus' refusal to adopt the most misogynistic attitudes to women that were available in his culture. But theologians like Daphne Hampson warn us against making the unwarranted leap from this to proclaiming Jesus as a feminist:

> True he was not, as far as we know, misogynist: there is
> evidence to the contrary. But it must not be thought that he was
> in this alone in his society: there were others also who were not
> ... There is no positive evidence that Jesus saw anything wrong
> with the sexism of his day. He did not, as far as we know, see
> the necessity for structural change to remedy the oppression that
> women were under. One may make a comparison here with his
> attitude towards the poor; one could evidently make out a case
> that, in relation to the poor, he preached the need for revolution
> ... His parables never challenge male privilege ... Nor,
> significantly, in the realm of religion does Jesus appear to have
> done anything to counter the inferior position in which women
> were placed ... That Jesus was personally kind to women there
> is no reason to doubt. That he freed people to be themselves
> and to be present for others is the undeniable witness of the
> texts. But that he had a feminist analysis of society is something
> for which there is no evidence.[9]

It is undoubtedly true that the focus of Jesus' message and ministry was not the liberation of women, it was the kingdom of God. However, it does seem to me to be clear that Jesus was aware, to some extent at least, of the implications of his message for women, and certainly there is evidence to suggest that after his death female followers grasped hold of the implications and applied them to themselves as women today are still doing. Yet, as in the Hebrew scripture, there is a distinction between direct teaching and story.

Jesus' teaching on sexual ethics, or at least the teaching which is attributed to him, illustrates this point. We have already seen that the teaching on adultery in Matthew's Sermon on the Mount, which has sometimes been claimed as being 'pro-women' by attempting to protect them from being reduced to mere sexual objects of lustful eyes, in fact reinforces the tenth commandment, 'you shall not covet your neighbour's . . . wife' (Exodus 20.17). What about the other teaching ascribed to Jesus on marriage and divorce? The teaching of the Torah on this issue was reasonably clear:

> Suppose a man enters into marriage with a woman, but she does not please him because he finds something objectionable about her, and so he writes her a certificate of divorce, puts it in her hand, and sends her out of his house; she then leaves his house and goes off to become another man's wife. Then suppose the second man dislikes her, writes her a bill of divorce, puts it in her hand, and sends her out of his house (or the second man who married her dies); her husband, who sent her away, is not permitted to take her again to be his wife after she has been defiled.

> (Deuteronomy 24.1–4)

So only a man may initiate divorce, if he finds something objectionable about his wife, and he must issue her with a certificate of divorce and not remarry her at a later date. In Jesus' day there was dispute among rabbis as to what might constitute 'something objectionable'. Rabbi Hillel had suggested that spoiling a meal was sufficient grounds for divorce. Rabbi Shammai, on the other hand, believed adultery to be the only legitimate ground upon which a man could divorce his wife, a view also taken by the Qumran community. In Mark 10.1–12 Jesus is placed in the midst of this dispute. He fails to align himself with either side in the dispute but comes up with an answer altogether more radical:

> But Jesus said to them, 'Because of your hardness of heart he [Moses] wrote this commandment for you. But from the beginning of creation, "God made them male and female. For this reason a man shall leave his father and mother and be joined

to his wife, and the two shall become one flesh." So they are no longer two, but one flesh. Therefore what God has joined together, let no one separate.' Then in the house the disciples asked him again about this matter. He said to them, 'Whoever divorces his wife and marries another commits adultery against her; and if she divorces her husband and marries another, she commits adultery.'

(Mark 10.5–12)

Adrian Thatcher comments on this passage: 'This teaching, within the context of easy divorce of women is little short of amazing. The law allowing divorce is not revised or tightened; it is abolished. In the reign of God men are forbidden to divorce women at all.'[10] And he claims, as several feminist critics have, that this passage affirms that women are not to be treated as goods to be disposed at will. There is certainly something radical in Jesus' teaching as it is presented in Mark. Against the Jewish tradition he asserts that a man can commit adultery against his own wife and not simply against another man and he affirms the absolute indissolubility of marriage, basing his teaching on Genesis. This no doubt would have the effect of protecting women from the dangerous vulnerability which came with divorce and singleness. However, as Gareth Moore has noted, the focus of this passage is not women but men. The central question is 'can a man divorce his wife?' Jesus' reply utilizes Genesis, which teaches that a man leaves his family to be joined to his wife, and the stark answer is 'no', 'Hence Jesus' teaching is again about what a man may do with his wife, and is aimed at protecting the wife.'[11] So we are in a slightly different position to that of the Sermon on the Mount. The wife is no longer reducible to the mere chattel of the husband. However, she is still the passive object of this teaching. She is protected rather than empowered.

Thatcher reads enormous significance into Jesus' use of Genesis,

Jesus interprets the passage by drawing out a particular meaning of 'one flesh'. This term is a metaphor which has its home in the Hebrews' unabashed acceptance of the body and bodily union

... Yet to become 'one flesh' with the marriage partner is to become one in being with him or her and so to undergo a transformation of one's own being as an individual person. But Jesus' comment on the passage is: 'It follows that they are no longer *two individuals* [his emphasis]: they are one flesh.' The insertion of 'individuals' in the New English and Revised English Bibles draws out a missing emphasis in earlier versions. Jesus' vision for women and men in marriage is a full sharing of each life with and for the other such that the individual identities are transcended in the single shared life in which each is fully 'from' and 'for' the other and is fulfilled 'in' and 'through' the other.[12]

I think Thatcher overstates his case here. Certainly the Septuagint version of Genesis 2.24 which Mark appears to be drawing upon adds 'two' to the Hebrew phrase 'They shall become one flesh'. This may reflect a desire to endorse monogamy but that is really all one can legitimately say; any other interpretation is speculative and reading into the text something which may not be there. Paul also used a 'one flesh' argument in 1 Corinthians 6.12–20 when trying to convince his wayward flock why they should not resort to prostitutes:

> The body is not meant for fornication but for the Lord, and the Lord for the body. And God raised the Lord and will also raise us by his power. Do you not know that your bodies are members of Christ? Should I therefore take the members of Christ and make them members of a prostitute? Never! Do you not know that whoever is united to a prostitute becomes one body with her? For it is said, 'The two shall be one flesh.' But anyone united to the Lord becomes one spirit with him.
>
> (vv. 13–17)

This is a typically Pauline argument, in that it is actually not one argument but several, which creates the impression, as with so many of Paul's instructions on behaviour, that gut reaction comes first, rationalization second. The first argument is based upon Paul's conviction that through baptism a Christian becomes part of Christ's body—our bodies matter because they are 'for the Lord' and not for fornication. It appears that some of the Corinthians may have been appealing to the dualistic argument and Paul is probably quoting one of their slogans in 6.18: 'Every sin that a person commits is outside the body'—it is the internal motives of a person that matter, not their bodily actions. Paul stamps on this reasoning: 'But the fornicator sins against the body itself. Or do you not know that your body is a temple of the Holy Spirit ...?' Far from being detached from one's body, sinning using one's body is a sin against God because your body is God's temple. The taking of Christ to a prostitute is obviously a horrific thought to Paul and obviously wrong. He then turns to the 'one flesh' argument. In Hebrew thought 'flesh' usually referred to 'body', whether that be a human person or persons or a social unit. When a person uses a prostitute they become one body with her and this is unacceptable because a Christian is already one body with Christ. This seems to be the heart of Paul's argument—it is a matter of fidelity to Christ (note that it is not a matter of fidelity to a spouse). Indeed he goes on to point out that your body is not your own to give to someone else because (and here we are back to slavery language) 'you were bought with a price ...' (1 Corinthians 6.20).

Paul uses Genesis 2.24 differently to Jesus. Gareth Moore argues that in using the passage Paul is demonstrating that intercourse with a prostitute is a parody of the 'unity of a shared life which a man and his wife enjoy'.[13] However, Paul does not apply this passage from Genesis to marriage in the rest of this letter to the Corinthians and indeed it does not appear again in any of his undisputed letters. It does turn up in Ephesians 5 where it is cited as referring to the hierarchical relationship between Christ and his Church (Ephesians 5.31–32). In Corinthians Paul uses the passage out of its context to shock the offenders—two people who have sex become one flesh. Therefore, in going to a prostitute, the Corinthian Christians are not only taking Christ to that prostitute but also breaking the bonds of their slavery by giving their bodies to someone else. Jesus uses the passage to indicate that a man and woman come together and form a new social unit. This social unit Jesus proclaims as indestructible, and this is good news for women living in his day, but that is all that can legitimately be read into Jesus' teaching here. Thatcher's reading of this passage as a manifesto for equality within marriage is too optimistic a reading. Similarly, in noting that Jesus allows for the possibility that a woman might divorce her husband, an impossibility in the Judaism of his day, Thatcher asks: 'Does Jesus look forward to a time when equality of access to divorce was to become possible?'[14] But the more likely explanation is that this verse reflects the Roman context of Mark's community where women were permitted to initiate divorce. Mark is simply drawing out the implications of Jesus' teaching for his own community.

Luke and Matthew share a saying, probably from their common source, which is not in Mark. In both versions of this saying (Matthew 5.31–32 and Luke 16.18) remarriage after divorce is condemned. In Matthew, whoever marries a divorced woman commits adultery. In Luke, a man who divorces his wife and remarries is condemned as adulterous. There is no indication in these sayings that the adultery is committed against the woman; in fact the focus of the story is again the activity of men. Matthew 5 also adds an exception clause, which is repeated (19.1–12), where we find a direct parallel to the passage in Mark 10. In his version of the story Matthew significantly alters Jesus' teaching in Mark: 'And I say to you, whoever divorces his wife, except for unchastity, and marries another commits adultery' (19.9). The word translated as 'unchastity' here is *porneia*. Various explanations have been offered as to its meaning. Some have argued that it refers to adultery and that Matthew was trying to protect those Christians who were also citizens of the Roman Empire. Under Roman law a husband had to expose his adulterous wife or else face the death penalty. However, this clause almost certainly does not refer to adultery as there was a specific word—*moicheia*—for this. Others have argued that the term *porneia* translates the Hebrew *zenût* which refers to marriages between people forbidden by Jewish laws of kinship. Such marriages were more common in the Gentile world. Others have pointed out that Paul uses the word to refer to any sexual transgression and this could be its meaning here—any sexual relationship outside the marriage. The point to note is that by the time Matthew's gospel was written, Christians were finding Jesus' radical teaching as presented in Mark impossible to follow. Indeed Paul faced this problem much earlier. Paul knew Jesus' teaching as represented in Mark's gospel (1 Corinthians 7.10). However, he seems to have had to deal with some specific and difficult cases at Corinth. He instructs a wife to resist the separation that her husband appeared to want (vv. 10–11; the passive tense is used here), but if she should be forcibly divorced she should remain single or endeavour to be reconciled to her husband. Paul would not allow Christian converts to separate from their non-Christian partners. However, 'if the unbelieving partner separates, let it be so; in such a case the brother or sister is not bound. It is to peace that God has called you' (v. 15).

Jesus' teaching on marriage was no doubt radical and may have served to protect women, but that this was its original intent or that this teaching expresses a vision of marriage based upon equality and mutuality is extremely doubtful. As Matthew and Paul demonstrate, Jesus' teaching was soon recognized as capable of causing more harm than good, a fact that has been attested to by millions of his subsequent followers.

So far then we have built up a picture of Jesus as a body-loving, body-affirming person who certainly stretched the bounds of social and sexual convention to some degree. His limited teaching on matters relating to sexual ethics are actually not teachings on sexual ethics at all but on the institution of marriage, which he shores up by dissolving divorce as an option. There are some other relevant passages that now need to be considered. Attention must be paid to a block of teaching which Matthew attaches to Jesus' major statement on divorce but which is not paralleled in any other gospel.

His disciples said to him, 'If such is the case of a man with his wife, it is better not to marry.' But he said to them, 'Not everyone can accept this teaching, but only those to whom it is given. For there are eunuchs who have been so from birth, and there are eunuchs who have been made eunuchs by others, and there are eunuchs who have made themselves eunuchs for the sake of the kingdom of heaven. Let anyone accept this who can.'

(Matthew 19.10–12)

This passage has been held up for centuries as Jesus' endorsement of celibacy. In fact, if read in context, the passage takes on a completely different meaning. The disciples are taken aback by Jesus' teaching on marriage. The almost complete ban upon divorce leads them to ask with exasperation whether it would be better not to marry. Jesus's reply is difficult. It is unclear whether 'this teaching' refers to the previous teaching on marriage or the teaching he is about to give. If the former, and this would make sense as this is the teaching the disciples are questioning, then Jesus acknowledges that not all will be able to abide by his radical teaching on marriage and divorce. Thus 'eunuchs' could refer to those who do limit themselves to one spouse—some are naturally inclined to this way of life, others are forced into it, and others choose it as a commitment to the kingdom. However, if we take the traditional reading, then it is amusing that Jesus' justification for celibacy seems to be a reversal of Paul's. Paul argued that celibacy is the ideal, marriage the concession. Here Jesus advocates celibacy for those who cannot cope with his radical teaching on marriage! Harvey interprets the passage as Jesus restoring dignity to those incapable of marrying:

Those who were physically incapable were treated as inferior to full citizens. Those women who failed to find a husband were mocked or pitied. Those who were widowed (of whom there were always many) were dependent on charity. Jesus chose the most offensive of the words that described any of these catagories ('eunuch') and declared that it was a state that could be deliberately chosen for the sake of the kingdom. By implication, he restored dignity and respect to them all. The startling character of his language reinforced his startling conclusion: incapacity for marriage, or free renunciation of marriage, may offer an honourable passport to the kingdom of heaven.[15]

Gay scholars have pointed out that, in the ancient mind, eunuchs were regarded as a third sex who engaged in passive sex with other men.[16] They were certainly not associated with celibacy. Could Jesus have been advocating the unthinkable for those who could not enter marriage? It is very unlikely and the passage is far too ambiguous. But we should not overlook the fact that eunuchs were associated in some ancient Israelite traditions with Canaanite cults, and the Deuteronomists order their exclusion from the community (Deuteronomy 23.1). Jesus' teaching in Matthew echoes Isaiah 56.4. In the new age those formerly excluded will be welcomed in. This is taken up in Acts 8.26–39, where an Ethiopian eunuch is baptized into the new community. The message of this teaching is that marriage is not the only relationship compatible with God's reign.

The next passage is the story of the healing of the centurion's servant which is found in Matthew (8.5–13), Luke (7.1–10) and John (4.46–54). As the story which may come closer than any other passage to indicating Jesus' views on homosexual behaviour, it is notable by its absence from most books and church documents on the subject. John's version is very different to that of the synoptic gospels but the story is broadly the same. In both synoptic versions of the story Jesus is besought to heal the servant of a centurion. The centurion wins Jesus' admiration by refusing to allow Jesus to enter his own home and declaring his faith that all Jesus has to do is 'say the word' and he will be healed. Luke uses two words to describe the one who is sick: *doulos* and *pais*. Matthew, however, only uses one word: *pais*. *Doulos* definitely refers to a slave, but *pais* has a more ambiguous meaning. It can mean 'child' of either sex (and in John the child is the official's son—*huios*) but it was also the word used in Hellenistic culture to refer to a man's slave lover. Gerd Theissen in his fictional account of the ministry of Jesus has his narrator probing the Pharisee Gamaliel about his attitude to Jesus. The Pharisee acknowledges that most of Jesus' teaching is in perfect accord with that of the Pharisees but that is not the problem:

> Yes, this Jesus could be my pupil. He could put forward all his views. But I would compel him to think through the consequences for our people and for everyday life. Let me mention another instance. One day a Gentile centurion living here in Capernaum came to him. He asked him to heal his orderly. Of course you have to help Gentiles. But why this one? Everyone knows that most of these Gentile officers are homosexual. Their orderlies are their lovers. But Jesus isn't interested in that sort of thing. He didn't ask anything about the orderly. He healed him—and the thought didn't occur to him that later someone might think of appealing to him in support of the view that homosexuality was permissible.[17]

In addition to slave lovers it was also possible and very common in the Roman world for a man to have female and/or male concubines. Concubines were not owned like slaves but maintained for long-term relationships, sometimes alongside wives. (1 Kings 11.3 proudly proclaims that Solomon had seven hundred wives and three hundred concubines.) However, many of the extant marriage contracts required the husband to get rid of male concubines at least. In the Gentile world that surrounded and encroached upon Palestine and the early Christian world, same-sex love between men was idealized, often specifically because it was based upon friendship—upon equality and mutuality. Boswell notes how in ancient romances male lovers (often with a difference in age) enjoy permanent relationships with each other, often alongside marriage but precluding relations with other men, and there is evidence of the existence of rituals to celebrate these relationships.[18] We must be very careful about what we try to make of this gospel story. It may well have had absolutely nothing to do with a sexual relationship between the two men. The very most we can claim is that Jesus was not interested in whether this centurion was having sexual relations with his slave, despite the possibility of a common assumption that this would have been the case. If the word *pais* does refer to a slave then there are power issues in the relationship which we would, I hope, not want to idealize. However, the main point is that Jesus shows no interest in the sexual ethics of the man, only in his faith.

The second passage of interest is the story of Jesus' encounter with the Samaritan woman in John 4.1–42. This is one of the stories about Jesus that portrays him as a breaker of all kinds of social convention. The disciples are shocked to find their master talking to a woman (v. 27), reflecting the view of some Jews contemporary with Jesus that women should not be addressed in public and should be avoided because of the danger that they might ensnare the unvigilant. Interestingly the disciples do not express surprise at the fact that Jesus is talking to a Samaritan. Relations between Jews and Samaritans were as sour as only relations between two groups can be, when they share a common religious heritage but have come to diverge on matters of belief and practice. A regulation which the author of John may well have been familiar with warned Jews that they should never assume that a Samaritan woman was ritually pure since they menstruated from babyhood.[19] When the fact that Jacob's well seems to have been a favourite courting site is added to our reading of the story, the reason for the disciples' alarm and the shock value of the story become obvious. Against this background it is all the more remarkable that Jesus engages in a quick-fire theological discussion with the woman that operates according to the typically Johannine fashion of statement, misunderstanding and elucidation. Suddenly, Jesus changes tack:

> Jesus said to her, 'Go, call your husband, and come back.' The woman answered him, 'I have no husband.' Jesus said to her, 'You are right in saying, "I have no husband"; for you have had five husbands, and the one you have now is not your husband. What you have said is true!' The woman said to him, 'Sir, I see that you are a prophet.' (vv. 16–19)[20]

There is some evidence to suggest that Jews at least were only permitted three marriages.[21] If that is so then the implication is that this woman has broken the law in the past and in the present by living with a man who is not her husband (presumably that means that she is living with a man to whom she is not legally contracted through a bill of marriage). The woman is honest with Jesus and he acknowledges it, but there is no hint of condemnation in what Jesus says, he simply states the facts. The woman begins to wonder at the nature of the person before her—could this be the prophet looked for by the Samaritans who would vindicate Samaritan worship on Mount Gerizim? The dialogue moves forward, and slowly the Samaritan woman comes to appropriate faith in Jesus. In this story, then, we are presented with a Jesus who breaks social and sexual convention to bring to faith and apostleship a woman whose whole life breaches such convention. Her coming to faith does not involve any repentance for her past life or apparent change in her behaviour. Indeed, it is her amazement that Jesus knew about her life that propels her out to spread the news to others.

The third passage occurs in Mark 12.18–27 and portrays Jesus in dispute with some Sadducees over resurrection, the possibility of which the Sadducees rejected. They endeavour to demonstrate the absurdity of the idea by invoking the laws of levirate marriage: a woman is married seven times to seven different brothers: 'In the resurrection whose wife will she be? For the seven had married her.' Jesus' reply is clear: 'For when they rise from the dead, they neither marry nor are given in marriage, but are like angels in heaven.' This is an interesting passage from our point of view because Jesus appears to state clearly that, when the glorious reign of God is brought in, marriage will no longer exist. This is important because many have interpreted his reference to Genesis 2.24 in his teaching on marriage as an expression of a belief that when the kingdom came human beings would be restored to their original married state in paradise. The mention of angels should not be assumed to be a reference to some kind of sexless state. Jewish understandings of angels were usually very bodily. Indeed, this tradition is continued in the work of John Milton who has an angel explain to Adam:

> Whatever pure thou in the body enjoy'st
> (And pure thou wert created) we enjoy
> In eminence, and obstacle find none
> Of membrane, joint, or limb...[22]

Ferdinand Mount, writing about Christianity and the family, has noted:

> It is not and never has been the Church's restrictions on sexuality which have constituted the basic threat which Christianity poses to the family. It is the carefree attitudes of the Sermon on the Mount ... The Sermon on the Mount is a wonderful, intoxicating sermon, but it is a sermon for bachelors.[23]

Despite centuries of Christian apologetic to the contrary, it cannot be denied that Jesus' teaching and behaviour as it is presented to us in the four gospels is hardly conducive to family life. He is portrayed as demanding that people leave all their social and familial obligations behind them and follow him immediately (Mark 1.16–20). Not even the most sacred familial obligations are considered important enough even to postpone following Jesus:

> To another he said, 'Follow me.' But he said, 'Lord, first let me go and bury my father.' But Jesus said to him, 'Let the dead bury their own dead; but as for you, go and proclaim the kingdom of God.' Another said, 'I will follow you, Lord; but let me first say farewell to those at my home.' Jesus said to him, 'No one who puts a hand to the plough and looks back is fit for the kingdom of God.'
>
> (Luke 9.59–62)

Jesus is consistently presented as demanding that people deprive themselves of their wealth, status and home to follow him. In fact he demands that his disciples learn to 'hate' their families (Luke 14.26–27). His attitude to his own family is consistent with this:

> Then his mother and his brothers came; and standing outside, they sent to him and called him. A crowd was sitting around him; and they said to him, 'Your mother and your brothers and

sisters are outside, asking for you.' And he replied, 'Who are my
mother and my brothers?' And looking at those who sat around
him, he said, 'Here are my mother and my brothers! Whoever
does the will of God is my brother and sister and mother.'

(Mark 3.31–35)

The old bonds of kinship were dissolved and replaced by new
ones. Elisabeth Schüssler Fiorenza has drawn attention to the
interesting fact that in the gospels, when Jesus speaks about the
need to leave behind blood relatives in order to gain new
brothers, sisters and mothers, he never mentions fathers.[24]
Blood fathers are people to be left behind but not to be replicated in the new order:

> Truly I tell you, there is no one who has left house or brothers
> or sisters or mother or father or children or fields, for my sake
> and for the sake of the good news, who will not receive a
> hundred fold now in this age—houses, brothers and sisters,
> mothers and children, and fields with persecutions—and in the
> age to come eternal life.

(Mark 19.29–30)

No fathers because there is only one father—God. And no
fathers because patriarchal structures are antithetical to the
kingdom. (Virginia Ramey Mollenkott refers to this as God's
kindom, thereby avoiding the male, monarchical overtones of
kingdom but still capturing the essence of Jesus' use of *basileia*.[25]) We know that this radical reworking of notions of
family operated in the early Church. Rosemary Radford
Ruether, in surveying the effect of Christianity on the family,
has noted:

> Christianity disrupted the family, because household and state
> were so closely linked in ancient society. To follow a religion
> contrary to that of the family—a religion, moreover, which
> declared the official religion to be false and demonic—was to
> strike at the heart of the social order of both the family and the
> state. It meant that wives could dissolve their allegiance to their
> households, children to their parents, slaves to their masters.
> These persons, in turn, no longer reverenced the state whose
> prosperity was founded on the favour of the ancestral gods.

Thus we should not minimize the seriousness of the assault on society posed by early Christianity.[26]

It is undoubtedly true that Christianity had particular appeal to women because of this freedom it gave them from the family and many heroic stories survive from the early centuries of Christianity attesting to the bravery of women who resisted persecution from their families and the state for their new faith. This bravery united them often with their slaves, and with members of the lower classes, an alliance that further exasperated those who regarded Christianity as socially and politically subversive. I think particularly of the Christian noblewoman Perpetua and her slave Felicitas, who were martyred together in Carthage around 203 CE and who became the object of enormous adulation for later centuries.[27] In the epistles of the New Testament, however, we find evidence of another tradition, a tradition which sought to play down the subversive implications of Christianity for the family. Paul typically struggles between what he knows are the radical demands of the Gospel and his own conservative instincts, but he tentatively begins to suggest that marriage and the family can be a locus for living out the way of Christ. Other writers faced with the problem of households divided by Christianity advocate a kind of dualism: you are inwardly free but do not cause scandal by living this freedom; accept physical oppression for the sake of Christ.

> Slaves, accept the authority of your masters with all deference, not only those who are kind and gentle but also those who are harsh. For it is a credit to you if, being aware of God, you endure pain while suffering unjustly ... because Christ also suffered for you, leaving you an example, so that you should follow in his steps ... Wives, in the same way, accept the authority of your husbands, so that, even if some of them do not obey the word, they may be won over without a word by their wives' conduct.
>
> (1 Peter 2.18–19, 21; 3.1)

This is an approach mirrored in early Christian apologetics. The conflict between attitudes towards family life eventually resolved itself into two separate ways of life: monasticism and what Ruether calls 'the Christianization of the patriarchal family and Roman empire', leaving the family largely unscathed by the radical Christian vision embodied in Jesus: 'By making the Christian egalitarian counterculture a monastic elite, outside of and unrelated to the family, the Christian church retrenched from the possibility that this radical vision itself could lay claims upon and transform the power relationships of society and family.'[28]

This Christianization of the family continues today, particularly among fundamentalist groups and politicians of the Right. Lesbian and gay people have been at the receiving end of such apologetics, their lives branded as antithetical to family values and therefore to Christianity. The Hebrew scriptures are actually subversive of modern attempts to idolize the 'family' in terms of married mother and father, plus children. Paul Ballard, in a discussion of Christianity and the family, has noted that 'the heart of the matter is that the Gospel has burst through the limitations of accepted human relationships'.[29] In terms of the family it means that the covenant of inclusive friendship desacralizes inherited patterns of family to be replaced by universal bonds of kinship. Virginia Ramey Mollenkott has identified forty different forms of family 'mentioned or implied' in the Hebrew and Christian scriptures. These include: patriarchal extended families (Genesis 14.14); polygamous marriage (Deuteronomy 21.15); female-headed extended family (Rahab, Joshua 6.17, 25); single-parents and children (2 Kings 4.1–7; Luke 7.11–12); monogamous marriage (Genesis 2.24; Matthew 19.5); cohabitation without marriage (Samson and Delilah, Judges 16.4ff.); surrogate motherhood (Hagar, Genesis 16.1–15; Bilhah, Genesis 30.1–7; Zilpah, Genesis 30.9–13); unrelated adults sharing a home (the widows, Acts 9.36–39); women married by force (Judges 21); cross-cultural adoptive families (Exodus 2.10); cross-class adoptive families (Genesis 15.2–3) and even 'commuter marriages' (Peter travelling about with Jesus, leaving his wife and mother-in-law at home, Matthew 8.14; and Joanna, wife of Chuza, who did the same thing, Luke 8.3)![30] The Hebrew and Christian scriptures actually speak a great deal more accurately and honestly about family life than most Christian Churches. They do not idealize or sentimentalize but present us with a quilt of images which we can recognize in our own experience of family life and which cries out in defiance of those who seek to claim it as the source and demander of 'traditional family values'. Jesus' behaviour is the most outrageous of all. And again we who find his attitude to the family liberating must not ignore the pain it must have caused. In a play about the 'unnamed, the unsung, the un-mentioned' women in Christian history, written by Irene Mahoney OSU and performed by Roberta Nobleman, Simon Peter's wife talks about the abandonment of herself and her children by Simon who has now even changed his name under the influence of 'the master':

> He would work miracles himself! The Master had told him so—he would pick up vipers and not be harmed, drink poison and not die. He would preach and teach and heal. (And what about me?) He would journey from place to place telling of the kingdom of God. (And what about me?) And when that kingdom came he would have one of the highest places. (And what about me?)[31]

The play as I saw it goes on to show the devastating effects upon Augustine's mistress, a medieval priest's wife, Anne Donne (wife of the poet and clergyman John) and Maria von Wedemeyer (fiancée of the theologian and martyr Dietrich Bonhoeffer) as their husbands/lovers tried to follow Jesus' demands. And yet the message of the play is not that all these men should have stayed at home but that these women were imprisoned by the institution of family and Church and locked behind masks—the Mistress, the Wife, the Mother, the Fian-cée—that prevented them from living out of their passion. They were expected to stay at home. As Peter's wife concludes in the epilogue, 'I grew to love the Lord myself, God knows, and Peter did the right thing I haven't a doubt. And yet I say the same thing now as I said then: What about me? What about us? What about all of us?'[32]

This brings us to the issue of Jesus' own model of relating. As has already been pointed out, we have no evidence with which to establish whether Jesus was married or not. Whether he was or not, none of his surviving teaching regarding marriage draws upon his personal situation or experience. The only model of relating that we can definitely see operating in the life of Jesus, as presented to us by the gospels, is friendship—and it is a way of being friends which exposes the passion behind friendship. One could say that the essence of Jesus' ministry was simply befriending—the forming of mutual, equal, loving, accepting and transforming relationships. The equality dimension is emphasized by Jesus' refusal to make any claims about himself despite pressure to do so, his refusal to play the 'master role' (John 13.1–11) and his constant concern to encourage others to do what he does: teach, preach, heal and take responsibility themselves for bringing in the reign of God. Celia Hahn has drawn attention to the fact that this is particularly obvious in the stories of the feeding of the five thousand where Jesus initially refuses to act, endeavouring to prompt his disciples themselves to do something: 'But he answered them, "You give them something to eat"' (Mark 6.37). Jesus almost always emphasizes that it is 'your faith' that has saved those healed.[33] The mutuality element is emphasized by his desire to be fed by those he helps, by his acceptance of physical ministry of women and in the glorious story of his disputatious encounter with the Syrophoenician woman whose challenge to Jesus' theology prompts him to alter his behaviour (Mark 7.24–30). The author of John's gospel makes explicit this central dimension of Jesus' ministry. During their last night and last extended conversation together, Jesus delivers a deeply moving monologue on the relationship between himself and his disciples. Again and again John's Jesus employs the verb *menein* to describe the relationship. This word is usually translated 'remain' or 'abide', but also means 'stay' or 'dwell on'. It is the word that lies behind the following sample of phrases from the Farewell Discourse:

Do you not believe that *I am in* the Father and the Father is in me? (14.10)

You know him, [the Spirit of truth] because he *abides with you*, and he will be in you. (14.17)

Abide in me as I *abide* in you. Just as the branch cannot bear fruit by itself unless it *abides* in the vine, neither can you unless you *abide* in me. (15.4)

As the Father has loved me, so I have loved you; *abide* in my love. If you keep my commandments, you will *abide* in my love, just as I have kept my Father's commandments and *abide* in his love. (15.9–10)

We must not assume that this is a dualistic concept of an internal experience of God and Christ—an equivalent to the 'kingdom of God is within you' theory. The word *menein* does not automatically convey this meaning. The word rather conveys an intimate relationship in terms of remaining with, or staying on with, the person concerned. I think we could be quite near to our model of two bits of clay meeting. When two bits of clay meet they impress their image on each other, each is changed, their encounter remains with them for ever. It is the same with people. Jesus' relationship with his Father has impressed itself upon him; and now he in turn impresses that image on his disciples and they in turn abide in him, that is, they have impressed their image on him. It is the language of mutual encounter. Something similar may be meant by the language of the Last Supper in the synoptic gospels where the disciples are asked to eat and drink bread and wine held up by Jesus as symbols of his body and blood. The food and drink become part of you: they change and affect you. The proof of this encounter lies not in some kind of internal attitude but in external behaviour, as Brown notes: 'To remain in Jesus, or in the Father, or in one of the divine attributes or gifts is intimately associated with keeping the commandments in the spirit of love (John 15.10; 1 John 4.12, 16), with a struggle against the world (1 John 2.16–17), and with bearing fruit (John 15.5)—all basic Christian duties.'[34]

Positive mutual encounter and influence which results in transforming behaviour: this is the language of friendship and this is quickly made explicit:

> This is my commandment, that you love one another as I have loved you. No one has greater love than this, to lay down one's life for one's friends. You are my friends if you do what I command you. I do not call you servants any longer, because the servant does not know what the master is doing; but I have called you friends, because I have made known to you everything that I have heard from my Father. You did not choose me but I chose you. And I appointed you to go and bear fruit, fruit that will last, so that the Father will give you whatever you ask in my name. I am giving you these commands so that you may love one another.
>
> (John 15.12–17)

Here we find a tradition in almost direct contradiction to that of Paul. We are not called to be in servant–slave relationships with Christ or with each other, but to friendship (friendship which essentially involves mutual service and sacrifice). John may be reflecting and referring to an often overlooked theme in the Hebrew scriptures, where those with whom God enters into formal covenants are thereafter referred to as God's friends (Exodus 33.11; Isaiah 41.8)—an unusual description, considering that covenants were, as we have already noticed, usually made between superior and inferiors.[35] It is surely significant that the gospels portray Jesus' last meal with his disciples as a Passover meal, the meal which was to become the central feature of Christian worship. Passover meals were usually very much family affairs. Once again we see Jesus broadening out the lines of kinship on the basis of friendship, not blood or ownership.

All the gospel writers are acutely aware of the tragedy and frailty of friendship. Those who remain faithful to Jesus are those who needed friendship most (particularly women), but the reader is constantly aware how precarious the relationship between Jesus and his disciples is. Most of them seem to be constantly bewildered by his behaviour, but the bond between them keeps them together. Peter tries so hard to get everything right and gets it all wrong. Nevertheless mutual love manages to transcend mutual exasperation. In the figure of Judas we have the tragedy of a passionate friendship in which the passion has not died but has transformed itself into a force for mutual destruction. We do not know the reasons, but we can recognize the experience. In the fourth gospel the author introduces another character, the anonymous 'Beloved Disciple', who in contrast with all the disciples, but particularly with Peter, remains close to Jesus, physically, emotionally and theologically, throughout Jesus' last days, trial and crucifixion. He is the perfect friend. Speculation as to the identity of the Beloved Disciple has been rife for years. Some, for example, have argued that it is Lazarus, who earlier in the gospel was referred to as 'he whom you [Jesus] love' (11.3), and, indeed, in John's story of the raising of Lazarus, we see a passionate friend deeply disturbed by the death of his friend. Other candidates include John Mark and John, son of Zebedee. Some believe he represents the Johannine community which was in dispute with the Jerusalem Church represented by Peter. However, the most likely explanation is that the Beloved Disciple is a literary creation, the ideal disciple. I would never argue that Jesus had 'sexual relations' with the Beloved Disciple for reasons I have already outlined in connection with David and Jonathan and Ruth and Naomi, but also because I do not believe the Beloved Disciple existed as a historical individual. He represents perfect intimacy with Jesus to which the author of John believes we should all aspire. At the Last Supper he is depicted as 'reclining on Jesus' bosom' (13.23), which picks up a description of Jesus in 1.18 as 'the one who is in the bosom of the Father'. The mutual encounter between the Father, Jesus and his friends is exemplified in this man.

It may also be helpful to dwell for a moment on a verse from John's resurrection narrative which has long troubled scholars. In the course of a conversation with Mary Magdalene in the cemetery the risen Christ says to her: 'Do not hold on to me, because I have not yet ascended to the Father' (20.17).

Scholars have questioned why Jesus appears to instruct Mary not to touch him whereas a week later he invites Thomas to place his fingers in his wounds. Some predictably misogynistic interpretations have been offered and some other far-fetched theories, such as that Jesus' wounds were still sore! However, the issue is confused by faulty translation. Mary is not forbidden to touch Jesus, she is forbidden to 'cling' to him. In the Septuagint version of the Hebrew scriptures, the verb used here, *aptesthai*, translates the Hebrew *davak*, which as we saw is used to describe the behaviour of man to woman in Genesis 2.24, and of Ruth to Naomi. In fact there may well be deliberate parallels with the latter story, for Jesus' following statement, 'But go to my brothers and say to them, "I am ascending to my Father and your Father, to my God and your God"', does contain echoes of Ruth 1.16.[36] Jesus cannot be clung to in this way; he has to go away in order that the Paraclete/Spirit can be poured out on his disciples; it is they who must cling to each other. It is a complex and heart-rending climax that acknowledges that friendships often have to end for the good of at least some of the friends. In a very real sense Jesus will remain with them for ever, his image embedded in theirs, but he has to leave in order that the Spirit may come. There may well also be poignant echoes in this story of the Song of Songs—a man and a woman seeking each other in a garden—but the story is not to have a happy ending.

The authors of the four gospels present us with an image of Jesus as a man of passion whose own primary network of relating was through friendship, with a passionate concern for people as embodied beings in need of loving touch. Much (but not all) of his own behaviour defies sexual convention and the institution of the family. It is all structured upon a unitary understanding of human nature; there is no trace of dualism. In many respects Jesus, as he is depicted, is very much a child of his heritage. In his behaviour and teaching he continues a tradition that runs through the Hebrew scriptures which locates the implicit presence and purposes of Yahweh in acts of sexual subversion.

I hope that this survey of Hebrew and Christian scriptures has thrown up the following insights:

- Whenever marriage is held up as a model or metaphor for the relationship of God, or Christ, with God's people, it contains explicit images of female submission that make it impossible for many of us to accept it as a model or ideal for sexual relationships.

- It is only in friendships that the scriptures present us with models of equal, mutual and just relationships. In these relationships God is present in the passion between the persons. Interestingly, Matthew, Luke and John all tell of Jesus appearing among his disciples after the resurrection. In Luke's Emmaus story the two disciples recognise Jesus' presence only when they share a meal, an act of friendship (Luke 24.28–35).

- Even though these friendships may not have involved 'genital expression' they are most certainly presented as bodily and passionate relationships, and so it may be appropriate to use them as models of passionate relationships including marriage.

- Neither the Hebrew nor Christian scriptures present a unified, monolithic theology, so that both contain traditions which provide clear teaching on sexual ethics and other traditions which defy those ethics. The theme of sexual subversion is an important one in both sets of scripture. There is a consistent difference in attitudes to relational ethics between 'pure' teaching and the story of salvation history. The latter often depends upon a subversion of the former. We could characterize this as the difference between Logos and Sophia. Too much attention has been paid to Logos and not nearly enough to Sophia. However, we must not idealize this subversion either. It often involves incest, adultery or deception. We can learn from the tapestries woven by our ancestors whilst recognizing the flaws through which Sophia escapes to lead us deeper into the dance of truth.

John, Thatcher, Williams and other critics of lesbian and gay people who do not want to identify their relationships as marriage have not sufficiently wrestled with the patriarchal construction of marriage. When Williams compares the arguments against incorporating lesbian and gay people into marriage with the arguments for excluding women from the priesthood he brings the issue to a head. I do not think there are any sound theological or ecclesiastical arguments for excluding women from the priesthood and no one could fail to be impressed by the logic of his argument for incorporating gay men and lesbians into marriage. However, like many campaigners for the ordination of women, I have come to question the ultimate value of incorporating women into the institution of priesthood. I wonder whether the very idea of setting apart a select group of people to perform sacred functions is fundamentally patriarchal and disempowering for the majority whose own priesthood, conferred by virtue of baptism, is played down or denied? The fact that feminist historians have pinpointed the development of priesthood as a vital step in the march of patriarchy disturbs me even more. I wonder whether adopting women into the priesthood is simply a way of silencing dissent and bolstering the institution in one fell swoop. Some hoped that incorporating women into the priesthood would eventually lead to the deconstruction of the priesthood itself, but there is little evidence of this happening, even in Churches where women have been ordained for a relatively long period of time. Being denied the ordained priesthood, women began to meet together, write and enact their own rituals and found that the concept of an ordained priesthood was no longer relevant or necessary. So I would want to ask the same question of lesbian and gay people and marriage: there may be no fundamental theological reasons for excluding them from it, and if there was a possibility of any church hierarchy incorporating lesbian and gay relationships into marriage I would fight for it, as I did and do for the ordination of women. But what is the ultimate value of incorporation into an institution which even heterosexuals are asking serious questions about, an institution which was born, formed and structured for and by patriarchy? This is not

to deny that marriages can be happy, empowering and subversive of patriarchy, just as priests can subvert the priesthood
by empowering the laity. It is to ask whether we should be
aiming at something better; whether we who are sitting around
the edge of the dance floor should simply be asking to be
included in the dance or whether we should be demonstrating a
different dance which leaves no one on the edge? It is an
annoying aspect of Christianity that we are not called into the
comfortable realm of equal rights, because one person's rights
are usually attained at the expense of another's, as the gay
theologian Michael Clarke has noted:

> With great irony we realise that the process of legally and
> democratically extending rights—first to African Americans,
> then to women, and to some as yet all-too-limited extent to
> endangered species and the environment—is nothing but a so-
> called liberal progression that has conveniently passed over
> certain groups—most Native Americans, the poor and the
> homeless, and gay men and lesbians—that are deemed invisible
> at best and aesthetically or morally undesirable at worst and that
> therefore remain disenfranchised.[37]

We must always be looking for models that encompass all, are
liberating for all, and that includes the non-human world. An
impossibility, maybe, but it does mean we have to get into the
habit of looking beyond that which is immediately available.
Some lesbian, gay and bisexual people barred from the institution of marriage began to define their relationships in their
own terms and have come up with friendship. Thatcher is no
doubt right that making a distinction between marriage and
same-sex relationships will lead to the latter being regarded as
inferior to the former, but only if we leave marriage out of the
redefinition. Thatcher and Williams have, I think, proved their
case: committed, monogamous lesbian and gay relationships
are, within the terms of the Church's own theologies, *de facto*
marriages. If lesbian and gay people desire to define their
relationships in these terms then they have a right to do so. My
point is simply that there might be a better model. John is not

really concerned with marriage, but with 'monogamy': 'One may have many friends; one may not, within any moral framework which remotely links with Christian teaching, have many sexual partners.'[38] It is time to explore the ethical implications of a theology of friendship.

*next weeks
lecture*

Notes

1 Leo Steinberg, *The Sexuality of Christ in Renaissance Art and in Modern Oblivion* (New York: Pantheon, 1983), p. 13.

2 Steinberg, *The Sexuality of Christ in Renaissance Art*, p. 91.

3 Augustine, *De Nuptiis et Concupiscentia*, 1.6.

4 Joan H. Timmerman, 'The sexuality of Jesus and the human vocation' in James Nelson and Sandra Longfellow, *Sexuality and the Sacred: Sources for Theological Reflection* (London: Mowbray, 1994), p. 93.

5 Gareth Moore, *The Body in Context: Sex and Catholicism* (London: SCM, 1992), pp. 14–15.

6 Moore, *The Body in Context*, p. 19.

7 Graham N. Stanton, *The Gospels and Jesus* (Oxford: Oxford University Press, 1989), pp. 197–8.

8 Patrick Kavanagh, 'Lough Derg', cited in Stephen Pattison, *A Critique of Pastoral Care* (London, SCM, 1988), p. 192.

9 Daphne Hampson, *Theology and Feminism* (Oxford: Blackwell, 1990), pp. 87–90.

10 Adrian Thatcher, *Liberating Sex: A Christian Sexual Theology* (London: SPCK, 1993), p. 86.

11 Moore, *The Body in Context*, p. 147.

12 Thatcher, *Liberating Sex*, pp. 86–7.

13 Moore, *The Body in Context*, p. 152.

14 Thatcher, *Liberating Sex*, p. 119.

15 A. E. Harvey, *Promise or Pretence? A Christian Guide to Sexual Morals* (London: SCM, 1994), p. 109.

16 Wayne R. Dynes, *Encyclopedia of Homosexuality* (London: St James Press, 1990), pp. 376–8.

17 Gerd Theissen, *The Shadow of the Galilean* (London: SCM, 1987), p. 106.

18 John Boswell, *Same-Sex Unions in Premodern Europe* (New York: Villard Books, 1994), pp. 72–107.

19 Raymond E. Brown, *The Gospel According to John*, vol. 1 (London: Geoffrey Chapman, 1982), p. 170.

20 There is a deliberate play on words here. In Greek the words for 'husband' and 'wife' are the same for 'man' and 'woman'.

21 Brown, *The Gospel According to John*, vol. 1, p. 171.
22 John Milton, *Paradise Lost*, VIII, 612–625.
23 Ferdinand Mount, *The Subversive Family* (London: Jonathan Cape, 1982), p. 28.
24 Elisabeth Schüssler Fiorenza, *Discipleship of Equals: A Critical Feminist Ekklesia-logy of Liberation* (London: SCM, 1993), p. 220.
25 Virginia Ramey Mollenkott, *Sensuous Spirituality: Out from Fundamentalism* (New York: Crossroad, 1993), p. 21.
26 Rosemary Radford Ruether, 'An unrealized revolution: searching scripture for a model of family', *Christianity and Crisis: A Christian Journal of Opinion*, vol. 43 (31 October 1983), p. 400.
27 As Boswell has pointed out, such adoration may have verged on the pornographic as the descriptions of their tortures and death are horribly vivid.
28 Ruether, 'An unrealized revolution', p. 403.
29 Paul Ballard, 'The social context of the family today—a Christian reflection', *Contact*, no. 114 (1994), p. 11.
30 Mollenkott, *Sensuous Spirituality*, pp. 194–7.
31 Irene Mahoney OSU, *All That I Am*, published by the author, 39 Willow Drive, New Rochelle, NY 10805 (1987), p. 7.
32 Mahoney, *All That I Am*, p. 41.
33 Celia Allison Hahn, *Sexual Paradox: Creative Tensions in Our Lives and in Our Congregation* (New York: The Pilgrim Press, 1991), p. 72.
34 Brown, *The Gospel According to John*, vol. 1, pp. 511–12.
35 At this point it is important to consider whether John in his use of different words for love—*agapē* and *philia*—meant different things. This is a particularly important point to grapple with in the conversation between Jesus and Peter in chapter 21 which most scholars regard as an appendix to the original gospel. Twice Jesus asks Peter, 'Do you love [*agapan*] me?' Peter replies using *philein*. Then Jesus asks the same question but using *philein*. Some have tried to argue that *agapan* refers to a higher, superior, purer, God-like love that Peter knows he cannot mirror, so eventually Jesus recognizes this. However, Brown has found that a detailed study of the use of the two words for love in the gospel 'shows that the verbs are often used interchangeably' (*The Gospel According to John*, vol. 1, p. 498) and Fenton believes that in the case of chapter 21 there is no more significance in the change of word for 'love' than in the variation between 'lamb' and 'sheep', and 'feed' and 'tend': John Fenton, *The Gospel According to John* (London: Oxford University Press, 1979), p. 210.
36 Brown, *The Gospel According to John*, vol. 2, p. 1016.
37 J. Michael Clark, *Beyond Our Ghettos: Gay Theology in Ecological Perspective* (Cleveland: Pilgrim Press, 1993), p. 12.
38 Jeffrey John, *'Permanent, Faithful, Stable': Christian Same-Sex Partnerships* (London: Affirming Catholicism, 1993), p. 18.

6   Passion: the ecstasy and the agony

In a workshop I was facilitating on the themes of this book a middle-aged Catholic woman, Mary, told the group that when she was a young girl and her teachers told her that we must love everybody just like God did, she took it all very seriously and fell passionately 'in love' with all sorts of people, believing that in doing this she was simply being a good Christian and getting a wonderful insight into the love of God. It did not take very long for her to realize that this was not exactly what the religious sisters and priests had in mind, and her conclusion was that they did not actually mean what they said about love. As she told her story I observed many heads nodding in recognition of the experience. One of the heads was mine. I remember the extraordinary efforts everyone around me made to quell my passion when I was young. Not only my passion for people but for every hobby or cause I took up, and for religion. I remember going through my Bible and underlining every reference to love. My ancestors in faith were validating my way of being but around me people who claimed the same ancestors regarded my passion as a disability: I was not balanced; I felt things too deeply; I cared for people too much; I was far too physically affectionate. It became very clear that I was not actually supposed to love people. I was supposed to package away my passion for some future man whilst cultivating a 'healthy' stoic indifference to the rest of the world. It was OK to like but not to love. I resisted the pressure because I knew that to capitulate to it would be to sacrifice richness for poverty. I would not cage my passion and so I was regularly punished for it; now I am so glad they failed.

The experience of bisexual people is shamefully ignored by all sections of our society. Lesbian and gay people can be particularly scathing in their dismissal of bisexual people as 'wanting to have their cake and eat it', portraying them often as moral cowards who identify with heterosexuals when the going gets rough for the lesbian and gay community. In hetero-reality bisexuals, when their existence is acknowledged, are often portrayed at worst as complete moral degenerates or at best people who are heterosexual really but also have an eccentric habit of being attracted to the same sex. Bisexuality is tolerated far more than homosexuality among people who are expected to be eccentric: pop stars, actors, sports players. Bisexuals very rarely make appearances in church documents and when they do the level of understanding of bisexuality is often embarrassingly weak. The Church of England bishops dismissed bisexual experience in one paragraph:

> [Nevertheless] it is clear that bisexual activity must always be wrong for this reason, if no other, that it inevitably involves being unfaithful. The Church's guidance to bisexual Christians is that if they are capable of heterophile relationships and of satisfaction within them, they should follow the way of holiness in either celibacy or abstinence or heterosexual marriage.[1]

The reason why both heterosexual and lesbian and gay people often find the phenomenon of bisexuality so threatening is that it undermines the neatly cut-and-dried categories with which we define ourselves and others. They threaten the whole system in which some of us rest so comfortably. And yet what if Freud was right, that we are all initially bisexual, born with the capacity to relate passionately with everyone? Freud, of course, regarded this as an infantile state to be matured and civilized out of. But if he is right then we have to accept that we are not born heterosexual or homosexual but become so. From day one we are initiated into a massive programme to turn us into heterosexuals. As Rosemary Radford Ruether has pointed out, this conditioning does not only focus on the 'correct' choice of gender for one's 'sexual' partner:

> but also persons of the 'right' race, culture, and social class. Indeed as our society sees it, it is as much a 'perversity' to be sexually attracted to persons of another race, religion, or social class as to be attracted to persons of the same gender. Most of us have deeply internalized this conditioning. Although we might feel sexually attracted to a person of the 'wrong' race or culture, we might also feel a physical loathing and disgust at our own feelings. This indicates how much our sexuality is a social product.[2]

One of the principal tools of conditioning is the use of the 'natural'. Some relations are considered 'natural', some are 'unnatural'. It is patently obvious how such arguments bolster patriarchy by binding women in relations with men, in which they are inferior partners with predefined roles which serve to confine and control them. It is less often acknowledged how this conditioning serves capitalism.

> The heterosexual couple and nuclear family are also essential to the maintenance of patriarchy/capitalism. Far from having arisen 'naturally', the widespread desire for one's 'own', supposedly freely-chosen spouse, own children, own home, has been relentlessly orchestrated and marketed for the benefit of capitalist society: families bond together and consume. The pressure to live in a traditional family unit is also enforced at a practical level: the organisation of housing and economics makes it much easier in our society to live as part of a nuclear family. And because this is the case, other forms of social existence and the structures to support them—for example, different types of housing—are presumed to be neither desirable nor desired.[3]

Some people, of course, manage to resist this relentless heterosexual conditioning: some by being happy to be primarily heterosexually oriented but recognizing that this is not the only legitimate way to relate; others by failing to turn out heterosexual at all. How and why some do so is not clear, but we find ourselves continually drawn to members of the 'forbidden' gender. We are reluctantly given an identity of our own:

'homosexual'. Now I wonder whether we are dealing with a kind of reverse discourse here. We are all taught that it is 'natural' passionately to desire one sex only, so that when some of us find that the heterosexual conditioning has not worked with us we assume, and indeed are taught, that we too desire one sex only. I wonder if bisexual people are people who have managed to resist almost all conditioning on this issue. Slowly bisexual people are beginning to claim a voice for themselves. As well as pinpointing the problems of being bisexual they are making available to the rest of us some insight into the joys of bisexuality:

> I love having no limits on who I can get close to, and having several people who are 'special'. I love the richness of my experience and life. It can be a way of expressing a sexuality which sees the person rather than the gender; it can be a way of having relationships which do not rely on stereotypes; it can be a way of relating more closely to people of both sexes; it can encompass many types of sexuality and many different people. Ideally, bisexuality is a way of forming relationships without putting boundaries on them because of gender.[4]

There can be no doubt that sexuality is a great deal more fluid than we have been led to believe or would often like to believe. It is interesting to observe that the great excitement in the gay male community when a scientist claims to have discovered some biological difference between gay men and other men is not mirrored in the lesbian or bisexual community. Women are only too aware of the dangers of the 'biology is destiny' approach to sexuality and gender, and lesbians and bisexual people are generally much more conscious of the fluidity of sexuality and the possibility of making choices about who to relate to sexually.[5] Some of us get extremely uncomfortable when prominent gay men refute the government's accusations that we are out to 'promote' homosexuality, by arguing that no one can choose their sexuality, they are 'born that way'. Even in the gay community there is fear of unfettered passion.

The idea that our passion, our sexuality, is like some

monstrous untamed beast living inside us is one deeply embedded in Christian history and consciousness. Augustine's
principal problem with sex, you will remember, is that in sexual
activity the person's will, their rationality, is taken over by lust,
lust which blocks God from the mind. This understanding of
sexuality has passed into orthodoxy. When making love, we are
out of control, irrational, even barely conscious. The roaring
beast inside us threatens to take us over. It is interesting to note
that Augustine saw the problem in very male-centred terms: 'I
feel that nothing more casts down the masculine mind from the
heights than female allurements and that contact of bodies
without which a wife cannot be had.'[6] It has passed into orthodoxy as well that male sexuality is 'naturally' or 'biologically'
difficult to control. Men are capable of restraint, for they are
above all else strong and rational, as long as they get co-
operation from women in this task. The problem is that loose
women tempt and goad them at every turn, threatening to
unlock the beast. Such an understanding of passion is riddled
with dualism. It is based upon the assumption that the
mind/will/reason is something separate from the body and that
passion/sexuality is something separate again. This whole
mindset gives licence to irresponsible sexual behaviour, particularly male sexual behaviour for which women pay the price.
Women are objectified as dangerous sirens. They are then
blamed for male irresponsibility. In Europe and North
America the Catholic Church is being forced to face up to the
fact that some priests have passionate relationships with
women (and indeed some with men) and that sometimes these
relationships produce children. Often when the woman
becomes pregnant she is abandoned by the priest (sometimes
under pressure from his bishop or superior). It has become
clear that the easiest way of avoiding the issues that this situation evokes is to blame the woman for 'leading Father into sin'.
In notorious cases most public sympathy seems to be directed
at the man. A similar resistance to accepting male responsibility
is seen in our attitude towards rape. Our society continues to
regard rape as primarily a sexual act (not an act of violence,

which is how the victims experience it), and so we are used to the claims that the victim 'asked for it' by dressing 'provocatively', being out alone at night, being too beautiful or too ugly, too obviously heterosexual, too obviously lesbian, and so on. Just by being a woman we are considered 'rapeable'—we can say 'no' till we are blue in the face but we still mean 'yes'—and are considered guilty until proven innocent.[7]

Passion once awakened is an extremely powerful force in our lives but it is not actually irrational or beyond our control. When we are making love (whatever that may involve) we are constantly making choices; we are always conscious. We may well decide not to weigh up the consequences of what we are doing, but that in itself is a rational, conscious choice. When enjoying intimate bodily contact with my partner I am not oblivious to the arrival of a hungry cat intent on nibbling my toes until I get up and feed him. We can choose to ignore him, just as we can choose to ignore the door bell, the window cleaner, the telephone, the neighbours making a noise downstairs; but we are conscious of them. Similarly, one of the possible joys of intimate bodily contact is that we are communicating with someone. We can decide to treat that person as a piece of flesh to be used for our own gratification, but that in itself is a conscious rational choice to ignore the reality of the person before us. They can be pleading with us to stop doing whatever we are doing to them; we can ignore them but we cannot be unconscious of them and still be acting. As for orgasm, the French refer to it as a 'small death' and Augustine evidently regarded it as the supreme moment of loss of will. But again, is this actually true? Gareth Moore comments:

> His [Augustine's] talk of being dragged down, overpowered, and so on, gives the impression that all this is happening against one's will, whereas the reverse is true. If you are in any sense held by this pleasure, it is not against your will. Sexual pleasure is often intense, and it belongs to the notion of intense enjoyment that you are fully engrossed in what you intensely enjoy; you do not want to tear yourself away from it, are not easily distracted, and maybe want more of it. We would only 'be

able' to think (i.e. want to think) at the climax if the pleasure was less intense.[8]

I choose to focus intensely on the pleasure of intimate bodily contact with someone I want to have that contact with. I want to savour the experience, focus on the pleasurable sensations, on the person's reactions to my touch. I do not want to be distracted into thinking about the hungry cat or the message being recorded on to the answering machine. I want to enjoy this pleasure fully by concentrating on it; but even in the midst of orgasm I am conscious and rational. I may not want to think about God or work or anything else but I could and indeed would if God or my students suddenly appeared. Indeed, intimate bodily pleasure, whether experienced in embrace with another person or on your own simply luxuriating in a hot bath, is often impossible to sustain with distraction around you. The construction of passion as the uncontrollable beast has led to self-fulfilling prophecy. There is also a common assumption that sexual arousal has to be satisfied or the 'beast' will do some terrible harm, particularly to men. Again it is quite common to find women blamed for men's irresponsible behaviour because they fail to satisfy male desire. A friend of mine who went to her pastor for advice concerning her husband, who was addicted to drink and gambling and prone to violence, was told that her husband's behaviour was probably caused by pent-up sexual desire and she should go home and have sex with him more often. Her story is by no means rare. The need to control the raging beast has had a significant effect on Christian understandings of marriage as the only place where it can be untethered.

There is also a strong link, as Moore notes, between sexual control and social control:

> People sometimes talk about others being out of control in their sexual behaviour, and plainly they feel insecure about this. Perhaps the important point is that these other people are thought to be out of *social* control. They are said to be out of

control when they do things that are forbidden by the section of society to which the speaker belongs. They are out of our control; we do not know what they might do, sexually. And their sexual behaviour is held to be symptomatic of them as a whole. If they can do that, what might they not do?—Unless people are controlled, they are dangerous. These people whose sexual behaviour is unorthodox are often for that reason held to be a danger to society.[9]

Perhaps Augustine and the other great Christian ethicists unconsciously recognized that passion is a subversive force that had to be controlled for political reasons and the best way to gain control over such a force is to make people afraid of it, to image it as an alien, dangerous force. It is interesting that in British society there is a close connection in the national imagination between homosexuality and espionage: the enemy within, whose sexuality is beyond the normal means of societal control and whose presence poses a threat to the very structures of that society. In the 1980s, AIDS refuelled this connection. A piece in the *Guardian* in 1985 suggested that 'gay men are an insidious, all-pervasive, and *invisible* menace to the lives of ordinary human beings going innocently about their business'.[10] During the 1980s and 1990s, right-wing governments in Europe and North America associated homosexuality with what the Tory government in Britain labelled 'the loony left'— socialism which was out to destroy 'the family', free choice, national pride and defence and everything 'that made our country great'. In the 1990s, in Britain, single mothers have joined lesbian and gay people as the 'enemy within', with a small number of politicians attempting to lay responsibility for almost every evil at their feet. They are women out of control, not contained within marriage or the nuclear family, not attached to a man. They are a subversive force who, like lesbians and gay men, have to be punished for their perversity. I believe that governments and church hierarchies are quite right to worry about the subversive force of people whose passion cannot be contained in the established institutions of marriage and 'family' life. In a very real sense we are spies—'spies of God' Jim Cotter calls us, citing Lear. With very little invest-ment in the present system, and pushed to the margins of it, we become '"frontier scouts", ahead of the pioneering wagon train, exploring new territory, "the other country"'.[11] From the perspective of the other country we see with clarity what is going on back home; we ask questions which shake its foun-dations; by our very existence we question so many of the assumptions on which it builds itself.

Sally Cline, in her exploration of celibacy among women, demonstrates that some women regard celibacy as a liberation from the constraint they experience in sexual relationships:

> Passionate Celibacy is a form of female sexuality. It is the choice to be without a sexual partner for positive reasons of personal, political, or spiritual growth, freedom and independence. Passionate Celibacy is a sexual singlehood which allows women to define themselves autonomously, whilst still retaining a network of connections, rather than in terms of another person and his or her needs. It is a form of sexual practice without the power struggles of a sexually active relationship, which is neither maintained by nor supports the genital myth.[12]

In Cline's book women consistently talk of formalized sexual relationships (i.e. marriage or co-habitation) as disempowering them, by restricting their choices in such a way that their creativity and autonomy are sapped dry. In a moving series of poems written after the death of her husband who was a clergyman, Janet Elizabeth Chesney honestly charts her grow-ing realization that 'Peter's death offered me an unprecedented opportunity to begin again with my life and I have grown into a more wonderful human being than I ever dreamed possible. Perhaps I could say that he died that I might live more abun-dantly.'[13] She moves through anger—

> Angry at Peter because he gave so much of himself to
>   others
> There was so little left for himself ... and for me.
>
> Angry at myself because when I look back

> All that I can remember are the mistakes
> The misunderstandings
> Why can't I remember the happy times?
> Why did I feel undervalued, misused,
> Forced into a role of 'wife' that I was born to
> Yet despised?
> Trapped by society, my background and Peter who had to
>   be King.
> And I felt powerless to change it.

—to forgiveness and a recognition of happy memories, then to letting go, and, finally, to liberation:

> I come into Your presence
> And do not fall at Your feet, a sinner,
> But am lifted up!
> I see myself as I really am
> Made in the image of God at last
> A truly magnificent woman...

> Territory without directions or map
> No track, no road, for travellers to find
> No near, no far, no-one knows the way.
> There is no way—
> Only the spirit of adventure in each of us
> That rejoices to experience:

> The limitlessness of God...
> in a sparkling drop of dew
> The minute part of God
> that forms our Universe.[14]

This has been and still is the experience of many women: their male partners have had to die or leave before they can experience liberation. Cline, in suggesting that celibacy may be the best option for women, only echoes the views of the earliest feminists who also believed that true freedom for women involved a sex-less state.[15] Mary Daly has defined 'Virgin' as 'Wild, Lusty, *Never-captured* [my emphasis], Unsubdued Old Maid; Marriage Resister'.[16] Many women appear to find their passion captured, constrained and narrowly channelled, particularly within marriage. It is this experience of being taken over that makes many women uncomfortable with the 'one flesh' language used by Christianity to talk about marriage. This is yet another reason why lesbian and gay people should be extremely wary of being incorporated into the institution of marriage. It is interesting that sexual unorthodoxy is also associated with creativity, with occupations such as art, writing, acting, music, dance, designing and so on, as well as with 'caring' vocations such as nursing, and in many cultures is also associated with the holy.[17] Passion not controlled or confined by rigid relational structures flows out in a myriad of different forms, creating subversive counter-cultures, places where the Gospel naturally grows.

 We have already come across the most persistent objection to the possibility of redefining our 'sexual' relationships in terms of friendship: 'promiscuity'. Adrian Thatcher, though willing to consider the possibilities of the idea, still has serious reservations:

> Sexual friendships between married and unmarried people would be adulterous; between close relatives they would be incestuous; and with minors they would be exploitative and illegal. The great majority of close friends would, one assumes, be alarmed at the possibility of expressing their fondness for each other in a sexual way. 'Sexual expression' could cover everything from a lingering grasp of the hand to sexual envelopment. Christians have clear grounds for locating procreative sex firmly within the marriage bond, but procreative sex is fairly rare. Touching, embracing, hugging and kissing are usually socially acceptable gestures. Most friends do these at least in a ritual way. A few will do so in an overtly sexual way. Friends anxious about the extent of intimacy they are prepared to allow themselves may want to use the 'principle of proportionality'.[18]

Thatcher goes on to explain that this principle dictates that the degree of 'sexual expression' should be commensurate with the level of relational commitment. He draws upon the work of

Karen Lebacqz who, in an attempt to develop a Christian ethic
for single people, has developed a theology of vulnerability.
Passion, she points out, makes a person vulnerable to great joy
and great hurt. She takes the last line of the second creation
narrative—'And the man and his wife were both naked, and
were not ashamed' (Genesis 2.25) and states: 'In ancient
Hebrew, "nakedness" was a metaphor for vulnerability, and
"feeling no shame" was a metaphor for appropriateness. We
can therefore retranslate the passage as follows: "And the man
and his wife experienced appropriate vulnerability."'[19] Sexuality is therefore essentially about vulnerability and resistance
to the desire to control another person. When Adam and Eve
grasped for control they lost their vulnerability and found
themselves in structured enemy-hood. Any sexual behaviour
that violates a person's vulnerability by seeking to exercise
power and control over them is therefore sinful. However, this
does not mean that sexual expression should be confined to
marriage, although marriage 'at its best' does provide an appro-
priately safe setting for vulnerability.

> Singleness carries no such protections. It is an unsafe
> environment for the expression of vulnerability. No covenant of
> fidelity ensures that my vulnerability will not lead to my being
> hurt, foolish, exposed, wounded. In short, in singleness the
> vulnerability that naturally accompanies sexuality is also coupled
> with a vulnerability of context ... Single people will have to
> explore their own vulnerability to find its appropriate expression
> in sexuality.[20]

Unfortunately neither Lebacqz nor Thatcher offers insight into
what appropriate vulnerability might actually mean, although
Thatcher suggests that penetrative sexual intercourse should
be ideally confined to a life-long commitment.[21]

Some familiar problems have returned to haunt us. Those
who take fright at the revision of sexuality in terms of friendship
are still clinging to dualistic understandings that separate off
sexual passion from other forms of relationality and which
inject sexual acts with specific and inherent meanings. I know

two people who come together every so often to have penetrative intercourse. They are minimally vulnerable to each
other; it is a friendly gesture; they are well protected against
unwanted pregnancy and AIDS. But I know other people for
whom time spent in a passionate hug is an act of intense mutual
vulnerability because of the context of the relationship in which
it takes place. Taking one's clothes off need not have anything
to do with vulnerability. Indeed, it can sometimes be easier to
do that than talk. Very few theologians appear to understand
this.

Why don't we face the question square on: what is wrong
with promiscuity? In many ways the image of God as the
husband faithful to his bride (Israel or the Church) has always
existed side by side with an implicit image of God as the
promiscuous lover who loves everything and everyone
created—an idea which has constantly grated with many Jews
and Christians who would prefer their God to be strictly monogamous. The all-loving God is the God my friend Mary (whom
we met at the beginning of this chapter) knew and tried to
emulate. Elizabeth Templeton would perhaps regard Mary's
disposition to love passionately and widely as an eschatological
foretaste of what is to come for all of us. Writing about marriage
she regards it as a manifestation of our sinfulness, because

> it manifests our inextricable embeddedness in a limitation of
> love which cannot be projected as our hoped-for end state. For
> this reason, though I am, most of the time, glad to be married,
> and though I have no moral guilt about having chosen it, I hope
> that Jesus was right, or the redactor who gave him the line, that
> in the Kingdom of God, we neither marry, nor are given in
> marriage. For it seems to me that, however we envisage the state
> of redeemed co-existence, in or out of time, it cannot be
> properly envisaged as a place of excluding relationships, even if
> it is hoped for as a condition of transformed particularity, in
> which identity is sustained, recognisably continuous with our
> present identity.[22]

For virtually two thousand years Christianity has been dominated by a sexual ethic which was based upon the implicit

assumption that passion is an obstacle to salvation, a road-block, or at least a stumbling block along the way to the kingdom. Jesus' words in Mark 12.18–27 promised a future in which such distasteful activities would disappear. Even in 1991 the House of Bishops of the General Synod of the Church of England could use this passage to look wistfully towards the time when the 'physical expression of sexuality, which is required now because of our mortality in order that human life may continue', will no longer be needed and we will be able to enjoy 'the fullest possible relationship of love with all, being no longer restricted by the particularity of the flesh'.[23] Note the ambivalent attitude to the body and the reduction of sexuality to procreative purposes that this statement implies. Jesus does not look forward to a time without bodies; on the contrary, his very words indicate that the kingdom will involve an embodied existence. The bishops do not notice that Jesus commissioned his disciples to work to establish the kingdom of God on earth partly by living as if it had already arrived. Virginia Ramey Mollenkott has beautifully reworked the words of Marlowe's *Dr Faustus* to convey Jesus' teaching on the reign of God: 'Why this is heaven, nor am I out of it.'[24] Could it be that the vision of the kingdom is a vision of embodied love in which no barriers to relating will be necessary because all will treat each other with justice in friendship? In which passion no longer has need of formalized boundaries, an experience which perhaps bisexual people have more foreknowledge of than the rest of us? A place of touch, of intimacy, of intense pleasure, of good food and drink, a place to bask in the beauty of creation? Certainly many of Jesus' words point this way, and yet the concept is so alien to our body-hating, passion-avoiding heritage.

But the passion has never quite been crushed; it has often been kept alive by women. In the medieval period women mystics often experienced their prayer or liturgical encounters with the divine as intensely and physically passionate. Hadewijch described her experience at the Eucharist in these terms: 'He came himself to me, and took me entirely in his arms, and pressed me to him, and all my members felt his in full felicity, in

accordance with the desire of my heart and my humanity.'[25]
Literally holding Christ to them in the Eucharist was a passionate experience, such that for some of them they received his
physical imprint upon their own bodies: the marks of the
wounds of his crucifixion would appear upon them.[26] Nor
were such passionate encounters with Christ restricted to
women. Rupert of Deutz spoke of a vision he had of Christ in
these terms, 'I took hold of him whom my soul loved. I held
him. I embraced him, I kissed him for a long time ... in the
midst of the kiss he opened his mouth so that I could kiss more
deeply.'[27] The strong emphasis upon the doctrine of the incarnation, and a strong sacramental theology, made medieval
piety in general very physical and focused on the body. But
even though countless Christians have looked forward to a
union with the divine described in the language of passion, very
few have broadened that vision to include passionate union
with other people.

These days almost every official body of the Christian
Church would want to pay lip service to the goodness of the
body and the goodness of sexuality. They are scrambling over
themselves to denounce dualism, and yet the fact that most still
end up promoting marriage as the ideal and lesbian and gay
relations as at best a 'less than ideal' alternative for those who
cannot aspire higher, demonstrates the shallowness of the pro-
body, anti-dualism they proclaim. The need to develop a body-
affirming, passion-affirming Christian theology and ethic is
vital, if for no other reason than if we do not acquire one and act
on it soon the body on which we all depend, our planet, which
has suffered dreadfully from our dualistic thought, is going to
die. We need a fundamental revolution of the theological imagination, not a mere tinkering with old models. I suggest that
we start from the revolutionary position that passion is good. It
is the way in which God dances through creation; it is the
primary means through which human beings communicate
with each other; it is what we are made to be. The establishment
of God's reign on earth will be a glorious dance of passion. If we
begin here then we begin with Augustine's 'love and do what

you will': all passion is good and the onus is to prove why some form of relating is not passionate and therefore not good, and not on trying to prove why some forms of relating are not evil. Perhaps we need to hold in our mind not the 'thou shalt not' culture of distorted Christianity but the tradition found in the Talmud that God will hold us accountable for every permitted pleasure that we forfeit. This may sound like a plea for the return of the 'free love' culture of the 1960s, but it is not. What that period of our history taught us is that 'sexual freedom', that is the ability to sleep with who we like without being 'caught out' by things like pregnancy, was ultimately very one-sided. Women had even less freedom to choose, for the culture demanded that they be sexually available and that they take responsibility for birth control. I will shortly argue that in a theology of friendship, consent is not a firm enough moral basis to build a sexual ethic upon. Free love is not liberation: justice is liberation. To say that passion is good, of God, is not to argue that it must always be expressed in the most intimate of ways. It is to release passion as a force for good, for building up right relationship and, as we shall see, this always involves nego-tiation, balance and justice.

In an earlier chapter I argued that one of the reasons why I believe 'passion' is a much more helpful concept than the 'erotic' in talking about sexuality is that it contains within its established meaning a dimension of tragedy and pain. We have already observed the comment of one Asian theologian that some women's experience of the erotic is so negative that they have real problems making it the centre of their theology. In seeking to reclaim the body and passion as good, we must be ever vigilant not to ignore the pain which is often at the centre of people's experience of themselves as embodied relational persons. The 1980s and 1990s have seen a substantial number of new-generation lesbians flatly rejecting feminism. Feminism is regarded as the repressive mother; true freedom lies in following the example of gay men in assuming the role of sex radicals or outlaws, where everything from porn to sado-masochism is OK as long as it takes place in a context of mutual consent.[28] (Ironically, at the same time articles are beginning to appear in the British gay press by men in which they lament the lack of a philosophical basis like feminism amongst gay men from which to begin to fight their oppression.[29]) I am sure that there are all sorts of complex reasons for this lesbian disenchantment with feminism, but I am certain that one of the reasons lies in feminism's failure to deal effectively with the tragedy and failure and pain of all sexuality, not just heterosexuality: the failure of relationships which should have been empowering and joyous because they were between two women endeavouring to relate to each other in mutuality and justice. It is the tragedy of the human condition that we are socially constructed, that we are all (no matter how subversive) formed by our environment. When we looked at the theme of sexual subversion we found the biblical stories extremely realistic in this regard; David and Jonathan and Ruth and Naomi were unable to transcend the demands of their social context. As Beverly Harrison and Carter Heyward have observed, the history of sexuality which we have inherited and which has played its part in forming us

> is embedded in social structures of patterned power relations such as institutionalized heterosexism, racism, and cultural imperialism. To explore how senses of personal power and eroticism have been linked historically in heterosexist patriarchy is to begin also to see that the self–other relation which elicits strong erotic desire frequently is one of domination and submission. As such, sex is often experienced as a dynamic of conquest and surrender rather than as power in mutual relation. In such 'eroticization of domination', sexual desire is linked with either self-oblivion or self-assertion. It would be ahistorical and naive to imagine that *anyone's* eroticism in this culture could be untouched by this dynamic.[30]

We have all been formed in a culture which has at its relational heart domination and submission. We have all been taught that this is 'natural' and that we act out domination or submission according to our racial, class, gender and sexual roles. Nor does being victims in one context prevent us from assuming roles of domination in another; on the contrary, the desire to experience power in the midst of powerlessness often serves to reproduce relationships of domination and submission among victims. Toinette Eugene, in her analysis of gender relations in the black community, has noted that black men often exhibit 'a kind of compensatory black male chauvinism ... in order to restore the "manliness" of the one who had traditionally been humiliated by being deprived (according to a white patriarchal model) of being the primary protector of his family'.[31]

When sexuality and gender are defined in these terms by the society that has formed us and is around us we are virtually trapped into this way of relating. Being a man or a woman, a boy or girl, is to be dominant or submissive; sex is domination and submission. This is why rape is primarily a sexual act in our consciousness, and why pornography, which depicts women as objects of men's desire and as aroused by violence, is regarded as harmless erotica. This is why the language of sexuality is also the language of violence—'fuck', 'bugger', 'screw', 'cunt' have entered our vocabulary as the language of everyday abuse. It is also the language of the school playground, the place of most sex education. It is a horrifying fact that pornography is the principal source of sex education for boys.[32] Marie Fortune, who has done extensive research on sexual violence, has argued that in European and American society male sexuality is constructed so that it seeks for its object the powerless, the passive and the submissive. It is not conditioned to find equality erotic nor to search for intimacy.[33] Pornography must play its part in this construction. In a survey of women conducted in 1991, 91 per cent of them found 'adult' magazines offensive. 81 per cent of them saw pornography frequently, but two-thirds of them did not freely choose do so but did so because of pressures from their partner. Although they were sexually aroused by pornography they were also offended by it.[34] One of the reasons why pornography goes largely unchallenged is that it makes an enormous amount of money and in a capitalist society it is illogical to interfere in such a money-spinning business.

Yet, just as some people manage to resist heterosexual conditioning so do some men manage to resist 'macho' conditioning. A very small number of these men come to believe that they are women trapped in a man's body, that what they are essentially is different to what they are physically. I do not want in any way to underestimate the psycho-social complexities of those people who experience themselves this way, but in a society that constructs gender on such rigidly narrow lines, lines that demarcate male and female feeling, movement, clothes, behaviour, thoughts, it is highly likely that a small number of men who manage to resist macho conditioning, and whose way of being in the world is regarded as 'feminine' by patriarchy, will conclude that they are the wrong sex. I was struck by a remark from one of the most famous of male-to-female transsexuals, the British writer Jan Morris, who said that 'if society had allowed me to live in the gender I preferred' she would not have submitted to a sex-change operation.[35] What would living in her preferred gender have meant—being gentle rather than aggressive, wearing skirts instead of trousers? In patriarchy men wearing clothing designated 'female' are unacceptable because women's clothes represent powerlessness. Men who do so are gender traitors: they are perverted. The number of female-to-male transsexuals has always been much smaller in the West (though there are signs that this is changing) and although the aggressive woman, the woman who wears 'male' clothes, has always been regarded as dangerous, her desire to climb the heights and become 'like a man' is understandable. It is in places where gay or lesbian identities are not acknowledged at all that the phenomenon of transsexuality is most common. Janice Raymond has shown in a study of the transsexual industry that it simply serves to perpetuate the rigid patriarchal construction of gender.[36] The Church, particularly in its Catholic manifestations, has often been a place where men have felt able to escape the pressures of macho conditioning, to take on 'caring' roles and dress up in glorious vestments (although this has often been combined with a virulent misogyny). Whilst we live in a gender-rigid culture there will be people who feel so alienated from the role they are expected to play because of their biological sex that they can only conceive of being happy in the body of a person of the opposite gender. These people deserve our compassion and support, but they also deserve our commitment to undermine such destructive dualism, to create a world in which people's just behaviour is not restricted by a system of rewards and punishments because of their biological sex.

What about drag? Drag artists are (usually) men who dress up in women's clothes and assume a female persona, usually for the purpose of entertainment. Marilyn Frye neatly summarizes many feminists' discomfort with drag:

> For the most part, this femininity is affected and is characterized by theatrical exaggeration. It is a casual and cynical mockery of women, for whom femininity is the trappings of oppression, but it is also a kind of play, a toying with that which is taboo ... the mastery of the feminine is not feminine. It is masculine. It is not a manifestation of woman-loving but of woman-hating.[37]

It is an issue of what men do with the sacred image of women. According to the Judeo-Christian tradition women are made in the image and likeness of God. We therefore have a holy responsibility for what we do with each other's images. However, not all drag artists are the same. Some do portray strong, feisty women. Women have the right to judge all these men and call them to account for what they do with our image. However, there is another dimension to this that cannot be dismissed, and that is the demonstration that there is more than one way to be a man/woman. Drag artists, so-called 'butch dykes', and gay men whom others judge 'effeminate'—in their clothes, in their body movements, in their approach to life—subvert the rigid gender distinctions upon which patriarchal order is based. It is these people who have always been at the front of the gay and lesbian liberation movements and borne the harshest oppression, because they have been the most visible. The gay and lesbian liberation movement's creation myth begins at the Stonewall Inn in New York in 1969 when drag queens and bull dykes fought back against a routine police raid. These people are our heroes and heroines. In other cultures, people who defy gender roles are often regarded as particularly close to the divine. They point towards the 'other country'.[38] There is a difference between subverting concepts of what constitutes a man or a woman and falling into models of relating which take their cue from stereotyped heterosexual models of domination and submission.

Harrison and Heyward, along with many feminist theologians, believe Christianity has played a central part in forming this construction of relationality. The good news has been preached as an ill-disguised form of sado-masochism. At the heart of our faith is the brutality of the cross, which various theologies of atonement envisaged as the supreme moment of grace: the perfect, sinless, innocent son is sacrificed by the loving father for the good of us all. We have a case of what Rita Nakashima Brock calls 'cosmic child abuse' at the heart of our faith.[39] The message is clear: salvation comes through pain. This theme continued in the life of the believer, in whom the battle between good and evil raged fiercely; salvation was to be sustained by fiercely resisting the urges of the 'evil' body; 'depriving' oneself of food, touch, beauty, comfort was essential. One had to conquer 'oneself', beat the body into submission now in order to be able to enjoy 'pie in the sky when we die':

> We learn to experience the deprivation of pleasure—the pain of being hurt, hungry, or rejected; of feeling weak, stupid, bad in the immediate present—as a moment filled with intense anticipation of pleasure that is yet to come. In short, Christians learn theologically to equate the anticipation of pleasure with pleasure itself.[40]

For the pleasure we do experience we have to pay; we must humiliate ourselves and pray for mercy. Christian women as embodiments of the 'wrong' side of dualism are only saved by submitting themselves to the authority of the embodiment of the 'right' side—men. 'The inability of so many women even to imagine that they should be well-treated in a relationship with a man or that they deserve physical and emotional pleasure is conditioned by the demand that we have our being for others.'[41] Harrison and Heyward point out that amongst women the most common form of sado-masochism is eating disorder. Pleasure and pain mingle in a destructive cocktail. Women are put under immense pressure in our society to be a certain body shape. They are taught to hate their bodies. In starving herself or making herself sick a woman seeks to gain control over her own body, perhaps by seeking to take control of a body that someone else abused or by seeking to punish a part of herself which she has 'allowed' to be used by others. There are plenty of explanations for this phenomenon:

> An anorexic woman, for example, wants to be thin since thinness is a virtue, and a pleasure, in men's eyes (and, thereby, her own). She is willing to starve herself, literally to death if need be, to become thin enough to enjoy herself. Another woman, who is bulimic, takes pleasure in eating—and wants to be thin. She experiences tension between pleasing herself with food and pleasing men (and, thereby, herself) with a trim figure. This tension generates a pattern of compulsive eating finally more painful than pleasurable, to be followed by compulsive elimination of the food. For the bulimic the pleasure of eating has become painful, and the pain of induced vomiting becomes a relief and a pleasure. Rather than make public challenge to institutions that teach misogyny, or embody this protest in her work and relationships (perhaps more common today), the woman internalizes the misogyny and punishes herself for daring to dream of her own liberation.[42]

Against this background the whole notion of 'consent' which has become central to liberal discourse about sexuality has to be reassessed. Sheila Jeffreys analyses the concept:

> A model of sexuality based upon the idea of consent is a male supremacist one. In this model one person, generally male, uses the body of another who is not necessarily sexually interested and possibly generally reluctant or distressed, as a sex aid. It is a dominant/submissive and active/passive model. It is not mutual.

It is not about the sexual involvement of both parties. It bespeaks not equality, but the absence of it. Consent is a tool for negotiating inequality in heterosexual relations. Women are expected to have their bodies used but the idea of consent manages to make this use and abuse seem fair and justified. In certain situations where this use might seem particularly and obviously unwelcome, such as street rape, women are given a limited right to object, but in general the idea of consent allows the sexual use and abuse of women to remain invisible as harm or a contravention of human rights ... Women's consent, the kind that can cause them to undergo furiously resented sexual intercourse in marriage, or just to accept that they should be used as a masturbation aid, is constructed by the pressures exerted upon women throughout their lives. Such pressures include economic dependency, sexual abuse, battering, and a cultural barrage of propaganda about what women are good for. They can induce a profound lack of self-determination. [43]

The so-called 'lesbian revolution' which has seen some sections of the lesbian community producing and using lesbian 'erotica', reclaiming strict role-construction of lesbian relationships and taking part in sado-masochism, is in my opinion very much to be regretted, although I acknowledge the role that such 'erotica' have in promoting lesbian visibility. I find the explanations and justifications offered unconvincing, particularly the argument that by assuming certain roles from heterosexual society lesbians are deliberately subverting them, parodying them, mimicking heterosexual ideology to undermine it. There is little evidence that this 'mimicry' has the desired effect of subverting the system. Yet, before those of us who are lesbian feminists become too judgemental about all this, we might reflect upon the possibility that it has been our failure to provide a realistic alternative to domination/submission in our own relationships that has left many women disillusioned by the experience of lesbian relationships. What has become clear is that women do not automatically relate to one another with justice, but come into a relationship with another woman as socially conditioned as anyone else. Lesbian relationships are not a magical forest of equality. Research is just beginning to address the issue of violence in lesbian relationships. A study of 104 lesbians found that 39 of them had been assaulted by a partner. Alcohol and drugs were associated with 64 per cent of these incidents. Generally, levels of alcohol abuse are up to three times higher among lesbians than heterosexual women.[44]

I do think, however, that Jeffreys is quite right when she says 'If your oppression turns you on you have a much harder time fighting your oppression.'[45] This is why we need a strong ethical basis from which to approach issues of sexuality. We need what Dorothee Soelle calls a *phantasie*, which is more than a mere fantasy. It is a collective vision of what things could be like, not in some far distant and utopian future, but now. A vision that empowers us to work for its realization because it is both enticing and realistic. What has become very clear is that the dualism between public/private, which has dishonestly relegated sexuality to the private sphere, has to be overcome. The personal is political, but the political is also personal. Seeking to change the way people relate to one another 'privately' is not enough, although it is important. Because people are caught in wider social relations and models of relating, change must include cultural, legal and social policy change. The word 'ethic' comes from the Greek *ēthos* meaning ethos or character it relates to the character of the person rather than to whether specific actions are right or wrong. Alasdair MacIntyre, in one of the most influential works of philosophy published this century, *After Virtue*,[46] argued that the Enlightenment beguiled Western humanity into believing that moral issues could be solved by rational discourse. This has proved to be completely erroneous and moral debates have simply become interminable: 'I do not mean by this just that such debates go on and on and on—although they do—but also that they apparently can find no terminus. There seems to be no rational way of securing moral agreement in our culture.'[47] What the Enlightenment destroyed was the ancient belief that morality, that is right behaviour, depended upon virtues, that is the right mind and disposition to the world, which are nurtured in moral communities.

> Human beings and the communities they forge are governed by a narrative unity. We live our lives through a narrative structure ... 'man is in his actions and practice, as well as in his fictions, essentially a story-telling animal ... he becomes ... a teller of stories that aspire to truth.' Beliefs are held and intentions and intelligible actions all take place within specific practices. These, in turn, develop traditions and become established in social institutions. Such practices enable the good for ourselves and the good for others to be realised. It is a symbiotic relationship: the virtues sustain the practices, and the practices continue to sustain the virtues.[48]

In the light of what we have learnt about the social construction of sexuality, it seems to me that the virtue needing to be recovered and cultivated above all others is one that is already held in high regard among women and gay men, and has held a venerable place in the Christian tradition and amongst ancient philosophers—friendship. Indeed, although Aristotle was wrong to dissect and order friendship, he was quite right to claim friendship as the fundamental relationship in society, the source of all justice. We should not underestimate the difficulty of working to achieve and sustain friendship in the webs of patriarchy. That is why we have to cling to the notion of *passionate* friendship.

I am my friend

Friendship with one's self is vital. We are not taught to love ourselves, indeed our whole society turns on the basis that we are not whole, not likeable, not lovable, not beautiful, unless and until we have bought this thing, done that thing, been on that diet. We are taught to see a distinction between 'ourselves' and our bodies. Our bodies are alien, wild things which have to be controlled and tamed, they are associated with decay and death. We are taught to be ashamed of them. Christianity has played its part in promoting such self-hatred. Part of the wonder and tragedy of human experience is that we literally hold each other in our hands, we form each other. Our passion for ourselves, our friendship with ourselves, can only be awakened by the loving touch of another and once awakened can be destroyed by the unloving touch of another. We encounter each other in various states of broken-heartedness. But once our passion is born, once we begin to be friends with ourselves, we become demanding:

> We begin to give up, of necessity, being satisfied with suffering, and self-negation, and with the numbness which so often seems like their only alternative in our society. Our acts against oppression become integral with self, motivated and empowered from within ... I become less willing to accept powerlessness, or those other supplied states of being which are not native to me, such as resignation, despair, self-effacement, depression, self-denial.[49]

Passion therefore gives us energy actively to dismantle the forces which lead to self-hatred. In finding a passion for your body-self you also discover what Virginia Ramey Mollenkott delightfully calls a 'shiver of solidarity'[50] with all bodies, a desire to bring all into the dance of passionate friendship. Young people need to be taught to love themselves, and very few can rely on their family to provide this. Teachers, youth leaders and other mentors are vital in this regard. It is particularly important that gay and lesbian young people, black and Asian young people, and all those children who grow up doubly oppressed, have mentors, role models, friends to teach them to value themselves. It is a tragic irony that the boundaries erected to protect young people from harmful touch, violation and pain may also serve to bar them from the friendship of teachers and mentors which they need to blossom in a positive sense of self.

This is true of adults as well, and has been brought out by Carter Heyward in her book *When Boundaries Betray Us*, which deals with her experience in therapy and demonstrates, first, the appalling, destructive effects of the tension of attempting to live out relationships of justice and mutuality in a religious, work and world context which operates on entirely opposite terms. Heyward and her partner Beverly Harrison embody that tension in the self-destructive behaviour of alcoholism and, in Heyward's case, bulimia. Secondly, the book illustrates for me some of the tensions between feminism and psychotherapy. Psychotherapy, in so far as it locates 'the problem' and the solution in the self rather than in social structures, can perpetuate the private/public dualism that feminism seeks to subvert. Heyward goes into therapy, but what she is actually seeking is a friend to reawaken her passion. The therapist responds to this implicit task, but when it becomes explicit she seems to become panicked and confused about 'professional boundaries'. Yet she will not let Heyward go, and Heyward's desire for friendship comes to be seen as a pathological smoke screen for some deeper trouble: memories of childhood abuse, which later Heyward comes to believe were 'false memories'. Heyward is eventually saved from complete emotional destruction by a network of friends. Heyward claims that the very boundaries which feminists fought for in order to protect the vulnerable from abuse can in turn become abusive. Yet Heyward must know that often therapists, teachers and mentors need protecting from the broken-heartedness of their 'clients', and vice versa. This is part of the pain of passion: only friendship can heal our broken-heartedness, but in some relationships we need to be protected from our or another's broken heart. All we can do is live with this terrible tension in our own lives whilst fighting on the social and political stage to dismantle the forces that cause our broken-heartedness in the first place and prevent mutuality.[51]

The discovery of passion is a form of resurrection which, as I said earlier, can sometimes be literally observed in the bodily posture. It also makes a person dangerous and threatening, particularly to those who get and sustain power from keeping us in the tomb of self-hatred. Maya Angelou's magnificent poem 'Still I Rise' brings out all these dimensions of the discovery of passion:

.. Does my sassiness upset you?
Why are you beset with gloom?
'Cause I walk like I've got oil wells
Pumping in my living room...

... Does my haughtiness offend you?
Don't you take it awful hard
'Cause I laugh like I've got gold mines
Diggin' in my own back yard...

... Does my sexiness upset you?
Does it come as a surprise
That I dance like I've got diamonds
At the meeting of my thighs?...[52]

Masturbation

Gareth Moore, commenting on masturbation, cites Woody Allen's famous comment: 'Don't knock it, it's sex with someone you love', and goes on:

> This is witty, but false. The most obvious fact about masturbation is that it is not sex with anybody, let alone with someone you love; this means that it has limited possibilities for pleasure ... if Peter masturbates, however much he loves himself, he does not normally delight that it is just *this* hand that is grasping his penis, precisely *he* who is doing it with or to himself.[53]

Moore is no doubt right that the pleasure of touching someone else is different from the pleasure derived from touching yourself, but I think he is wrong to denigrate the pleasure that can be gained from touching yourself as an act of love for yourself. Learning to love yourself is the most difficult and the most important task we have, and masturbation can play an important part in that. I am sure that the taboo surrounding masturbation (less powerful than it was concerning male masturbation, but still shadowing female masturbation, no doubt because the idea that women can give themselves pleasure without need of relationship is deeply threatening) has a great deal to do with the general taboo about enjoying our body-selves. Perhaps for

women especially, whose bodies are objectified and despised
by society at large, expressing passion for yourself through
touch can be a self-saving act. It is also worth reminding
ourselves that masturbation is sometimes the only way women
can experience orgasm. The Hite survey of female sexuality
found that 70 per cent of women could not achieve orgasm
through vaginal intercourse, which is still presented by the
Churches as the only legitimate way to have sex.[54] Touching is
a sign of friendship; touching yourself in ways that give you
pleasure, that build you up, that unlock your passion is a good
thing to do.

Fantasy

Undoubtedly a great deal of masturbation is accompanied by
sexual fantasies. We have been conditioned to think that we can
only enjoy our bodies if they are being shared with someone
else. Pornography is sometimes used in the creation of fantasy.
Some women do have fantasies involving rape. When making
love to one person, people sometimes fantasize about making
love to someone else. Our capacity to fantasize is important. To
dream impossible, subversive dreams, to imagine something
different from today's reality, is vital for kick-starting and
energizing ourselves to do something or simply helping us to
survive where we are. However, our fantasies, as much as any
other part of us, are at least partly formed by the social structures in which we move. It should come as no surprise to us that
we might fantasize about rape, about domination and submission (sometimes playing the opposite role to the one assigned to
us by our gender), and that these thoughts should 'turn us on':
they are sexy, they are sex as we have been taught it. Fantasy is
not simply a private, neutral space; it draws its images and
power from understandings of sexuality 'outside' and beyond
the individual and tells us something important about our
intentions, our orientations towards others and ourselves.
When fantasies involve the objectification and use of another
person, when mutuality and equality are absent from them,

they are antithetical to the ethos of friendship. What we desperately need are writers, artists, film-makers, teachers who can portray mutuality as sexy, who can eroticize equality. We need prophets and visionaries who can transcend the mindset that sex equals domination and submission. Our fantasies need feeding positive images. We should also be questioning the free availability of literature and visual material which presents women and children as passive sexual objects open to abuse and violence. I know that there are 'grey' areas around the question of what constitutes pornography. This grey area is often invoked in the argument against any kind of restrictions at all. It would seem to me that the way forward to a just solution must be to allow women some control over how their image is used. This seems to me to be a sacred right if we believe that woman is made in the image and likeness of God. Women should demand the right not just to be represented but to be in control of the mechanisms that review what 'erotic' material should and should not be legally available. Of course, women will disagree over specific material. It is not an instant solution to the problem of pornography, but it would be a step in the right direction. Similarly, we should look for a society in which women and men are not pushed by economic necessity into selling their bodies.

Disability and old age

One of the sad and unjust consequences of identifying 'sex' with reproduction and 'sex' with penis in vagina has been the failure to acknowledge the sexual feelings and needs of our senior citizens and people with disabilities. A well-informed and sensitive statement from the Office of the General Assembly of the Presbyterian Church in the USA on persons with disabilities noted the sinful effects of this kind of attitude:

> When persons are desexualized through silence or rejection concerning their sexuality, their self-esteem is undercut, their sense of person power diminished, and they are dehumanized. In such situations, they may experience loneliness, anxiety,

anger, depression, and behaviour problems. When these things are caused, there is an affront to God's inclusive justice.[55]

It goes on to point out that, since the likelihood is that we will all experience some form of disability in our lives, it is in all our interests to address this issue. Families, doctors, nurses, hospitals, and homes for the disabled and the elderly must recognize the basic human need of all people for physical warmth and touch. Our inherited disgust with our bodies and their needs are often projected on to people whose bodies do not fit in with the 'ideal' image we are bombarded with. Many people feel physically disturbed by the idea of disabled people or older people enjoying physical intimacy, and this has an effect on the self-image and behaviour of these two groups of people. The societal belief that older and disabled people cannot or should not function sexually becomes a self-fulfilling prophecy. The Hebrew scriptures are full of stories which recognize and honour the sexuality of the old. The Presbyterian Church in the USA was one of the first mainstream Christian Churches to produce a report which honestly addressed issues of sexuality unrestricted by the constraints of the traditional Christian body-hating mindset. It had this to say about older people:

> We must be open to a range of possibilities if we are to secure sexual justice for older adults. The traditional norm of 'sex only in marriage, celibacy in singleness' is extremely limiting for older adults. Remarriage is a near-impossibility for many persons due not only to the lack of available partners, but also to welfare and social security restrictions that make marriage financially burdensome. Thus we must continue to resist restrictions on welfare and Social Security benefits to older adults regardless of marital status. In addition, we must eliminate ideas of strict age limits for appropriate partners of older adults and redefine family in a broader, Christian sense. These efforts would reduce the isolation of older adults by providing a greater variety of human contacts from which intimacy might grow including recognition of gay and lesbian relationships among older adults.[56]

It is not only lesbian and gay people who have suffered from the idolatry of marriage. All Christians would accept that it is a Christian duty to care for the sick, the old and the disabled, but when we are prepared to recognize that such care involves making sure that they are able to experience intimate bodily pleasure and relationships if that is their desire we will know that we have finally conquered two thousand years of disastrous dualism.

Celibacy

It will be obvious, I hope, that a body-affirming theology of passionate friendship does not in any way devalue the vocation or state of celibacy. On the contrary, the celibate stands proud against the 'genital myth' that has caused so much pain and confusion in Western (including Christian) thinking. For much of its history the Church valued celibacy as the ultimate ideal state because of its pathologically negative attitude to the body. That attitude still hangs on, of course, as is obvious in the Roman Catholic Church's insistence that most of its clergy accept mandatory celibacy; other Churches desire that those who cannot enter into the institution of marriage live a celibate life. When I was in the process of writing a book about gay Catholic priests it became very obvious that a great deal of psychological harm was being done to Catholic priests and religious because of the general assumption that to be celibate is to be asexual, beyond the need for close companionship and physical affection.[57] This is, of course, not true. Indeed, we can only expect vowed celibates to stay celibate if we do offer them the love, affection and care—the friendship—that every human being desires and deserves. In the context of a theology and ethic of friendship, a person who chooses to be celibate is someone who sacrifices the relationship of passionate radical vulnerability in order to commit themselves completely to the building up of a community of friendship. This means that their experience and practice of intimacy will be different. While most of us intensify our friendship into a handful of close relationships, the celibate's intensity will be spread much further. Just as most of us constrict the expression of our passion because of our finiteness, so celibates constrict their experience of radically vulnerable relationships in order to be able to be faithful to a community. Note that this takes the emphasis off celibacy being defined as 'not having sex' because, as we have seen, there are all sorts of problems determining what is and what is not sex.

The challenge facing all of us as we try to make sense of sexuality within the context of the Christian vision is how to hold to a fundamental delight in the divine gift of sexuality and passion whilst recognizing that we do live in a situation of structural sin that affects all our relating. How do we be friends in this situation?

Notes

1 *Issues in Human Sexuality* (London: Church House Publishing, 1991), para. 5:8.
2 Rosemary Radford Ruether, 'Homophobia, heterosexism, and pastoral practice' in James Nelson and Sandra P. Longfellow, *Sexuality and the Sacred: Sources for Theological Reflection* (London: Mowbray, 1994), p. 393.
3 Sue George, *Women and Bisexuality* (London: Scarlet Press, 1993), p. 12.
4 George, *Women and Bisexuality*, pp. 165, 182.
5 Many men and women who recognize that it is possible for them to relate passionately to members of both sexes choose to label themselves 'lesbian' or 'gay' as a means of claiming some visible space for their same-sex relationships and also to indicate where their primary emotional, passionate and political energy is directed. Some believe that the label 'bisexual' actually serves to perpetuate the invisibility of same-sex love.
6 Augustine, *Soliloquies*, 1.10.
7 See Helena Kennedy's analysis of women and the British justice system in *Eve Was Framed: Women and British Justice* (London: Chatto and Windus, 1992).
8 Gareth Moore, *The Body in Context: Sex and Catholicism* (London: SCM, 1992), p. 49.
9 Moore, *The Body in Context*, p. 49.
10 Cited in Jim Cotter, *Good Fruits: Same-Sex Relationships and Christian Faith* (Sheffield: Cairns Publications, 1988), p. 50.
11 Cotter, *Good Fruits*, p. 60.

12 Sally Cline, *Women, Celibacy and Passion* (London: André Deutsch, 1993), p. 21.

13 Janet Elizabeth Chesney, 'Peter's Death' in Susan Durber, *As Man and Woman Made: Theological Reflections on Marriage* (London: United Reformed Church, 1994), p. 133.

14 Chesney, 'Peter's Death', pp. 134–5, 139.

15 See Michael Mason, *The Making of Victorian Sexuality* (Oxford: Oxford University Press, 1994).

16 Mary Daly and Jane Caputi, *Websters' First New Intergalactic Wickedary of the English Language* (London: The Women's Press, 1988), p. 176.

17 For example, among several Native American tribes, men and women whose principal passion is for members of their own sex act as shamans. See Judy Grahn, *Another Mother Tongue: Gay Words, Gay Worlds* (Boston: Beacon Press, 1984), p. 55.

18 Adrian Thatcher, *Liberating Sex: A Christian Sexual Theology* (London: SPCK, 1993), p. 173.

19 Karen Lebacqz, 'Appropriate vulnerability' in Nelson and Longfellow, *Sexuality and the Sacred*, p. 259.

20 Lebacqz, 'Appropriate vulnerability', pp. 260–1.

21 Thatcher, *Liberating Sex*, p. 108.

22 Elizabeth Templeton, 'Towards a theology of marriage' in Durber, *As Man and Woman Made*, p. 17.

23 *Issues in Human Sexuality*, para. 3:26, p. 30.

24 Virginia Ramey Mollenkott, *Sensuous Spirituality: Out from Fundamentalism* (New York: Crossroad, 1993), p. 27.

25 J. Giles Milhaven, 'A medieval lesson on bodily knowing: women's experience and men's thought', *Journal of the American Academy of Religion*, vol. 57, no. 2 (Summer 1989), p. 347.

26 Milhaven, 'A medieval lesson on bodily knowing', p. 346.

27 Milhaven, 'A medieval lesson on bodily knowing', p. 344.

28 For a thorough though controversial exploration of this phenomenon see Sheila Jeffreys, *The Lesbian Heresy: A Feminist Perspective on the Lesbian Sexual Revolution* (London: The Women's Press, 1994).

29 See, for example, Felix Cascara, 'Gay men need an agenda', *Our View*, no. 5 (June–July 1994), p. 36.

30 Beverly Wildung Harrison and Carter Heyward, 'Pain and pleasure: avoiding the confusions of Christian tradition in feminist theory' in Nelson and Longfellow, *Sexuality and the Sacred*, p. 133.

31 Toinette M. Eugene, 'While love is unfashionable: ethical implications of Black spirituality and sexuality' in Nelson and Longfellow, *Sexuality and the Sacred*, p. 108.

32 Thatcher, *Liberating Sex*, p. 188.

33 Marie Fortune, *Sexual Violence* (New York: The Pilgrim Press, 1983), p. 20.

34 Anne Borrowdale, *Distorted Images: Christian Attitudes to Women, Men and Sex* (London: SPCK, 1991), pp. 83–4.
35 Elaine Showalter, *Speaking of Gender* (New York: Routledge, 1989), p. 2.
36 Janice Raymond, *The Transsexual Empire* (London: The Women's Press, 1982).
37 Marilyn Frye, *The Politics of Reality: Essays in Feminist Theory* (New York: The Crossing Press, 1983), pp. 137–8.
38 See Grahn, *Another Mother Tongue.*
39 Rita Nakashima Brock, *Journeys by Heart: A Christology of Erotic Power* (New York: Crossroad, 1991), p. 56.
40 Harrison and Heyward, 'Pain and pleasure', p. 136.
41 Harrison and Heyward, 'Pain and pleasure', p. 138.
42 Harrison and Heyward, 'Pain and pleasure', pp. 139–40.
43 Jeffreys, *The Lesbian Heresy*, p. 46.
44 Nicole Houseman, 'Domestic violence: the lesbian dimension', *Lip* (Summer 1994), p. 17.
45 Cited in Sue Wilkinson and Celia Kitzinger, 'Theorising heterosexuality' in *Heterosexuality: A Feminism and Psychology Reader* (London: Sage Publications, 1993), p. 17.
46 Alasdair MacIntyre, *After Virtue: A Study in Moral Theory* (London, Duckworth, 1981).
47 MacIntyre, *After Virtue*, p. 6.
48 Peter Vardy and Paul Grosch, *The Puzzle of Ethics* (Fount, 1994), pp. 115–16.
49 Audre Lorde, 'Uses of the erotic' in Nelson and Longfellow, *Sexuality and the Sacred*, p. 78.
50 Mollenkott, *Sensuous Spirituality*, p. 162.
51 I am not here dealing with the other central issue of Heyward's book, the so-called False Memory Syndrome, which she endeavours to explain in terms of some sort of mystical connection with the pain of the world which translates itself into false memories. This seems to raise all kinds of serious issues which she does not attempt to address.
52 Maya Angelou, *And Still I Rise* (London: Virago Poetry, 1986), pp. 41–2.
53 Moore, *The Body in Context*, p. 57.
54 Shere Hite, *Women as Revolutionary Agents of Change: The Hite Reports: Sexuality, Love and Emotion* (London: Sceptre Books, 1994), p. 35.
55 Office of the General Assembly, Presbyterian Church (USA), 'Persons with disabilities' in Nelson and Longfellow, *Sexuality and the Sacred*, p. 283.
56 Office of the General Assembly, Presbyterian Church (USA), 'Older adults' in Nelson and Longfellow, *Sexuality and the Sacred*, p. 302.
57 Elizabeth Stuart, *Chosen: Gay Catholic Priests Tell Their Stories* (London: Geoffrey Chapman, 1993).

7 Being a friend

There is ... a time to embrace, and a time to refrain from embracing.

(Ecclesiastes 3.5)

Com-passion

It is a central contention of this book that lesbian and gay experience teaches us that the dynamics of sexuality and passion are experienced in all our relationships. Viewing our so-called 'sexual' relationships as separate from our 'normal' relationships, and our 'sexual acts' as fundamentally different from all other acts, leads to a distorted understanding of all human relationships and a privatizing of passion that renders this potentially world-transforming force tame, domesticated and beyond the jurisdiction of justice. Christians are called to be promiscuous with their love. The message of the gospels is that our love is called out beyond our families, into the world. Nor is this love something 'merely spiritual' or intellectual—it is embodied, it involves us taking our bodies to other people's bodies. In the Eucharist we are reminded in the eating and drinking of the bread and wine that Jesus of Nazareth gave himself bodily, and his voice summons us as the body of Christ on earth to do the same. We are called to relate to the world in friendship: a relationship which as it grows between people results in mutual and equal acceptance, respect and delight, it is an embodied relationship with social and political reper-cussions. In other words, we are called to delight in the world around us, to approach it in a positive rather than negative manner. We are called to engage with it, not fly from it; we are called to work for justice within it. Our delight in our own embodiment should give us a 'shiver of solidarity' with all other bodies and a desire to work to ensure that all bodies are treated justly: all bodies are well fed, have access to good health care, are well sheltered and so on; and that the body upon which all depend, the body of the earth, is also treated justly. This means using our bodies to ensure that this is done. We are finite creatures and have to learn to balance our friendships and our responsibilities; we have to make choices about where we channel our energies. However, this sense of finiteness can often lead to a paralysis. Embodiment comes in many forms. Very few of us are able to devote our whole lives to famine relief, ecology, justice issues in our own country and abroad, but we have a duty of friendship to support those who do, in whatever way we can—by giving money, by doing some kind of voluntary work, by lobbying politicians, by educating ourselves about the origins of the clothes we wear, the food we eat, the materials we use and the justice issues that lie beneath them, and so on. We are called to 'compassion'. Matthew Fox has noted the violence done to the concept of 'compassion' when it is reduced to 'pity' or 'mercy', because that is to reduce it to a hierarchical concept: someone has mercy or pity upon someone less powerful than themselves.[1] Com-passion means to have passion with, to share passion with others. It is the word used to express the feelings we have when we see our friends rejoice or suffer pain; we share that feeling with them, a feeling which propels us towards action. Carter Heyward has put it well:

> Compassion is that attitude or quality of being that people of passion reflect in their relationships and work. A compassionate person lives in such a way that her passion for life, for human dignity, for God's justice manifests itself as a sturdy, unbreakable connection to other people. Passion *with* others ... To be involved, sharing the same world, the same dilemma,

realizing that each person's destiny is bound up with one's own. The point at which radical self-interest and the willingness to give oneself/one's life, if necessary, coincide. Compassion, in which love is actually the love of one's neighbour as oneself.[2]

To be a friend to the world involves being dragged into the heart-breaking process of balancing the needs of individuals or groups against one another, of often being part of a process that decides which people live and which die, whilst working for structural social and political change that will endeavour to ensure that such choices no longer have to be made so often. We need to be aware that we are involved, however passively, in these kinds of decisions. It may feel too much to bear, but if we force ourselves to look into the eyes of a starving or abused child, a homeless person, animals subjected to degrading and torturous treatment, a family ravaged by unemployment and poverty, a swath of land turned to desert through continuous exploitation, we may see in all of these our friend. To feel a 'shiver of solidarity' is the only hope we have of eliciting and mobilizing true compassion. We are called to be shamelessly, hopelessly, promiscuous in our love. That also means, of course, loving 'the enemy', loving those who perpetuate injustice actively or passively (and we all do the latter). How do you be friends with such people? How do you balance your friendship to the victims with your friendship to the oppressor? I think it most importantly involves refusing to play by the rules of oppressors, refusing to dehumanize or demonize them as they have done to you or to others; all the time recognizing them as embodied beings made in the image and likeness of God. This means refusing to give up on them and, most important of all, refusing to be afraid of them, challenging them constantly with their actions, calling them to account, always alive to possibilities of change. Sometimes when the evil is so great and shows no sign of relenting, when there is no reasonable hope of change, sometimes friendship with the vulnerable may force us into destroying the oppressor. These macro issues are beyond the scope and competence of this book but I mention them to place our embodied passion in a proper perspective. It is not something that should be confined to two consenting adults in private; it is about our relationship to the whole of God's earth.

As on a macro so on a micro scale, we are called to be 'promiscuous' in our embodied passion, to love those around us with a fierce, joyous, just passion. But once again we have to recognize the constraints we are under in this vocation. We are finite and our energy is finite, and is constrained even further by the structures in which we live. We do not have the time or energy to love every one around us with passion—not even Jesus did that. We are also a broken-hearted people, formed by our previous relationships, which again affects our relationships with others. We find many people unlikeable, quite apart from unlovable, because of their and our brokenness. Because of the constraints we are under there is a difference, in terms of the energy we can and want to put into such relationships, between our primary relationships of friendship and the friendliness we are called as Christians to exhibit to all around us. In view of our lack of safety in the world in which we live, we must also have the right to choose not be someone's friend if we feel that such a friendship would endanger ourselves or them or the balance of our other friendships. Most important of all, we live in an all-pervading context in which relationships are conceived in terms of domination and submission. This has two chief repercussions: first, it means that it is actually unsafe to enter into passionate relationships; second, we are conditioned to behave unjustly towards one another and to break that conditioning is extremely hard. This is the tragic painful dimension of passion, it is the cross at the heart of the relational world. Susan Thistlewaite has said: 'There is *both* connection and destruction, creativity and evil at the heart of the cosmos.'[3] It is in the nature of friendship that we should be honest about and seek to be aware of the dynamics operating in our lives. Bearing this in mind, can we begin to sketch out some of the right-behaviour that will result from cultivating the ethic of friendship in our lives?

Negotiation

One of the appalling consequences of our negative attitudes to the body, to sexuality and to relationships, is that we do not talk about them with each other. We do not talk about our 'mere' friendships, because to do so would attribute to them an importance we do not think they deserve. Most people do not talk about their 'sexual' relationships until they are in trouble. It is a mark of friendship that we take a relationship, and the other person involved, seriously enough to talk about it: we negotiate boundaries; we are honest when things are going wrong; we are aware of each other and the baggage, needs and expectations each brings into the relationship. It is true that most of us fall into friendships by accident—suddenly, almost unconsciously we find ourselves in a relationship that matters a great deal to us—but that is no excuse for not talking about it. Paying attention to the friendship and negotiating it is particularly important if we find ourselves in a relationship with someone who is broken-hearted (in Rita Nakashima Brock's sense of that phrase), whose passion has never been awakened or has been destroyed. Inequality in terms of emotional wholeness, and in other terms as well, has to be acknowledged and worked through if we are going to learn to treat each other with justice and work towards mutuality. Negotiation of physical affection is also vital. For some friends this never becomes an issue. Though extremely fond of one another, the extent of their physical intimacy is a letter or card, perhaps the rare kiss or brief hug; this particularly applies to heterosexual men. We should want to touch our friends, we are embodied beings, our bodies are our primary means of communication. But, of course, we are broken-hearted, many of us have been damaged by touch and friends need to respect each other's brokenness. Unwanted touch is violence. I recently heard a group of women discuss how much they hated it when men, like their local vicar, colleagues and so on, kissed them without asking their permission. They experienced it as just another form of sexual harassment.

But if two friends find themselves moving towards mutuality in their relationship then physical affection is going to be a part of that. We all come to relationships with preconceived notions about what physical gestures mean, but these may be different notions. I may think that certain physical expressions of affection establish a certain kind of commitment between us, you may not, which is why it is so important to talk. I am not implying or suggesting that all friends should or could 'have sex' with one another. All physical gestures are important, but their significance has to be established by the friends together if pain and confusion is not to result. It would be wrong to imply that all negotiation is or must be verbal; we communicate with our bodies as well as our words and body language can be an effective and more gentle way of establishing boundaries. I am also aware of the dangers of what Martin Luther King called 'the paralysis of analysis', when endless talking and analysing of relationships can actually overtake the relationship itself. It is a matter of balancing our responsibility for our relationships with a due acknowledgement of the mystery of passion.

The great strength of Adrian Thatcher's theological reflection upon sexuality is that he acknowledges what other Christian reflections upon relationships very rarely acknowledge: that there are numerous ways to 'have sex'. So much of the Churches' discussion of AIDS has been embarrassing because it has been along the lines of 'AIDS is caused by promiscuity, therefore we have been right all along, monogamy is the only answer'. Promiscuity does not cause or transmit AIDS: certain types of sexual behaviour do. You can go to a bar with a 'back room' and mutually masturbate tens of different people and be under no real risk of catching HIV. You can have penetrative sex with one person who has had penetrative sex with one person, or received infected blood, and catch HIV. As we observed earlier, when you cease to define sex purely in terms of penetration or goal (orgasm) it becomes increasingly difficult to establish what is and what is not sex. I am convinced that we have got to stop thinking in terms of sexual and non-sexual, moving instead to terms of affection and intimacy, mutual respect and communication. Of course, people aware of the responsibilities of friendship will not engage in irresponsible behaviour which could result in the endangering of health or unwanted pregnancy. Friends too will want to be alert to the possibilities of unconscious relationships of domination and submission seeping into the friendship and turning it into something else. This commitment to pay attention to the relationship, to negotiate it as it develops is, I believe, primarily what it means to be 'faithful' to a relationship. Carter Heyward expresses it well:

> Fidelity is tenacious trust in our relational power to strengthen us to move with friends and lovers into new, sometimes fearful, places of intimacy and struggle. Fidelity is our daring to say YES to the power of mutuality in a world, and in relationships, in which it is usually safer to say NO. To be faithful to our commitments is to honour pledges we have made to certain people or tasks in the course of our love and work. Commitment involves investing ourselves in purposeful ways to particular people or processes. No two commitments are ever entirely the same because no two relationships or occasions for love or work are the same ... we are obligated to honour, rather than abuse, one another's feelings. This requires us to be really present, rather than acting out roles we have been socialized, professionalized, or otherwise taught to play.[4]

The sin of friendship is betrayal. We betray our friends, we are unfaithful to them, when we abuse their trust in us, when we succumb to patterns of relating we know to be sinful. We live out our relationships in a context of structural sin and we are formed in that context. It is our 'original sin' stamped onto us at a frighteningly early age. In this context it is quite understandable why we should have veered between the two extremes of submitting mindlessly to socialization and ringing ourselves with 'thou shalt nots'. We need 'thou shalt nots', but when those commandments prevent rather than promote justice being done, something has gone wrong. It is always wrong to abuse another person, always wrong to treat another person with injustice; but if fear of doing that actually dries our passion

and paralyses our relationality, that is wrong too. Part of being
an adult is that we learn that risk is an essential part of life. We
are right to be ever vigilant of abuse; we are right to seek to
protect the vulnerable from any risk of relational abuse. If we
fail to do so we are literally passing on original sin and being
unfaithful to them. However, it can also be sinful and abusive to
shrink from right-relationship with someone, not to touch
someone justly when it is what they need and we are in a
position to reach out. A proper commitment to justice, to
negotiation, to honesty should make touch much safer and
therefore more available.

Balancing friendships

Friendships are relationships in which we become most fully
what God intends us to be. We should therefore be striving to
be as open to as many as possible, for this is how the divine
reign will be established on earth. However, our finitude, our
broken-heartedness, and our own sense of safety may lead us to
decide that we will limit the possibilities of complete vulnerability to one person alone. Every friendship we make is a
triumph over the forces of sin, the various forces in our society
that conspire to keep us apart from each other, to assume masks
and play roles, to treat each other unjustly. And every friendship takes place within that context and the context of our own
finitude. I believe that in the secret places of our lives we yearn
for relationships based upon mutuality, justice, compassion
and complete affirming acceptance. But for that yearning to be
fulfilled, complete and utter vulnerability, radical vulnerability,
must exist between the friends. We long to 'jump about stark
naked', to use a phrase of Kierkegaard's, to be completely
ourselves with another person and for them to be so with us and
to grow from that vulnerability into the best that we both can
be. But within the sinful context in which we live, and in which
we have been formed, the attainment of such radical vulnerability requires enormous effort and a great deal of time.
Because radical vulnerability is a process, not a moment,

achieved above all through a journey into deeper and deeper trust, based upon mutual exposure of ourselves, we need some assurance that the other person will be there tomorrow to reaffirm us as we are and will struggle through the inevitable problems and tensions that arise in relationships.

Intimacy usually involves a great deal of pain. Christopher Rowland has pointed out that in the gospels Jesus' moments of intimacy with God are always moments of agony and terror because they are moments of 'confrontation with the reality before which all hearts are open'.[5] That reality is present in all relationships of radical vulnerability. It also takes an extremely long time to deconstruct our 'inherited' patterns of relating. In many respects all friendships are based upon implicit assurances, as Gareth Moore has noted,[6] but in a relationship of radical vulnerability these are not enough. For the safety of both people, explicit commitment, a covenant, is necessary. This covenant need not be pledged with great ceremony, and certainly does not depend for its validity on the willingness of the Church to approve and bless it, but it needs to be explicit and negotiated. And there is something important about making a public declaration of a commitment like this which formally notifies other friends of a change in the balance of your web of friendships and asks for their support in sustaining this particular relationship. In such a context it seems entirely reasonable to me to pledge such a commitment in life-long terms. It is in the very nature of friendship that it is a relationship constituted on infinite terms: 'You cannot set a deliberate term to a friendship, because you cannot make a decision to stop liking somebody by such and such a date. The bonds of friendship stretch into an indefinite future.'[7] If this is true of friendships in general, then it seems to me sensible that people in relationships of passionate radical vulnerability make such a commitment explicit, that for their own safety they declare their intention to maintain such a relationship for life.

Sometimes we will find ourselves falling into a relationship of radical vulnerability almost by accident and wake up one day and realize that this is what we are dealing with. Then we ought

222 Just good friends

to begin to negotiate the boundaries of it. This will include the question of whether either person wishes to be free to establish a relationship of radical vulnerability elsewhere. To say that this cannot happen and does not happen successfully is to be dishonest, and Churches should take time to listen to people who believe they have successfully achieved such relationships, precisely because they *may* have a more definite foretaste of the kingdom than most of us. But the energy and effort in balancing two relationships of radical vulnerability in a society which is constructed to prevent such relationships should not be underestimated. All parties would have to be strong, with an extraordinarily determined passion and heroic commitment to honesty and self-examination. I have to be honest and say that I think such relationships are virtually impossible; the constraints and risks are too great, the balancing act virtually impossible. Concepts of 'ownership' have no place in relationships of friendship and are particularly antithetical to many women who have been at the receiving end of them, particularly in the constructions of marriage down the ages. Doing away with the concept of ownership does not give friends the licence to treat each other irresponsibly or unjustly. We may not be 'one flesh' but we do hold each other in our hands.

Where there is an intention to conceive or adopt children in such a relationship the need of all children to be brought up in a loving, stable, passionate environment must be a consideration in negotiating the boundaries of relationships. A parent's relationship with a child is a *de facto* life-long one, and when two people enter into an agreement to have children together (by whatever means) they have a right to expect of each other life-long commitment to and responsibility towards that child. Parenting is a full-time co-operative job. I wonder whether it would be humanly possible to sustain two relationships of radical vulnerability at the same time as responsibly parenting a child. Parenthood is the relationship above all others 'not by any to be enterprised, nor taken in hand, advisedly, lightly, or wantonly', to use the words of the Book of Common Prayer on marriage. A. H. Halsey's research into the development of children whose parents have divorced reminds us again of how we hold each other in our hands. Halsey found that such children tend to die earlier, suffer more illness, be educationally, socially, and financially disadvantaged and are more likely themselves to become divorced parents than are children of non-divorced parents.[8] One of the consequences of Christianity for so long permitting sexual activity only if it led to reproduction is that we have been socialized to think we should all want and have children (although a few of us have managed to resist). It is in the essence of passion that it spills over from the relationship; it is creative. But there is no reason why that creativity should be confined to the creation of children. And we in the northern hemisphere of the world who consume most of the earth's resources need to think much more carefully than we are accustomed to about how we balance our friendships with each other, with the planet, and with our friends in the South. In an overpopulated world we need to think very seriously about what responsible parenthood means. This also means working for a society in which other forms of creativity are taken more seriously and valued more dearly.

Lesbian and gay people have proved themselves as capable of forming permanent, stable and committed relationships of radical vulnerability as anyone else. In a context in which it is unsafe to be a lesbian or gay man and in which most of us are broken-hearted by the homophobia that teaches us to hate ourselves, it seems to me to be nothing short of a miracle that most of us manage to find one another and love each other into passion and then establish relationships of radical vulnerability. To me this is testimony above all else of the passionate presence of God in the world, sweeping through and knocking down the obstacles to our relating.

Do relationships of radical vulnerability exclude other relationships of physical intimacy? Carter Heyward thinks not. For her, fidelity is not primarily about restricting genital acts to one person, as Christianity has come to believe, but about fidelity to the friendship and the boundaries established within it. She comments:

To be nonmonogamous is not necessarily to be, in the pejorative sense, 'promiscuous'—wanton and nondiscriminatory—in our sexual practices and choices of sexual partners. It may be rather a way of participating in the embodied fullness of different special relationships ... Fidelity to our primary relational commitments does not require monogamy. But learning to value sexual pleasure as a moral good requires that we be faithful to our commitments. This is always an obligation that involves a willingness to work with our sexual partner, or partners, in creating mutual senses of assurance that our relationships are being cared for. Thus we are obligated to be honest—real—with each other and to honour rather than abuse each other's feelings.[9]

I dislike using the term 'monogamy' because of its obviously patriarchal origins—it means 'one wife', and therefore seems an inappropriate word to use in this context. There would seem to be nothing inherently wrong with friends who are not involved in relationships of radical vulnerability enjoying intimate physical relations, as long as these are negotiated honestly with all concerned. If we accept, as surely we must, that acts of physical intimacy have no inherent meaning, then the onus is on the friends to establish the boundaries of their relationship. However, in seeking to nurture a culture of *friendship* one must always be aware of the dangers of falling into a pattern of simply using people and their bodies for our own personal pleasure.

This is where Sheila Jeffreys' analysis of the whole notion of consent is useful. Consent and friendship are not synonymous, although consent is a vital part of friendship. Consent in matters of negotiating relationships is not enough from the perspective of those advocating an ethic of friendship; friendship is the key. It is, for example, part of the tragedy of relating in a society centred upon money that human relationships are often structured around concepts of ownership and debt.[10] An ethic of friendship does not permit such interpretation and will not accept sexual activity as some kind of payment. However, when parties are involved in relationships of radical vulnerability, then the issue is altogether different, precisely because for relationships to survive and thrive they need complete, single-mindedness commitment, which is what the much abused word 'chastity' means. Such single-mindedness will include a level of physical intimacy which both partners agree is an appropriate expression of their friendship of passionate radical vulnerability. It is the nature of single-minded commitment that such a level be confined to that relationship. This single-mindedness also applies to the expenditure of other forms of energy (emotional infidelity is as damaging to such relationships as physical infidelity). It means that all our primary energy is devoted to our primary relationship; it does not mean that absolutely all our energy should be devoted to such a relationship. Indeed it is a quality of all friendship that it generates energy, it does not sap it. In friendships of radical vulnerability we experience ourselves as we are meant to be. This is a profoundly empowering, gracious experience; it generates overflowing love; in Christian terms it incarnates the presence of the passionate God. It becomes, therefore, the source of deeper friendships for others. Fidelity to relationships of radical vulnerability means that this relationship will come before others if that choice has to be made. Some people, gay and straight, would argue that relationships of radical vulnerability are in a class of their own and should therefore be labelled and treated differently to all our other friendships. Applying a different language to them (for example, the language of marriage) creates an important safety barrier around the relationship which gives it space to grow and flourish. I can see the advantages of this but want to resist it strongly because it seems to me that one of the chief problems with marriage has been its elevation above friendship. It is important that people, perhaps particularly Christian people, should regard their relationships of radical vulnerability as part of the wider project of friendship, which is the divine method of world transformation, and that the same ethic of justice should be applied in all our relationships. Soft boundaries are certainly more dangerous, but their advantage is that they demand we take full responsibility for all our relationships.

I have said that one of the reasons why I prefer the term

'passion' to the term 'erotic' is that it contains within it ac-knowledgement of the frailty, pain and tragedy of relating. Vulnerability inevitably brings massive risk, risk which cannot be avoided. I know of women who therefore choose to parent a child with someone with whom they are not seeking a relation-ship of radical vulnerability because they want the child to be brought up in a secure, more or less guaranteed, life-long relationship. They are aware of how fragile a passionate re-lationship can be and do not want children to suffer from the break-up of such a relationship. They therefore seek a co-parent with whom they are not passionately involved in the hope that this person will always be around for the child. It is for this reason that a small number of lesbians and gay men choose to parent together rather than with a same-sex partner. Part of the problem of idealization/idolization of marriage is that men and women have been led to expect that marriage guarantees the creation of a relationship of passionate, radical vulnerability and, of course, it does not. In fact, the construction of marriage in our society actually acts as a huge block to forming friend-ship. This has led to an enormous amount of pain. Esther Rothblum and Kathleen Brehony, a psychologist and psycho-therapist respectively, undertook a study of lesbian women who lived together. Some parented children together, regarded this relationship as their primary one in terms of radical vul-nerability and yet did not 'have sex' with one another, that is, they did not enjoy much physical intimacy, if any at all. There were many reasons for this. Some had begun their relationship as lovers but particular forms of physical intimacy had slowly discontinued, not to the chagrin of either person. Some re-searchers in seeking to explain this phenomenon have suggested 'that because women are the "emotional glue" that holds heterosexual relationships together, when we love each other, there is enough emotional bonding at every level that the ritual of sexual intimacy is less essential to maintaining the relationship'.[11] Some chose celibacy, in that spirit so eloquently outlined by Sally Cline. Some had been badly damaged by previous sexually abusive relationships. Some had physically intimate relationships with other people, whilst being very honest with them as to where their primary commitment lay. What was particularly disturbing, however, was the failure of society around these women to take their primary relationships seriously. We equate committed relationships with 'sex' and where 'sex' does not exist we are apt to dismiss the relationship as 'not real' or dysfunctional. This is particularly the case with those of us—lesbians, gay men and bisexuals—who are defined by our sexuality. One sex therapist, having read the text of the book, recognized the mistakes she had made in making this assumption:

> Sex therapy currently assumes that the goal is to be sexual. *Boston Marriages* has made a subtle shift in my thinking about this assumption. There are wide paths to explore in the land of relationships, and we make a mistake by automatically pathologizing those paths which may not include sex.[12]

It may well be that the phenomenon of 'serial monogamy', probably the most common form of relationship in Europe and America today, owes its prominence to the fact that we assume that, when certain types of physical intimacy cease, the relationship must be over, and our narrow definitions of what constitutes 'proper sex' simply exasperate this situation.

One of the most moving essays in the *Boston Marriages* book is the personal story of Ruth (a bisexual woman married to a man) and Iris (a lesbian in a partnership) who have found a passionate friendship with each other and negotiated a level of physical intimacy with each other which honours their commitment to one another and their commitment to their partners. Listen to them speak (I have blended their voices):

> I've never been in love with anybody so deeply. I never knew it could exist. When we go there, nothing else is there but us and something like heaven ... I know her. I know her in a way that I've never known anyone. Part of why I know her, part of why we can do this, is because this is not sex ... We do feel sexual feelings come up when we do this. There is a point at which I consciously move that feeling up from my vagina up into my

heart. It just flows into her heart and it's a connection like
nothing I've ever experienced ... Bliss is a sort of emanation. I
find myself using medieval and Renaissance Christian concepts
to describe some of what happens. It's a spiritual experience
...There is a physical experience too. Our skin changes when
we are with each other ... We have an experience being one,
becoming each other. While still maintaining autonomy ... I
don't fear losing myself ... There is no map, we're doing
without a map. This feels really dangerous. It's emotionally
terrifying to be this open to someone who is committed to
someone else ... This relationship, as far as the impact of
passion on my soul, is the most important relationship I've ever
had in my life ... People need to take it seriously. We've had
trouble with people taking it seriously—lesbians, straight people.
therapists ... It's important to say that we're very much in love
with our partners. In the beginning of our relationship, our not
being sexual was a lot about keeping our commitments to our
partners. But now our not being sexual is about being on a
journey together that's incredibly important ... Imagine saying,
'just lovers', like some people say, 'just friends.' What if people
said: 'We're not friends, we're just lovers.'[13]

This is the relationship of Ruth and Naomi, David and Jonathan, Jesus and his disciples, Christian women and men down
the centuries, and yet the Church has had nothing to say to
these people, no language, no theology to interpret the most
important relationship in their lives other than negatively.

Part of the pain of passion that leads to relationships of
radical vulnerability is that some people have children, buy
houses, and have sex, get married if they can, because they are
frightened of the fragility of the passion and want some sort of
guarantee, some extra glue to bind them, only to find that all
these things act as an anti-glue if they are not properly negotiated. Sometimes the pain of mutual broken-heartedness is too
great to bear; sometimes one person loves the other into
passionate knowledge and with that passionate knowledge
comes the realization that the relationship which awakens it
cannot contain it. Sometimes two broken-hearted people meet
and believe that they have the ability to love each other into a

relationship of passionate, radical vulnerability, and formally commit themselves to endeavouring to love each other, because they believe they can, but find despite years of trying that they cannot, and one of them finds that empowering love elsewhere.[14] Or the relationship is suffocated by social structures which invade from outside and from within the relationship where they are incarnated in the persons involved. Joanna Trollope's *The Rector's Wife* is a brilliant portrait of all of these factors colliding in the person of Anna Bouverie and the inevitable pain and destruction caused to everyone around her (except the other women who are empowered by her courage in seeking passion wherever it leads her).[15] And people change. We are in a constant state of flux and transformation, this is the glory and danger of being human. Sometimes two people change through no wrongdoing of their own into people who cannot sustain relationships of radical vulnerability any more. When a covenant becomes a positively oppressive force in people's lives, causing misery to all involved, then people should be allowed out of the tomb into the possibility of resurrection. It seems to me that perhaps the ultimate test of fidelity, as Heyward defined it, is knowing when to let go of the covenant and each other and when to attempt to ride out the inevitable storms of relationships. Relationships do end, passion does die, hearts do turn cold. We spend our lives trying to balance our friendships; it is no accident that justice is often portrayed as a person with a balancing instrument in her hands. How are we to be just to all our relationships, and to ourselves? This is the essence of relational ethics. It is inevitable that we will fail because we are not living in justice nor are we taught to be just. Because we are broken-hearted people in a context which defines relationship in a particular way, many of us do not seek friendship in our most intimate of relationships. We do not want equality; we want an uneven distribution of power. One person may feel the need to be looked after and led in a relationship, whilst another may feel the need to take control. When people with complementary needs find each other their relationship can be strong and happy. However, the Christian vision is that people grow into beings 'fully alive', able to realize their full potential through the empowerment of love. Relationships which are based upon clearly defined and prescribed roles are vulnerable to destruction if one partner grows beyond their role but the other does not. My experience of being involved in higher education and training of clergy has shown me how many relationships are based upon implicit roles and when a woman, in particular, moves beyond that role this often precipitates a profound crisis in the relationship. There are, of course, times in a relationship based upon friendship when power-shifts have to made, for example, in times of sickness, but the basic axis of the relationship remains the same and balance is restored in due course. Ruth and Iris (see above) found a relationship of radical vulnerability with each other, a relationship which did not come between themselves and their partners. In this sense their primary relationships have failed, but instead of simply leaving their partners for each other, they seek to be faithful to their commitments to them whilst exploring their passion together. This is the mess and muddle of many lives—lesbian, gay, heterosexual and bisexual—and those who endeavour to balance their relationships with justice in the midst of this mess should be applauded not condemned.

Forgiveness is an essential aspect of friendship. It is interesting that, despite protestations to the contrary, the one area in which the Church has always projected a very unforgiving image is sexuality. Jesus the passionate was Jesus the forgiving. It is part of letting go, of freeing ourselves and others to move on to greater possibilities of passion. A forgiving culture is not a 'soft' or 'anything goes' culture; on the contrary it is a culture that, whilst recognizing human frailty, demands that you should be free from disabling guilt in order that your future search for passion, for justice, be more successful. It is unresolved, unforgiven guilt that leads to compulsively unjust behaviour in relationships as elsewhere. Forgiveness is an essential part of the quest for justice.

One of the primary duties of friendship is to challenge the unjust behaviour of our friends and to accept and welcome the advice and challenges to our own behaviour by friends. We hold each other's consciences in our hands. The privatization of relationships, particularly coupled relationships, means that we tend to believe that our relationships are 'no one else's business', but this is simply not true. We live in a web of relationships; we are responsible for each other; it is our project to build up a web of just relationships. We do not have the right to wade into other people's relationships and interfere but we do have a responsibility to each other. If the Christian Church were to become the principal advocate of friendship as the primary ethical basis for relationships in the Western world, it could with integrity call people to right relationship. But it can only do this if it first establishes itself as a friend to the body, to just relationships, and to those struggling to establish such relationships in a context of injustice which historically the Church itself has helped to perpetuate. It needs to become a network of moral communities built upon and promoting the virtue of friendship.

An agenda for the Church

In the light of the theology of sexuality that I have outlined, what agenda would I want to put before the Christian Churches? I am not directing these remarks to the hierarchies of Churches but to the 'real' Church, particularly the laity who have yet to learn to claim their power in any church. We are the Church and we must act as Church and in the name of Church, even when that means opposing our 'fathers' (or even 'mothers') in God. Mary Hunt redefined Church as a coalition of justice-seeking friends. I would want to make that more specifically Christian and say that the Church is a coalition of justice-seeking friends working to incarnate the passion of God between themselves and in the world. So this is an agenda I set before you and before me.

1. We must fight in the name of Christ against the constructions of injustice in the world. This includes fighting against
   the construction of sex, and relationships in general, in

terms of domination and submission. The voice of the Churches is often heard on homosexuality, divorce, contraception and abortion, but rarely heard on rape, pornography, child abuse, harassment and social and economic inequality between men and women. Christians need to speak out on these issues and use their political power to make sure something is done about them. The Church should speak out and act up against the enforced heterosexual conditioning, and rigid gender conditioning imposed upon our children, because of the injustice and misery it creates. Some theologians talk about the need to develop an androgynous humanity in which 'male' and 'female' characteristics are balanced in each person. I dislike this term, first because it still shows itself dependent upon a Jungian dissection of maleness and femaleness, and second because it seeks to mould all of humanity into one image. Notions of gender must be subverted and children liberated from them, but that does not mean that there is an ideal human way of being which holds in balance all these different gendered characteristics. Difference and variety is the spice of life, the signature of creation. We should seek to liberate people to be different—a difference not dependent on gender roles but on personal development. The ancient Christian tradition of being 'born again' may be helpful here. What this tradition conveys is that it is possible in the infinite grace of a passionate God to enter into a new way of being and relating fundamentally different to that which we are socialized to accept. This is a relationship of friendship and passion which transcends boundaries of gender, class, race and so on. In Christ there is no Jew or Greek, slave or free, male or female, heterosexual, gay/lesbian or bisexual. The only boundaries to love are those of justice. Our children should be free to find the way in which they love best: gay, lesbian, straight, bisexual, celibate. We all should be free to do this, always within the bonds of justice and friendship; not only for our own sakes but for the sake of the Gospel which is incarnated and proclaimed in love.

In Christ, traditional concepts of family are dissolved to be replaced by the kinship of friendship. Lesbian, gay and bisexual people have an important insight into the reality of experiencing something like a universal family/kindom. It is the ethic of friendship that is the true 'family value' and the Church should be supporting all those who exist in bonds of friendship, not simply the 'nuclear family'. The ethic of friendship will ensure that Christians fight for equal access for lesbian, gay and bisexual people to the civil rights enjoyed by heterosexual people. This will include the opportunity to register domestic partnerships and thereby enjoy the same privileges and legal protection as heterosexual married couples.

In view of the ambiguous attitude to the family many people quite properly have, Christians need to think seriously about whether to continue to talk about the Church in terms of family. On the one hand, negative experiences of blood family can be redeemed by experience of a new form of kinship in Church. On the other hand, the rather negative attitudes to the family attributed to Jesus are not accidental; it is extremely difficult to combine friendship and family. Families exist in structured power relations; they are also closed institutions, and it is no accident that those churches which are keenest on promoting themselves as family are often the most hierarchically ordered.

Respecting the needs and dignity of lesbian and gay Christians involves graciously respecting the need of some of them to form their own Christian communities. Some of those exiled from their own churches have formed small communities of worship, ministry and political action. Sometimes people will combine membership of these base communities with membership of larger established Christian churches. When ministry to lesbian and gay people is often non-existent or flawed, it is natural and proper that we should seek to minister to each other and live out an alternative vision of a truly inclusive, body-affirming Church. The wider Church needs to learn to be less threatened by these alternative communities and recognize them as incarnations of judgement on their ministry but also as pools of grace able to enrich, teach and inspire other Christians.

2. Christians need to assess existing Church structures and practice according to the ethic of friendship. The redefining of marriage is crucial, as a relationship in which two friends of the opposite sex enter into a covenant of passionate radical vulnerability. The Church should not dictate the terms of that covenant but encourage and help specific couples to negotiate a covenant. The Church will continue to bless such covenants, but there will be no reason to deprive lesbian and gay people of that blessing. This is something the Church can and should be doing now. We are the Church, we all have the power to bless, to express our recognition of the presence of God in a relationship and entrust its future to God. We should use that power even when clergy and bishops refuse to use it. Lesbian and gay people have been blessing each other's relationships for years. Lesbian and gay people tend to wait until they are reasonably sure that a relationship of radical vulnerability is possible with their partner before seeking a public space in which to declare their covenant and ask for God's blessing upon it. An increasing number of heterosexual couples do the same: by the end of the century it is estimated that 80 per cent of couples will live together before marrying. The Church needs to remind itself that it has always taught that marriage is a sacramental relationship created by the partners themselves, not by the Church nor, indeed, by the state. Therefore the wedding ceremony has never been the beginning of the marriage, but the celebration of it. Liturgical ceremonies for heterosexual couples need to reflect this reality and desperately need to move away from the patriarchal notions of ownership which still remain in even the most modern versions. Lesbian and gay couples who have been writing their own ceremonies of commitment for years could offer help in this project. Reclamation of the goodness

of the body should actually inspire a complete liturgical revolution. Much of Christian liturgy is at present so head- and word-centred that people are not recognized as embodied, their bodies are not considered worthy or appropriate to be taken up in worship.

3. The Church should be there for people when relationships fail. Since we are dealing with passion, at the heart of which is always the cross, pain and failure, the Church should be there to enable people to bring their friendships to a close with forgiveness. When important chapters of our life close we usually wish to bring them to an end with some kind of ritual. The Church needs to develop prayers and liturgies to help people mark an end to their relationships. There is no time when we more urgently need to be assured of the presence of God and the friendship of God. People sometimes argue that the mere existence of such ceremonies, like the mere existence of divorce, serves in some way to promote separation. We do not deprive people of hospitals and medical centres because such things encourage illness, nor do Christians forbid funerals even though we believe in resurrection. We are called to offer friendship to one another in the midst of reality, which is painful and messy, and in which people do get sick, die and relationships fail. When I included some ceremonies for partings in a prayer book for lesbian and gay people, I was accused by some of thereby admitting or pandering to the view that lesbian and gay relationships fail more readily than heterosexual ones.[16] My answer was that I was attempting to deal with the reality of both heterosexual and lesbian and gay relationships. Calls for such liturgies have come primarily from heterosexuals. Jean Mortimer writes about her own divorce and the liturgy of release she devised:

> Nor do I think that an officially agreed order for the service of release from ... commitment would erode the Church's influence and ideals. If the love and forgiveness of God for

all people is to have any meaning, then the Church needs to move away from a theology of strength and success towards a theology of weakness and failure recognising that it is not a simple case of either/or but a far more complex situation in which the apparently contradictory nature of such false polarities can be challenged in the interest of developing a more holistic approach to doctrine, liturgy and pastoral care ... Though we in our fickleness and ever-present frailty may continue to bend or break our human promises, God's covenant of loving judgement never fails.[17]

4. In a similar spirit the Church needs to provide people with the opportunity to celebrate the presence of God not only in their primary relationships but in all their most significant friendships. Mary Hunt speaks of the need to 'sacramentalize' friendship:

> Friendships need reverence, candour, space, and specificity. Most of all they require some sort of periodic celebration to renew and refresh the bonds in a community of friends ... To sacramentalize is to pay attention. It is what a community does when it names and claims ordinary human experiences as holy, connecting them with history and propelling them into the future.[18]

Indeed, if we are to adopt an ethic of friendship we must sacramentalize friendship. This is because the way in which Christianity holds up what is important to it to the world is through liturgical celebration. Of course, in a very real sense the Eucharist is a sacrament of friendship, but it is the communal, universal friendship that we celebrate and long for, with our experience of the joys and pains of friendship. We also need words, symbols, music to celebrate the specific, what the Roman Catholic Church used to refer to as 'particular', friendships in our lives. John Boswell has proven that there are venerable, historic precedents for the Church liturgically celebrating friendships. Liturgical services to mark the annual lesbian and gay pride celebrations can serve this purpose.

5. One of the most solemn tasks of the Church is to press for

and provide body-affirming relationship (rather than 'sex') education which will include explicit information about the various possibilities for intimate bodily encounter, but will place all relationships in the context of friendship and encourage honest negotiation.

6. 'Love means not having to say you're sorry'—one of the biggest lies ever invented and one of the biggest causes of injustice, for this idea encourages irresponsibility by assuring people that they are not accountable for their actions. Love demands recognition and repentance from injustice. The Church will never convince the vast majority of lesbian and gay people, bisexual people, battered women, and all those victims of the demonic dualism that has distorted our attitudes to the body and relationships, of its friendship unless it first acknowledges its guilt and asks for forgiveness.

Notes

1 Matthew Fox, *A Spirituality Named Compassion* (San Francisco: Harper and Row, 1979).

2 Carter Heyward, *Our Passion for Justice: Images of Power, Sexuality, and Liberation* (New York: The Pilgrim Press, 1984), pp. 236–7.

3 Susan Brooks Thistlewaite, *Sex, Race, and God: Christian Feminism in Black and White* (London: Geoffrey Chapman, 1990), p. 107.

4 Carter Heyward, *Touching Our Strength: The Erotic as Power and the Love of God* (San Francisco: Harper and Row, 1989), pp. 130–1.

5 Christopher Rowland, 'Jesus, the gospels and intimacy', *Christian Action Journal* (Summer 1993), p. 7.

6 Gareth Moore, *The Body in Context: Sex and Catholicism* (London: SCM, 1992), pp. 113–14.

7 Moore, *The Body in Context*, p. 113.

8 *The Times* (3 July 1991).

9 Heyward, *Touching Our Strength*, pp. 136–7.

10 I am grateful to Professor Peter Selby for this point.

11 Leslie Raymer, 'What's sex got to do with it?' in Esther D. Rothblum and Kathleen A. Brehony, *Boston Marriages: Romatic but Asexual Relationships Among Contemporary Lesbians* (Amherst: University of Massachusetts Press, 1994), pp. 99–100.

12 Ellen Cole, 'Is sex a natural function: implications for sex therapy' in Rothblum and Brehony, *Boston Marriages*, p. 192.

13 Ruth and Iris, 'We have bliss' in Rothblum and Brehony, *Boston Marriages*, pp. 157–63.
14 It is surely significant that the marriage service does not ask couples 'do you' love but 'will you'.
15 Joanna Trollope, *The Rector's Wife* (London: Black Swan, 1991).
16 Elizabeth Stuart, *Daring to Speak Love's Name: A Gay and Lesbian Prayer Book* (London: Hamish Hamilton, 1992), pp. 95–106.
17 Jean Mortimer, 'Separation and divorce' in Susan Durber, *As Man and Woman Made: Theological Reflections on Marriage* (London: United Reformed Church, 1994), pp. 174–5.
18 Mary Hunt, *Fierce Tenderness: A Feminist Theology of Friendship* (New York: Crossroad, 1991), p. 117.

8 Friend God

Pure friendship is an image of the original and perfect friendship that belongs to Trinity, and is the very essence of God.[1]
(Simone Weil)

The search for new ways of speaking about God has been an urgent priority for feminist theology. All God-talk is metaphorical. Sallie McFague describes metaphorical thinking as

> seeing one thing *as* something else, pretending 'this' is 'that' because we do not know how to think or talk about, 'this', so we use 'that' as a way of saying something about it. Thinking metaphorically means spotting a thread of similarity between two dissimilar objects, events, or whatever, one of which is better known than the other, and using the better-known one as a way of speaking about the lesser known.[2]

God, by virtue of being God, is always beyond our mental and linguistic grasp. Rosemary Radford Ruether, in answer to a question about her theology being too immanent and not transcendent enough, replied that for her the notion of transcendence was not about God being completely 'other' than us and distant from us, but about God being uncatchable and uncontrollable by us. For whilst we can never throw a net around God, the only reason we speak about God at all is that we see her shadow cast across the faces of people, events and other things; we detect her trails; we smell her perfume on the wind; we see dim echoes of God's image impressed upon the wet clay of our world. We know all our theology begins in anthropology but it is in the mess and muddle of this world that we believe we perceive tantalizing hints about the nature of ultimate reality. Yet McFague emphasizes that metaphor is just that: all metaphors 'always contain the whisper, "it is *and it is not*"'.³ The problem is that the last part of the whisper tends to become inaudible and so metaphors become idols: that is, false images of God, made in human image, which serve to bolster the power of some whilst disempowering others. Feminist theology has exposed the part that imaging God as male and constructing his masculinity within the terms of domination–submission has played in oppressing women. Nor is feminist theology itself immune from wax in the theological ear that prevents us hearing 'and it is not'. At a feminist theology conference I attended I found myself as a non-maternal lesbian deeply disempowered by the enthusiasm for imaging God/ess as mother and idealizing pregnancy and childbirth. So I want to make it clear that in discussing the image of God as friend I am conscious that it is *only* a metaphor, but one I think worth adding to the pantheon of metaphors we need to develop to save us from our tendencies towards idolatry and help us luxuriate in the richness that is God.

Sallie McFague and Mary Hunt have both done some extremely creative work on the metaphor of God as friend. But neither of them starts where I want to start, in the Christian tradition itself and more particularly with the concept of the Trinity. Feminist theology has not made a collective priority of reclaiming the concept of the Trinity and one can understand why. In the way the doctrine of the Trinity was developed it became the golden calf of the idolatry of masculinity. Mary Daly mischievously described it as

the most sensational one-act play of the centuries, performed by the Supreme All-Male cast; 'sublime' (and therefore disguised) erotic male homosexual mythos, the perfect all-male marriage, the ideal all-male family. The best boy's club, the model monastery, the supreme Men's Association, the mould for all varieties of male monogender mating.⁴

Brian Wren notes that 'in worship, the traditional doxology pictures God as an all-male one-parent family with a whoosh of vapour'.[5] And yet the concept of the Trinity may be worth reclaiming because in its essence it does proclaim that at the heart of God there is *relationality*. Leonardo Boff and other liberation theologians have pointed to the dangers inherent in a radical monotheist God: the one God ruling from above establishes a model for human relating which is dictatorial. Trinitarian theology acts as a critique to this abusive model of human relating.[6] God is a 'community of persons-in-relation'[7] and, what is more, this is a community based upon radical mutuality. The problem is that the belief in and assertion of the radical mutuality at the heart of God, which was always an essential part of Christian orthodoxy, was hard to convey within the constraints of the Neoplatonic philosophy utilized in the formation of the doctrine of the Trinity. It was under the influence of Neoplatonic philosophy that the language of 'generation' entered Trinitarian theology. God the Father, source of all, 'generates' a Son; in Eastern Orthodoxy, the Father also generates the Spirit; in Western Christianity, Father and Son together generate the Spirit. The language of generation was considered essential in order to preserve the integrity, distinctiveness and uniqueness of the three 'persons' of the Trinity. But despite the fact that this language lay alongside a language of radical equality and mutuality, the language of generation and the metaphor of parenthood undermined it:

> From the asymmetry of trinitarian relations in the classical model a practical inequality follows, with neither Son nor Spirit attaining the authority of the Father. All originates from the first person, the apex of the divine pyramid. Such a model is clearly coherent with the existence of patriarchal structures in church and society, and is in functional rapport with them. It both reproduces and supports such structures.[8]

Augustine explicitly ruled out using the language of friendship to describe the relations within God because he felt it would blur the differences between the three persons, 'a friend is so called relatively to his friend, and if they love each other equally then the same friendship is in both'.[9] But to describe God as a community of friends does not necessarily involve the blurring of distinctions between the friends, any more than a human community of friends enjoying mutuality would be indistinct from one another. Differences are not dispelled but acknowledged and celebrated in friendship. In the Trinity we recognize God the creator, God embodied, and God the Spirit/Sophia existing in friendship. The language of generation was not the only language used to describe the relationship of the Trinity. In the seventh century, John of Damascus used the term *perichōrēsis* in his theology of the Trinity. It is a word that suggests a cyclical movement and is related to the verb *perichōreuō* which means 'dance around'. It conjures up a dynamic, non-hierarchical equal, mutual relationship, 'a beautiful intertwining, unending dance, whose movement flows to and fro between the dancers'.[10] What keeps these friends in this unending dance is passion for each other. The dance is an expression of that passion and a celebration of it. Their passion is the music to which they dance. Dancing is, of course, a bodily activity, it engages the whole person. Nor is dance necessarily confined to celebration; people also dance to express sadness, grief and anger. It is surely significant that dance has played a huge part in religious ritual in many different cultures and ages. And there is something particularly powerful about dancing in a circle, about being part of a larger movement. At the heart of God is a dance of passionate friendship.

It is amusing to observe what difficulty Christian theologians have always had in dealing with the third person of the Trinity. Indeed, whilst proclaiming the Spirit to be a person, the Spirit has usually been imaged in non-personal terms as a dove, hanging around or above the Father and Son. The Spirit has become the eternal gooseberry, not so much involved in the circle-dance as sitting on the side-lines as Father and Son waltz across the ballroom. Liberal feminists who have sought to inject an element of femaleness into the Trinity and identified the Spirit as the female principle have only compounded this image: now the gooseberry is female, typically marginalized from the male bonding, sent out into the world to do all the motherly work! Various attempts have been made to integrate the Holy Spirit into the Trinity. Augustine toyed with the images of Lover (Father), Beloved (Son) and Love (Spirit). Richard of St Victor believed that the Spirit was the receiver of the love that spilled over from the relationship between Father and Son: 'Shared love is properly said to exist when a third person is loved by two persons harmoniously and in community, and the affection of the two persons is fused into one affection by the flame of love for the third.'[11] John V. Taylor famously described the Holy Spirit as the 'go-between God'.[12] Brian Wren has adopted the model of Lover, the Beloved and the Mutual Friend: 'The Mutual Friend is their equal partner, delighting in their mutual love, knowing each and by each fully known, the whole effortlessly enclosing all creation and inviting all things to join the great ongoing dance.'[13] Wren thinks that it is quite right that we should use impersonal metaphors for the Spirit to protect ourselves from forgetting that these are metaphors. I would agree but I strongly suspect that Christian clumsiness in dealing with the Spirit has a lot to do with our discomfort with the concept of threeness in relationship. Our obsession with coupledom makes us incapable of dealing with a three-person relationship, even in God. The Spirit must be the love between the Father and Son or even the receiver of the outflow of love between the Father and Son, or the mutual friend of Father and Son but never the equal participant in the relationship. The doctrine of the Trinity conceived as three friends dancing a dance of passion serves to remind us that we are called to more than coupledom, that as Elizabeth Templeton noted the kingdom is about inclusive not exclusive passion.

One problem that many of us have with the Trinity is that it seems to portray God as self-sufficient; we can be left feeling like the wallflowers at the party. This is why it is essential to remember the ancient Christian tradition that we are the body of Christ on earth; we are part of God the incarnate; we are taken up in the dance of passion; we are part of the Trinity. Our just passionate, mutual dances with each other reflect and are taken up into the dance of God. Our task is to ensure that there are no wallflowers, that all are involved in this cosmic dance. Mary Hunt, although not explicitly utilizing the concept of the Trinity, does think it is vital that we image God as friends rather than friend, because friends never exist in the singular.[14]

Sallie McFague has noted that one of most appealing aspects of the metaphor of God as friend(s) is its underscoring of equality. God does not relate to us as parent to child but as 'adults':

> Becoming adult need not mean, although it often has in our society meant, becoming independent in the sense of becoming a solitary individual. On the contrary, in an ecological, evolutionary context, becoming adult must mean the movement from dependent status to interdependence: the recognition that mature perception and activity in our world demand interrelating not only with other human beings but also with other forms of being, both nonhuman and divine. It is, above all, our willingness to grow up and take responsibility for the world that the model of friend underscores. If God is the friend of the world, the one committed to it, who can be trusted never to betray it, who not only likes the world but has a vision for its well-being, then we as the special part of the body—the *imago dei*—are invited as friends of the Friend of the world to join in that vision and work for its fulfilment.[15]

We are called to maturity by our divine friend(s), to take responsibility for each other and our world, but we are not on our own. We are pushed and prodded and cherished and loved by a presence beyond our grasp, yet so familiar that it cannot be ignored. God will not allow us to 'sit out' the dance.

The metaphor of God as friend(s) has roots in the Hebrew and Christian scriptures. We have already observed the reference to those with whom God made covenants as 'friends' in the Hebrew scriptures. Hochma is portrayed as a friendly presence, immanent in the creation she loves, summoning us to justice whilst inviting us to share a meal with her. This image is taken up in the figure of Jesus who in God's name establishes a community of friends and invites all to join it. In his own body Jesus bears the tragedy of friendship failed, passion transmuted into destruction. Mary Hunt believes that it is important that we should not be afraid to take our experience of the frailty of friendship into our experience of God, and I think she is right. At a workshop I attended on our images of God, a collective sharp intake of breath greeted my revelation that I often experience God as an unreliable friend. Yet many of us have the experience of crying out to God 'why have you forsaken me?' Christianity, unlike Judaism, has always had problems in dealing with the experience of the absence of God and voicing the pain and betrayal felt in this experience. Sometimes when we need God most she is on the cross with us rather than in a position of strength to help us, or just achingly absent. It is right and proper, if we are seeking to exist in honest and mutual friendship with the divine, that we should call her to judgement as she calls us.

Another advantage of thinking of God as friend(s) is that 'friend' can contain within it multilayers of other images; parent, lover, wisdom, sister/brother can, and indeed should, also be friends. In worship it is one of the very few images of God that is truly inclusive.

Many Christian feminists have problems with the cross as the central image of our salvation. They think that the equation of salvation with suffering and death simply serves to reinforce and glorify suffering. Yet other Christian feminists see the cross altogether differently, as God's identification with their suffering, not as a passive acceptance of it but as a scream against it. For me, the cross has retained its centrality in my faith not as the central act in a great drama of atonement but as the sad, stark reminder that relationships fail, dreams die, embodied persons break; the structures of sin conspire to prevent and then destroy friendship and this experience is as much part of the heart of God as of ourselves. The resurrection is the pledge by the divine friend(s) that in the end the forces of disconnection and entropy will not triumph over the forces of friendship.

We often experience friendship as an experience of what some would call 'grace'. We are surprised by a blossoming love which we neither expected nor consciously sought. In this experience of the graciousness of friendship we touch the sacramental presence of God, of Sophia craftily weaving a web between us and then stretching the ends of the twine to bind us to others. Many no longer find anthropomorphic images of God helpful and we should remind ourselves of the biblical location of God in the betweenness of persons as the passionate power that bind them together. We must never forget, 'it is *and it is not*'. What we can detect in the shadows on the faces of those around us is that there is something of friendship in God, not idealized, sentimental friendship but real, messy painful friendship of which we are an integral part and which we incarnate in our own relationships. We become sacraments of God's wanton passionate love when we endeavour to relate in friendship. In relationships of radical vulnerability we experience and incarnate something of what it could be like in the reign of God. In the passion between us we experience the God who, according to John Chrysostom, is 'more erotic than bride and groom'.[16] In every generation, the Wisdom of Solomon assures us, Sophia passes into holy souls making them friends of God (7.27). We are called to be passionate friends to each other and to God who is Passionate Friend.

Notes

1 Cited in Elizabeth A. Johnson, *She Who Is: The Mystery of God in Feminist Theological Discourse* (New York: Crossroad, 1993), p. 218.
2 Sallie McFague, *Metaphorical Theology: Models of God in Religious Language* (London: SCM, 1982), p. 15.
3 McFague, *Metaphorical Theology*, p. 13.
4 Mary Daly, *Gyn/Ecology: The Metaethics of Radical Feminism* (Boston: Beacon Press, 1978), p. 38.
5 Brian Wren, *What Language Shall I Borrow? God-Talk in Worship: A Male Response to Feminist Theology* (London: SCM, 1989), p. 200.

6 Leonardo Boff, *Trinity and Society* (Tunbridge Wells: Burns and Oates, 1988).

7 Adrian Thatcher, *Liberating Sex: A Christian Sexual Theology* (London: SPCK, 1993), p. 55.

8 Johnson, *She Who Is*, p. 197.

9 Augustine, *De Trinitate*, 5.6.7.

10 Wren, *What Language Shall I Borrow?*, p. 202.

11 Cited in Thatcher, *Liberating Sex*, p. 55.

12 John V. Taylor, *The Go-Between God: The Holy Spirit and the Christian Mission* (London: SCM, 1972).

13 Wren, *What Language Shall I Borrow?*, p. 211.

14 Mary Hunt, *Fierce Tenderness: A Feminist Theology of Friendship* (New York: Crossroad, 1991), pp. 167–8.

15 Sallie McFague, *Models of God: Theology for an Ecological, Nuclear Age* (London: SCM, 1987), p. 165.

16 John Chrysostom, 'Homily 5 on Romans', cited in Kenneth Leech, *The Eye of the Storm: Spiritual Resources for the Pursuit of Justice* (London: Darton, Longman and Todd, 1992), p. 67.

Selected bibliography

Aelred of Rievaulx, *Spiritual Friendship* (Kalamazoo: Cistercian Publications, 1974).

James Ashbrooke, 'Different voices, different genes', *Journal of Pastoral Care*, vol. 46 (Summer 1992).

Paul Ballard, 'The social context of the family today—a Christian reflection', *Contact*, no. 114 (1994).

Judith Barrington, *An Intimate Wilderness: Lesbian Writers on Sexuality* (Portland, OR: The Eighth Mountain Press, 1991).

David Biale, *Eros and the Jews: From Biblical Israel to Contemporary America* (New York: Basic Books, 1992).

Leonardo Boff, *Trinity and Society* (Tunbridge Wells: Burns and Oates, 1988).

Anne Borrowdale, *Distorted Images: Christian Attitudes to Women, Men and Sex* (London: SPCK, 1991).

John Boswell, *Christianity, Social Tolerance and Homosexuality: Gay People in Western Europe from the Beginning of the Christian Era to the Fourteenth Century* (Chicago: University of Chicago Press, 1980).

Same-Sex Unions in Premodern Europe (New York: Villard Books, 1994).

Rita Nakashima Brock, *Journeys by Heart: A Christology of Erotic Power* (New York: Crossroad, 1991).

Peter Brown, *The Body and Society: Men, Women and Sexual Renunciation in Early Christianity* (London: Faber and Faber, 1989).

Raymond E. Brown, *The Gospel According to John*, 2 vols (New York: Doubleday/London: Geoffrey Chapman, 1982).

Vincent Brümmer, *The Model of Love* (Cambridge, UK: Cambridge University Press, 1993).

Christopher Burdon, *Stumbling on God: Faith and Vision through Mark's Gospel* (London: SPCK, 1990).

J. Michael Clark, *Beyond Our Ghettos: Gay Theology in Ecological Perspective* (Cleveland: The Pilgrim Press, 1993).

Sally Cline, *Women, Celibacy and Passion* (London: André Deutsch, 1993).

Janet Coleman, 'The Owl and the Nightingale and papal theories of marriage', *Journal of Ecclesiastical History*, vol. 38, no. 4 (October 1987).

Peter Coleman, *Gay Christians: A Moral Dilemma* (London: SCM, 1989).

Gary David Comstock, *Gay Theology Without Apology* (Cleveland: The Pilgrim Press, 1993).

Congregation for the Doctrine of Faith, *Letter to the Bishops of the Catholic Church on the Pastoral Care of Homosexual Persons* (London: Catholic Truth Society, 1986).

Jim Cotter, *Good Fruits: Same-Sex Relationships and Christian Faith* (Sheffield: Cairns Publications, 1988).

Yes ... Minister?: Patterns of Christian Service (Sheffield: Cairns Publications, 1992).

William Countryman, *Dirt, Greed and Sex: Sexual Ethics in the New Testament and Their Implications for Today* (London: SCM, 1989).

Mary Daly, *Gyn/Ecology: The Metaethics of Radical Feminism* (Boston: Beacon Press, 1978).

'Sparking: the fire of female friendship', *Chrysalis: A Magazine of Women's Culture*, vol. 6 (1978).

Pure Lust: Elemental Feminist Philosophy (Boston: Beacon Press, 1984).

Mary Daly with Jane Caputi, *Websters' First New Intergalactic Wickedary of the English Language* (London: The Women's Press, 1988).

J. P. DeCecco, *Gay Relationships* (New York: Harrington Park, 1988).

Emma Donoghue, *Passions Between Women: British Lesbian Culture 1668–1801* (London: Scarlet Press, 1993).

Susan Dowell, *They Two Shall be One: Monogamy in History and Religion* (London: Collins Flame, 1990).

Martin Bauml Duberman, Martha Vicinus and George Chauncey, Jr, *Hidden from History: Reclaiming the Gay and Lesbian Past* (London: Penguin, 1991).

Susan Durber, *As Man and Woman Made: Theological Reflections on Marriage* (London: United Reformed Church, 1994).

Andrea Dworkin, *Woman-Hating* (New York: Dutton, 1974).

Wayne R. Dynes, *Encyclopedia of Homosexuality*, 2 vols (London: St James Press, 1990).

D. J. Enright and David Rawlinson, *The Oxford Book of Friendship* (Oxford: Oxford University Press, 1991).

Lillian Faderman, *Surpassing the Love of Men: Romantic Friendship and Love Between Women from the Renaissance to the Present* (London: The Women's Press, 1985).

Odd Girls and Twilight Lovers: A History of Lesbian Life in Twentieth-Century America (London: Penguin, 1992).

Elisabeth Schüssler Fiorenza, *Discipleship of Equals: A Critical Feminist Ekklesia-logy of Liberation* (London: SCM, 1993).

Austin Flannery OP, *Vatican Council II: The Conciliar and Post-Conciliar Documents* (Leominster: Fowler Wright, 1980).

Carol Lee Flinders, *Enduring Grace: Living Portraits of Seven Women Mystics* (HarperSan Francisco, 1993).

Marie Fortune, *Sexual Violence* (New York: The Pilgrim Press, 1983).

Michel Foucault, *The History of Sexuality: An Introduction* (Harmondsworth: Penguin, 1981).

Matthew Fox, *A Spirituality Named Compassion* (San Francisco: Harper and Row, 1979).

Original Blessing: A Primer in Creation Spirituality (Santa Fe: Bear and Co., 1983).

Hildegard of Bingen's Book of Divine Works with Letters and Songs (Santa Fe: Bear and Co., 1987).

Breakthrough: Meister Eckhart's Creation Spirituality in New Translation (New York: Image Books, 1991).

Sandra Friedman and Alec Irwin, 'Christian feminism, eros, and power in right relation', *Cross Currents*, vol. 40 (Fall 1990).

Marilyn Frye, *The Politics of Reality: Essays in Feminist Theory* (New York: The Crossing Press, 1983).

Sue George, *Women and Bisexuality* (London: Scarlet Press, 1993).

Carol Gilligan, *In a Different Voice? Psychological Theory and Women's Development* (Cambridge, MA: Harvard University Press, 1982).

Lucy Goodison, *Moving Heaven and Earth: Sexuality, Spirituality and Social Change* (London: The Women's Press, 1990).

Robert Goss, *Jesus Acted Up: A Gay and Lesbian Manifesto* (HarperSanFrancisco, 1993).

Elaine Graham, 'Towards a theology of desire', *Theology and Sexuality*, vol. 1 (September 1994).

Judy Grahn, *Another Mother Tongue: Gay Words, Gay Worlds* (Boston: Beacon Press, 1984).

Mary Grey, *The Wisdom of Fools? Seeking Revelation for Today* (London: SPCK, 1993).

Julian Hafner, *The End of Marriage: Why Monogamy Isn't Working* (London: Century, 1993).

Celia Allison Hahn, *Sexual Paradox: Creative Tensions in Our Lives and in Our Congregation* (New York: The Pilgrim Press, 1991).

Daphne Hampson, *Theology and Feminism* (Oxford: Blackwell, 1990).

A. E. Harvey, *Promise or Pretence? A Christian's Guide to Sexual Morals* (London: SCM, 1994).

Gilbert Herdt and Andrew Boxer, *Children of Horizons: How Gay and Lesbian Teens Are Leading a New Way Out of the Closet* (Boston: Beacon Press, 1993).

Carter Heyward, *Our Passion for Justice: Images of Power, Sexuality and Liberation* (New York: The Pilgrim Press, 1984).

Touching Our Strength: The Erotic as Power and the Love of God (San Francisco: Harper and Row, 1989).

When Boundaries Betray Us: Beyond Illusions of What is Ethical in Therapy and Life (HarperSanFrancisco, 1993).

Shere Hite, *Women as Revolutionary Agents of Change: The Hite Reports: Sexuality, Love and Emotion* (London: Sceptre Books, 1994).

The Hite Report on the Family: Growing Up Under Patriarchy (London: Bloomsbury, 1994).

House of the Bishops of the General Synod of the Church of England, *Issues in Human Sexuality* (London: Church House Publishing, 1991).

Mary Hunt, *Fierce Tenderness: A Feminist Theology of Friendship* (New York: Crossroad, 1991).

Jo Ind, *Fat Is a Spiritual Issue: My Journey* (London: Mowbray, 1993).

Luce Irigaray, *Marine Lover of Friedrich Nietzsche* (New York: Columbia University Press, 1991).

Sheila Jeffreys, *The Lesbian Heresy: A Feminist Perspective on the Lesbian Sexual Revolution* (London: The Women's Press, 1994).

Jeffrey John, *'Permanent, Stable, Faithful': Christian Same-Sex Partnerships* (London: Affirming Catholicism, 1993).

Pope John Paul II, *Familiaris Consortio* (London: Catholic Truth Society, 1981).

Elizabeth A. Johnson, *She Who Is: The Mystery of God in Feminist Theological Discourse* (New York: Crossroad, 1993).

Brian Keenan, *An Evil Cradling* (London: Vintage, 1992).

Morton Kelsey and Barbara Kelsey, *Sacrament of Sexuality: The Spirituality and Psychology of Sex* (Warwick: Amity House, 1986).

Helena Kennedy, *Eve Was Framed: Women and British Justice* (London: Chatto and Windus, 1992).

Kwok Pui-Lan, 'The future of feminist theology: an Asian perspective', *The Auburn News* (Fall 1992).

Alice L. Laffey, *Wives, Harlots and Concubines: The Old Testament in Feminist Perspective* (London: SPCK, 1990).

Kenneth Leech, *The Eye of the Storm: Spiritual Resources for the Pursuit of Justice* (London: Darton, Longman and Todd, 1992).

C. S. Lewis, *The Four Loves* (London: Collins, 1960).

Graham Little, *Friendship: Being Ourselves with Others* (Melbourne: The Text Publishing Company, 1993).

Ann Loades, *Feminist Theology: A Reader* (London: SPCK, 1990).

Asphodel P. Long, *In a Chariot Drawn by Lions: The Search for the Female in Deity* (London: The Women's Press, 1992).

John McCarthy and Jill Morrell, *Some Other Rainbow* (London: Corgi Books, 1994).

Sallie McFague, *Metaphorical Theology: Models of God in Religious Language* (London: SCM, 1982).

Models of God: Theology for an Ecological, Nuclear Age (London: SCM, 1987).

Alisdair MacIntyre, *After Virtue: A Study in Moral Theory* (London: Duckworth, 1981).

Catharine MacKinnon, *Only Words* (Cambridge, MA: Harvard University Press, 1991).

David P. McWhirter and Andrew M. Mattison, *The Male Couple: How Relationships Develop* (London: Prentice-Hall, 1984).

Irene Mahoney OSU, *All That I Am* (published by the author, 39 Willow Drive, New Rochelle, NY 10805, 1987).

Michael Mason, *The Making of Victorian Sexuality* (Oxford: Oxford University Press, 1994).

J. Giles Milhaven, 'A medieval lesson on bodily knowing: women's experience and men's thought', *Journal of the American Academy of Religion*, vol. 57, no. 2 (Summer 1989).

Virginia Ramey Mollenkott, *Sensuous Spirituality: Out from Fundamentalism* (New York: Crossroad, 1993).

Gareth Moore, *The Body in Context: Sex and Catholicism* (London: SCM, 1992).

Colin Morris, *The Discovery of the Individual: 1050–1200* (London: Harper and Row, 1972).

Ferdinand Mount, *The Subversive Family* (London: Jonathan Cape, 1982).

Roland E. Murphy OCarm, 'Canticle of Canticles' in Raymond E. Brown SS, Joseph A. Fitzmyer SJ and Roland E. Murphy OCarm, *The New Jerome Biblical Commentary* (Englewood Cliffs, NJ: Prentice-Hall/London: Geoffrey Chapman, 1991).

James Nelson, *The Intimate Connection: Male Sexuality, Masculine Spirituality* (London: SPCK, 1992).

Body Theology (Louisville: Westminster/John Knox Press, 1992).

James Nelson and Sandra P. Longfellow, *Sexuality and the Sacred: Sources for Theological Reflection* (Louisville: Westminster/John Knox Press/London: Mowbray, 1994).

David Oliphant, 'Marriage—a union of equals? The 1991 Mary Body Memorial Lecture', *St Mark's Review* (Autumn 1992).

Helen Oppenheimer, *Marriage* (London: Mowbray, 1990).

M. Scott Peck, *The Different Drum: Community-Making and Peace* (London: Arrow, 1988).

The Road Less Travelled (London: Arrow, 1990).

Ken Plummer, *Modern Homosexualities: Fragments of Lesbian and Gay Experience* (London: Routledge, 1992).

Barbara Ponse, *Identities in the Lesbian World: The Social Construction of Self* (Westport: Greenwood Press, 1978).

Janice Raymond, *The Transsexual Empire* (London: The Women's Press, 1982).

A Passion for Friends: Towards a Philosophy of Female Affection (London: The Women's Press, 1986).

Esther D. Rothblum and Kathleen A. Brehony, *Boston Marriages: Romantic but Asexual Relationships Among Contemporary Lesbians* (Amherst: University of Massachusetts Press, 1993).

Christopher Rowland, 'Jesus, the gospels and intimacy', *Christian Action Journal* (Summer 1993).

Rosemary Radford Ruether, 'An unrealized revolution: searching scripture for a model of family', *Christianity and Crisis: A Christian Journal of Opinion*, vol. 43 (31 October 1983).

 Gaia and God: An Ecofeminist Theology of Earth Healing (London: SCM, 1992).

Kenneth C. Russell, 'Aelred, the gay Abbot of Rievaulx', *Studia Mystica*, vol. 5, part 4 (Winter 1982).

Peggy Reeves Sanday, *Female Power and Male Dominance: On the Origins of Sexual Inequality* (Cambridge, UK: Cambridge University Press, 1981).

Elaine Showalter, *Speaking of Gender* (New York: Routledge, 1989).

Dennis E. Smith and Hal E. Taussig, *Many Tables: The Eucharist in the New Testament and Liturgy Today* (London: SCM, 1990).

Carroll Smith-Rosenberg, *Disorderly Conduct: Visions of Gender in Victorian America* (New York: Alfred A. Knopf, 1985).

Arlene Stein, *Sisters, Sexperts, Queers: Beyond the Lesbian Nation* (New York: Plume, 1993).

Edward Stein, *Forms of Desire: Sexual Orientation and the Social Constructionist Controversy* (London: Routledge, 1990).

Leo Steinberg, *The Sexuality of Christ in Renaissance Art and in Modern Oblivion* (New York: Pantheon, 1983).

Elizabeth Stuart, *Daring to Speak Love's Name: A Gay and Lesbian Prayer Book* (London: Hamish Hamilton, 1992).

 Chosen: Gay Catholic Priests Tell Their Stories (London: Geoffrey Chapman, 1993).

Arlene Swidler, *Homosexuality and World Religions* (Valley Forge: Trinity Press International, 1993).

Donner M. Tanner, *The Lesbian Couple* (Lexington, MA: D. C. Heath, 1978).

John V. Taylor, *The Go-Between God: The Holy Spirit and the Christian Mission* (London: SCM, 1972).

Adrian Thatcher, *Truly a Person, Truly God: A Post-Mythical View of Jesus* (London: SPCK, 1990).

Liberating Sex: A Christian Sexual Theology (London: SPCK, 1993).

Gerd Theissen, *The Shadow of the Galilean* (London: SCM, 1987).

Susan Brooks Thistlewaite, *Sex, Race, and God: Christian Feminism in Black and White* (New York: Crossroad/London: Geoffrey Chapman, 1990).

Ann Belford Ulanov, *The Feminine in Jungian Psychology and in Christian Theology* (Evanston: North Western University Publishers, 1971).

Peter Vardy and Paul Grosch, *The Puzzle of Ethics* (London: Fount, 1994).

Veritatis Splendor: Encyclical Letter Addressed by the Supreme Pontiff Pope John Paul II to All Bishops of the Catholic Church Regarding Certain Fundamental Questions of the Church's Moral Teaching (London: Catholic Truth Society, 1993).

Sue Walrond-Skinner, *The Fulcrum and the Fire: Wrestling with Family Life* (London: Darton, Longman and Todd, 1993).

Heather Walton, 'Theology of desire', *Theology and Sexuality*, vol. 1 (September 1994).

Marina Warner, *Alone of All Her Sex: The Myth and the Cult of the Virgin Mary* (London: Picador, 1985).

Sue Wilkinson and Celia Kitzinger, *Heterosexuality: A Feminism and Psychology Reader* (London: Sage Publications, 1993).

Robert Williams, 'Toward a theology of lesbian and gay marriage', *Anglican Theological Review*, vol. 72 (1990).

William Williamson, 'People we're stuck with', *The Christian Century*, vol. 107 (October 1990).

Monique Wittig, *The Straight Mind and Other Essays* (Hemel Hempstead: Harvester Wheatsheaf, 1992).

Brian Wren, *What Language Shall I Borrow? God-Talk in Worship: A Male Response to Feminist Theology* (London: SCM, 1989).

Index

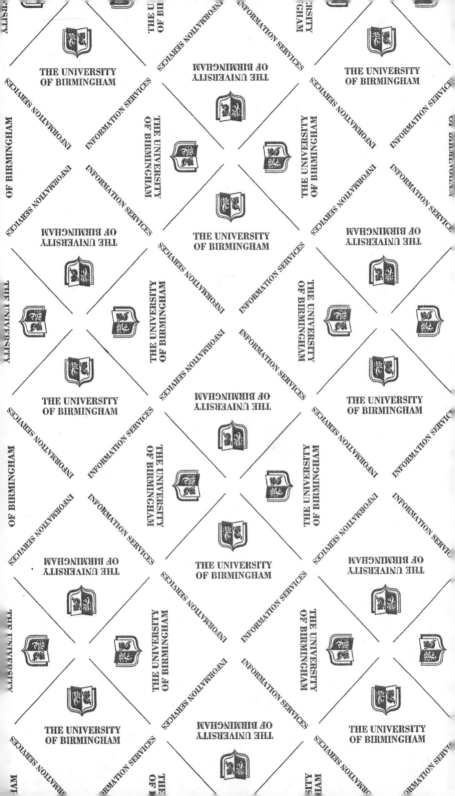